TRAFFIC JAM

Ten years of 'sustainable' transport in the UK

Edited by Iain Docherty and Jon Shaw

This edition published in Great Britain in 2008 by

The Policy Press
University of Bristol
Fourth Floor
Beacon House
Queen's Road
Bristol BS8 1QU
UK

Tel +44 (0)117 331 4054
Fax +44 (0)117 331 4093
e-mail tpp-info@bristol.ac.uk
www.policypress.org.uk

© The Policy Press 2008

British Library Cataloguing in Publication Data
A catalogue record for this book is available from the British Library.

Library of Congress Cataloging-in-Publication Data
A catalog record for this book has been requested.

ISBN 978 1 84742 072 5 paperback
ISBN 978 1 84742 073 2 hardcover

Cover design by Qube Design, Bristol
Front cover: image kindly supplied by www.alamy.com
Printed and bound in Great Britain by Hobbs the Printers, Southampton

To Dae Dawson, Kate Pangbourne, Andrew Carse, Julie Clark and Mags Currie, our splendid and industrious PhD students working on transport-related projects.

What follows is one of the reasons we haven't been as accessible as we would have liked. We hope you'll see it as a reasonable excuse, and also that you'll have a better story to tell one day.

Traffic jam

Damn this traffic jam
How I hate to be late
Hurts my motor to go so slow
Damn this traffic jam
Time I get home my supper'll be cold

Damn this traffic jam...

Well, I left my job about 5 o'clock
Fifteen minutes to go three blocks
Just in time to stand in line
Freeway looking like a parking lot

Damn this traffic jam…

Now, I almost had a heart attack
Looking in the rear view mirror
Saw myself the next car back
Looking in the rear view mirror
'Bout to have a heart attack

Damn this traffic jam…

Now when I die I don't want no coffin
I've thought about it all too often
Just strap me in behind the wheel
And bury me with my automobile

Damn this traffic jam…

I used to think that I was cool
Driving around on fossil fuel
Then I found what I was doing
Was driving down the road to ruin.

From Taylor, J. (1977) *JT*, New York: Columbia Records

Contents

List of tables, figures and boxes

Tables

Figures

Boxes

Foreword

Trying to find evidence of a coherent transport policy when examining the record of the first decade of the Labour government is rather like attempting to ring up a person whose obituary you have just read in a newspaper. There may have been something approaching a policy once, but there is precious little trace of it now.

Transport was the area in which the Blair governments least exerted themselves and there is little evidence that this is changing under Gordon Brown. There are good short-term political reasons for this. Transport is a long-term issue that delivers little in the lifetime of a politician. Order a shiny new underground line today, and some other bugger, possibly of a rival party, will open it. That, however, is an excuse, not a justification for a quite overwhelming failure. It is hard to point to any transport policy initiatives under Labour that have borne fruit. Most of the positive achievements have occurred in response to an emergency such as the replacement of Railtrack with Network Rail, or were the continuation of Conservative policies like the construction of High Speed 1 or were largely the work of devolved bodies, notably plans for Scottish rail expansion and the introduction of the congestion charge in London (although these were made possible as a result of different legislation introduced by the Labour government).

On the other hand, while the list of achievements can be counted on one hand, the number of missed opportunities resulting from timid policy making requires all digits and more. Of course transport is a difficult issue and there are strong lobbies in favour of the most environmentally damaging modes – car use and aviation. Nevertheless, Labour politicians have shown a quite extraordinary pusillanimity in addressing the most obvious failings of the market to deliver a sustainable transport policy. Where a bit of backbone was required in addressing the fundamental issues, there has been a total lack of vertebrae. Even where progressive policies have been considered or adopted, they have been abandoned in the face of the first hint of serious opposition.

Take, first, roads and driving. The Conservatives' annual 5% above inflation rise on fuel tax duty was briefly continued and, indeed, increased to 6%. Then, just as it was beginning to bear fruit in terms of reduced traffic growth, the policy was ditched. As for road-building, John Prescott scrapped dozens of schemes soon after coming to office and put almost all of the rest on ice, but before long that policy had been reversed. Bizarrely, too, the plan for a lorry road-user charging scheme, popular among domestic road hauliers because it would involve creating a level playing field with foreign trucks, was abandoned by Alistair Darling without any plausible explanation, and an overall national scheme has been kicked into the very long grass. Bus policy has been particularly timid given its potential to deliver improvements quickly. While recognising the failings of the deregulation of the 1980s, Labour has refused to make any serious attempts to reregulate the industry; legislation to allow local authorities to introduce Quality Contracts created so many hoops for councils to jump through that it has never been used. Light rail has quietly been abandoned as a solution to traffic congestion in urban centres, despite its clear regenerative effects and popularity.

As for railways, the bizarre structure of public control and private ownership has created a system so expensive that enhancement schemes are constrained. Given these huge costs, the refusal of Labour to undertake a root and branch overhaul of a structure – one which even Alastair Darling admitted was 'botched' during his tenure as Secretary of State for Transport – is puzzling to say the least. And rail and bus fares have been allowed to rise whereas motoring costs have stagnated in recent years. These above inflation rises have helped stimulate demand for domestic aviation, which is lightly taxed. (Aviation policy has at least been consistent and clear – there has never really been any attempt to deviate from 'predict and provide'.) I remember once asking Alistair Darling, when he was Transport Secretary, why he did not do more to encourage train travel rather than aviation, and he said it was not his job to influence modal choice, a virtual admission of the absence of a transport policy.

Possibly the nearest Labour came to any intellectual coherence on transport was early in New Labour's first term when John Prescott's White Paper *A new deal for transport* was published, but since then any attempts to draw up a strategy have foundered. To have to conclude that Prescott, a politician who towards the end was regarded by the public with both pity and contempt, was the best Transport Secretary of the New Labour administrations is depressing in the extreme. Yet, he was the only one even to attempt to define integrated transport and to address environmental issues. He created the Strategic Rail Authority, although ultimately its successes were limited. He promised 25 light rail schemes across the country, and it was not his fault that his successors were too short sighted to bring all but a couple to fruition. He helped establish the system of governance in London that enabled the congestion charge to be implemented and, crucially, for the revenue to be hypothecated for transport, a prerequisite for the success of any such scheme. He even pushed through the Public–Private Partnership (PPP) for the London Underground with the best of intentions – that he was desperate to see investment in the system – even if the scheme itself has turned out to be an expensive debacle.

In contrast, Prescott's successors have been political pygmies. Stephen Byers did take the sensible step of foreclosing on Railtrack (but failed to go for the obvious solution of renationalisation, which would have been a far cheaper option than the present structure), but otherwise he showed little interest in challenging the status quo. Alistair Darling made a virtue of doing nothing, sitting on his hands for four years overseeing a rail review that, strangely, abolished the Strategic Rail Authority, the only part of the structure created by Labour, and made sure that he made as little commitment as possible to major infrastructure schemes such as Crossrail and a second High Speed Line. Douglas Alexander did make some moves towards reregulating parts of the bus industry and was publicly supportive of a national road-charging scheme, but he always knew he would be promoted to another post by Gordon Brown and therefore he could afford to be more courageous than his predecessor. His successor, Ruth Kelly, like Darling, demonstrated scant interest in putting her head anywhere remotely near the parapet.

Intelligent left-of-centre politicians should of course be able to understand the importance of tackling current transport trends and their externalities. But the reality is that Labour has been scared of viewing transport in such a wider context. There are a variety of reasons for this – I have already mentioned transport's long-term nature. But there are also perverse appraisal assumptions used in the UK that can favour road development and actively seem to work against certain modes, especially light rail. In addition, there exists an obsession with ensuring that competition is possible and making sure that the private sector's scope for making profits is not reduced, even when these may largely be at the expense of the public purse. It is not an exaggeration to say that many civil servants and politicians are starstruck by the private sector and unable to recognise its limitations. Then there is a deep mistrust of the public sector, which results in a failure to consider the real choice between private and public sector options, as demonstrated by the disastrous decision to go for a PPP for the London Underground. Labour has shown itself to be terrified of powerful interest groups (just consider its readiness to acquiesce to Bernie Ecclestone's threat to take Formula 1 out of Britain if the tobacco advertising ban went ahead as planned), and there is the internal working of the government itself to take account of. Not only does the Treasury take a narrow economic view of social issues such as transport, but the dead hand of the civil service also cautions against risk and radicalism. Finally, there is, now, a reliance on consultants whose advice often favours the most complex schemes in order to ensure that further contributions will be required. Witness the wonderful irony that after the collapse of Metronet, which ran two-thirds of the London Underground PPP created largely on the recommendation of PriceWaterhouseCoopers (PWC), it was the same PWC that was called on to advise on how to proceed.

But merely listing these factors is not to understand them. That requires delving into history because these failings in fact have a deeper root, buried in Britain's political culture. In the railways, for example, British administrators and politicians have always favoured competition and light regulation rather than integration and tight control. It is no coincidence that in a country where the railways were developed without the active role of the state, they were subsequently privatised more quickly than almost anywhere else and with a structure designed to encourage competition for a mode of transport where coordination is clearly a more efficient ethos. British transport policy, therefore, is hidebound by history. It will take politicians who have a far greater understanding of this kind of context than New Labour's timid bunch to break the mould.

Christian Wolmar
London, May 2008

Preface and acknowledgements

This book is about transport developments in the UK since the publication of the landmark White Paper *A new deal for transport* in 1998 (DETR, 1998). The state of British transport had become unacceptable according to the incoming Labour government (and many others), and ministers were to improve considerably our transport systems and seek to change the way we travel. Key to this strategy was persuading us all to be more sustainable by using 'our cars a little less and public transport a little more' (DETR, 1998, p 3). Labour's theme song for the 1997 General Election was D:Ream's *Things can only get better*, and leitmotifs of Blair's (and now Brown's) governments have been to argue (a) that this has been the case and (b) how much better Britain is doing than its European competitors. We leave comment on other policy areas to colleagues,[1] but 10 years after the White Paper both of these statements are difficult to uphold in relation to transport, and particularly *sustainable* transport. Promoting sustainable transport is undeniably problematic and involves a mix of sometimes controversial 'sticks' (such as road user charging) to make people use their cars less, and 'carrots' (such as hugely improved public transport) to provide a realistic choice of quality alternatives. There also has to be a focus on reducing the need to travel, and key here are so-called 'soft' or 'smart' measures that can be very effective at increasing the frequency with which people walk, cycle or simply stay put.

For the purposes of illustration, let us take the particularly juicy carrot of major capital investment in public transport systems. A recent report by the consultants Grant Thornton (2008) lamented that British cities have been talking about light rail and other sizeable transport improvement schemes for longer than it has taken their European competitors to actually build them. In France, 2007 alone saw the opening of the second fully automatic metro line in Toulouse, a short extension to Line A in Lyon, a second extension to Paris' automatic Metro Line 14, the opening of the circumferential Tram T3 along the southern perimeter of the capital, the first lines of new tram networks in Le Mans, Marseille and Nice, Line D in Grenoble, Line E in Strasbourg and extensions to other modern tram networks in Bordeaux, Clermont Ferrand, Nantes and Valenciennes. And France is not the only European country investing hugely in public transport: in Spain the Madrid metro has just become the second largest by length in Europe; in Italy the first automatic metro line recently opened in Turin; and so on. Notwithstanding significant recent improvements in transport in London, British cities between them managed not a single tramway, light rail or heavy rail upgrade or extension in 2007 (the Docklands Light Railway spur to London City Airport opened in 2006).

Academics are often criticised, or at least teased, for having the easy job of highlighting deficiencies in the formulation and implementation of government policy. To an extent, of course, this is true, although at least in terms of public transport improvement our jobs on the above – and, for that matter, plenty of other

– evidence might be more difficult if we lived in France or Germany.[2] Besides, it seems to us right that academics, along with journalists and other investigators and commentators, take on the tasks of analysing and assessing government policy and practice to provide well-researched and justified criticism of longstanding systemic failure to deliver better policy outcomes. In the forerunner to this book (Docherty and Shaw, 2003), Phil Goodwin wrote that transport policy in Britain has degenerated to the point that the major political parties are effectively campaigning on the basis that they will 'make things worse more slowly than the other lot'. In our view, if things are going to get worse, then voters should have the opportunity to read some informed views on the reasons why.

For what it is worth, we think that under the right conditions it is possible for things to get much better, and certainly there are some positives to take from recent transport developments. November 2007, for example, saw the opening of the High Speed 1 (HS1) route from the Channel Tunnel to St Pancras International. What a pity, then, that the completion of HS1 was 13 years late, given that the equivalent infrastructure on the French side was ready when the Channel Tunnel opened in 1994. This delayed arrival is one of a battery of examples that suggests that Whitehall regards major capital investment in public transport infrastructure as at best an occasional extravagance, and at worst a heinous misuse of resources. (There is a less clear-cut picture in the devolved administrations.) Perhaps there is a grain of truth in the old jibe that consent for HS1 and St Pancras was only given after UK civil servants finally got fed up with the ridicule meted out by their continental counterparts after yet another late arrival for a Brussels meeting. Fans of high speed rail should not get carried away, however: although mentioned in passing in recent government despatches, the prospects for domestic high speed rail are precarious to the point that HS1 is likely to remain 'High Speed One and Only' for the foreseeable future.

Joking aside, proper investment in transport infrastructure is seen as a fact of everyday life in mainland Europe, not the immensely problematic test of public policy it has become on this side of the Channel. It is now impossible to think of France without the *train à grande vitesse* (TGV) (high speed train; HST), such has been its impact on the national psyche (and geography). No doubt the same will be true for Spain, which is energetically pursuing the construction of Europe's longest HST network at 7,200 kilometres; for Italy, which is well advanced in constructing two new 'spine' high speed routes (Turin-Milan-Venice and Milan-Florence-Rome-Naples); and for Germany, where *Deutsche Bahn* (DB) (German rail) continues to develop the InterCityExpress (ICE). Highly impressive and extremely well-patronised transport projects – large and small, operating across a range of spatial scales – are recognised as significant in securing economic (moving people and goods more efficiently to promote growth), social (tackling exclusion to give more people more access to life chances) and environmental (cutting emissions) advantages. It is possible through such means to pursue the prize of a high growth, low carbon economy.

So why is the UK government incapable of treating public transport travellers with the respect afforded to them by its European partners? Why do its ministers display an 'ostrich' mentality, which results in everyone else getting better than us at things we used to do well? And why – perhaps most irritatingly – do we remain good at diagnosing problems but seem incapable of implementing the right solutions? In the 1980s, for example, British Rail (BR) recognised that journey times on the West Coast Main Line (WCML) were in need of improvement. Being the UK, of course, no capital investment would be forthcoming for a TGV-style high speed line, but BR's engineers developed the concept of a tilting train to go around bends on the existing line more quickly. Alas, even this ended up being deemed a waste of money and the project was abandoned. How ironic that tilting trains now run on the WCML using Italian-designed rolling stock based on a British idea. Moving forward 15 years, in *A new deal for transport* New Labour provided a strong analysis of the problems besetting transport in Britain, but – at least in the view of those contributing to this book – has balked at actually doing much about them. Tram schemes have been abandoned, significant rail capacity expansions have failed to materialise (although Thameslink '2000' and Crossrail were *finally* – if grudgingly – given the go-ahead recently), large-scale road building is back on the agenda and road user charging, introduced against the wishes of the government by Ken Livingstone in London, runs the very real risk of being dropped altogether on a national basis. Even 'smart' measures, which hardly cost anything and can be very successful, have sat uneasily with Labour's broader approach and in this sense have yet to attain mainstream policy status. Again we state: promoting sustainable transport is by no means all about spending billions of pounds on expensive public transport schemes.

One curious aspect to all of this is the more-than-occasional perception of conceited self-congratulation among ministers, their civil service and costly array of special advisers. The view is often heard that British appraisal techniques are among the best and most sophisticated in the world, the implication being that we are more likely to be getting right what others are apparently getting wrong. This is a remarkable position, utterly irreconcilable with the situation 'on the ground' – outmoded and unsuitable infrastructure, an absurd project complexity fetish, resultant project cost inflation (witness the PPP debacle on the London Underground), more congestion and so on – but finds ongoing favour with those 'in the loop', especially ministers once they have gone native. Recently, in the House of Commons, rail minister Tom Harris appeared affronted that one of his colleagues 'said that few would claim that our network is the envy of Europe'. Harris continued to 'take him to task on that, because not only do many aspects of our rail industry outstrip performance in Europe, but the model of the British rail network is being examined by European governments who wish to privatise and restructure their own rail networks along our model' (*Hansard*, 2006, col 140). Can this be the same model of rail network the Labour Party savaged in opposition and exposed quite reasonably to be the laughing stock of Europe? Much clearly hangs on the way one chooses to interpret 'model', for it is difficult to believe that other European countries have now decided to undermine their existing railway systems at vast public expense.

It is against this background that we finalised the typescript for this book. We chose to do much of this in a rented apartment in Strasbourg, a city roughly twice the size of Plymouth but only half that of Glasgow (the places of our domicile), but which boasts five tram lines, an ingeniously extended and modernised railway station and a bus system of the quality only London among British cities enjoys. It also has a fully integrated ticketing system, something all but unheard of outside of the capital in Britain's deregulated public transport environment. We travelled to Paris on HS1 and continued on TGV Est, the fastest train in Europe. All of this brings sharply into focus the poor performance of much of Britain's transport compared with that of our major European partners – despite what the Commission for Integrated Transport (CfIT, 2007) might say – and it is perhaps understandable that we are disheartened about what successive British governments have achieved.

To a greater or lesser extent, this disappointment resonates in the texts of our fellow contributors, and we should like to take this opportunity to express our sincere thanks to them for writing excellent chapters and making our job as editors enjoyable as we strove to meet an extremely tight deadline. Phil Goodwin joined us towards the end of our *séjour* in Strasbourg for splendid discussions about the book, transport policy and, of course, the relative merits of French and German cheese. We are extremely grateful for his additional input to this project. Our commissioning editor at The Policy Press, Emily Watt, provided excellent administrative support and we also very much like the cover picture she sourced! On the subject of visuals, Jamie Quinn, of the University of Plymouth's Cartographic Resources Unit, seems perpetually to be drawing the short straw as this is the third of our books in the last couple of years for which he has produced the artwork. Thank you, Jamie. We will keep supplying the liquid incentives. Becky Skinner dug up more than we ever knew about walking and cycling, and Steve Bennett took time out from answering erroneous calls from the *News of the World* about his refereeing skills to cast a critical eye over the text. Finally, our friends and families – especially Andrea – are, as always, due great credit for all of their support and encouragement, despite the absences and hassles we really must stop imposing as we go about our jobs. At least we take you for nice meals occasionally.

We hope you enjoy this collection of essays, which, as is our editorial wont, we have done our best to fashion into a coherent story. If you are reading them on a journey in Britain, the chances are you will have plenty of time to ponder their contents.

Iain Docherty and Jon Shaw
Somewhere between Speyside and Islay, May 2008

Notes

[1] See, for example, Dorling (2006). He mentions D:Ream too, and calls for a budding lyricist to come up with words for Labour's 2010 campaign song! No doubt there will soon be a Prime Ministerial Decree on the matter from the Desk of the Supreme Leader.

[2] Perhaps less so if we researched other areas of public policy.

References

CfIT (Commission for Integrated Transport) (2007) *Are we there yet? A comparison of transport in Europe*, London: CfIT, www.cfit.gov.uk/docs/2007/ebp/index.htm (accessed 11 January 2008).

DETR (Department of the Environment, Transport and the Regions) (1998) *A new deal for transport: Better for everyone*, Cm 3950, London: The Stationery Office.

Docherty, I. and Shaw, J. (eds) (2003) *A new deal for transport? The UK's struggle with the sustainable transport agenda*, Oxford: Blackwell.

Dorling, D. (2006) 'Inequalities in Britain 1997-2006: the dream that turned pear-shaped', *Local Economy*, 21, pp 353-61.

Grant Thornton (2008) *Connecting for competitiveness: The future of transport in the UK city regions*, London: Grant Thornton LLP.

Hansard (2006) Volume 450, 11 October, col 140, www.publications.parliament.uk/pa/cm200506/cmhansrd/cm061011/halltext/61011h0011.htm (accessed 11 January 2008).

List of acronyms

ABP	Associated British Ports
ACOPS	Advisory Committee on Protection of the Sea
APD	Air Passenger Duty
AQMA	Air Quality Management Area
ATOC	Association of Train Operating Companies
BA	British Airways
BBC	British Broadcasting Corporation
BCR	benefit–cost ratio
BCV	Bakerloo, Central and Victoria (London Underground lines)
BERR	Department for Business, Enterprise and Regulatory Reform
BR	British Rail
BRT	Bus Rapid Transit
CBA	cost–benefit analysis
CEO	Chief Executive Officer
CfIT	Commission for Integrated Transport
CO_2	carbon dioxide
DB	*Deutsche Bahn* (German rail)
DfT	Department for Transport
DLR	Docklands Light Railway
DoT	Department of Transport
DRDNI	Department for Regional Development Northern Ireland
DUP	Democratic Unionist Party
EARL	Edinburgh Airport Rail Link
EC	European Commission
ECMT	European Conference of Ministers of Transport
EEA	European Environment Agency
ETS	Emissions Trading Scheme
EU	European Union
FDI	Foreign Direct Investment
GARL	Glasgow Airport Rail Link
GDP	Gross Domestic Product
GLA	Greater London Authority/Greater London Assembly
GLC	Greater London Council
GNER	Great North Eastern Railway
GOR	Government Office for the Region
GVA	gross value added
HGV	heavy goods vehicle
HLOS	High Level Output Specification
HS1	High Speed 1
HSR	high-speed rail
HST	high-speed train

IATA	International Air Transport Association
ICAO	International Civil Aviation Organization
ICE	InterCityExpress
infracos	infrastructure companies
IMO	International Maritime Organisation
IROPI	Imperative Reasons of Overriding Public Interest
ISC	Infrastructure Service Charge
JLE	Jubilee Line extension
JNP	Jubilee, Northern and Piccadilly (London Underground lines)
KLM	*Koninklijke Luchtvaart Maatschappij* (Royal Dutch Airlines)
km	kilometre
km/h	kilometres per hour
KSI	killed and seriously injured
LCC	low-cost carrier
LIP	Local Implementation Plan
LNG	liquid natural gas
LRT	London Regional Transport
LSP	London Service Permit
LTP	Local Transport Plan
LTS	Local Transport Strategy
LUL	London Underground Limited (*not* a rude word in Dutch)
M	motorway
MCA	Maritime and Coastguard Agency
MP	Member of Parliament
MtC	million tonnes of carbon
MTR	Mass Transit Railway
NAO	National Audit Office
NATA	New Approach To Appraisal
NCS	National Cycling Strategy
NIMBY	not in my back yard
NIR	Northern Ireland Railways
NO_2	nitrogen dioxide
NO_x	nitrogen oxides
NWS	National Walking Strategy
OEF	Oxford Economic Forecasting
OPRAF	Office of Passenger Rail Franchising
ORR	Office of the Rail Regulator/Office of Rail Regulation
PESTEL	political, economic, social, technological, environmental and legal
PDU	*Plans de Déplacements Urbains* (Urban Travel Plan)
PM_{10}	particulate matter under 10 micrometres in diameter
PPP	Public–Private Partnership
PSA	Public Service Agreement
PSO	public service obligation

PTA	Passenger Transport Authority
PTE	Passenger Transport Executive
PUG	Passenger Upgrade
QC	Quality Contract
QP	Quality Partnership
RCEP	Royal Commission on Environmental Pollution
RDF	Route Development Fund
RFA	Regional Funding Allocation
ro-ro	roll-on/roll-off
ROSCO	Rolling Stock Company
RSS	Regional Spatial Strategy
RTC	Regional Transport Consortium
RTP	Regional Transport Partnership
RTS	Regional Transport Strategy
SACTRA	Standing Advisory Committee on Trunk Road Assessment
SDP	Strategic Development Plan
SECA	Sulphur Dioxide Emission Control Area
SNP	Scottish National Party
SO_2	sulphur dioxide
SOFA	Statement of Funds Available
SPV	special purpose vehicle
SQP	Statutory Quality Partnership
SRA	Strategic Rail Authority
SSL	subsurface lines (London Underground)
STAG	Scottish Transport Appraisal Guidance
TEU	twenty-foot equivalent unit
TfL	Transport for London
TGV	*train à grande vitesse* (high-speed train)
TIF	Transport Innovation Fund
TOC	Train Operating Company
TPI	Target Programme for Improvements
TPP	Transport Policies and Programmes
TSI-PRM	Technical Specification for Interoperability – Persons with Restricted Mobility
UK	United Kingdom of Great Britain and Northern Ireland
US	United States
VAT	Value Added Tax
VED	Vehicle Excise Duty
WCML	West Coast Main Line
WelTAG	Welsh Transport Planning and Appraisal Guidance
WHO	World Health Organization

Notes on contributors

Iain Docherty and **Jon Shaw** have published four books together on various aspects of transport geography and policy. In addition to this volume and its predecessor, *A new deal for transport? The UK's struggle with the sustainable transport agenda* (Blackwell, 2003), they wrote (with Danny MacKinnon) *Diverging mobilities? Devolution, transport and policy innovation* (Elsevier, 2008) and edited (with Richard Knowles) *Transport geographies: Mobilities, flows and spaces* (Blackwell, 2008). They were also joint recipients of the Scottish Transport Award for Young Transport Professional/Researcher of the Year in 2006.

Iain is Senior Lecturer and Director of MBA Programmes at the Department of Management, University of Glasgow. His research and teaching addresses a wide range of issues affecting connectivity, institutional change and regional competitiveness. Iain also acts as an adviser on strategic policy issues to a range of private sector, governmental and other organisations, including his role as Non-Executive Director of Transport Scotland.[1] He is the author of *Making tracks: The politics of local rail transport* (Ashgate, 1999).

Jon is Reader in Human Geography and Director of the Centre for Sustainable Transport at the University of Plymouth. He is also the UK and Ireland editor of the *Journal of Transport Geography*. He researches issues associated with mobility, accessibility and transport policy and governance and he is widely published in the academic and policy literatures in these areas. His other books are *Competition, regulation and the privatisation of British Rail* (Ashgate, 2000) and *All change: British railway privatisation* (McGraw-Hill, 2000).

Pedro Abrantes is Lecturer in Public Transport at the Institute for Transport Studies, University of Leeds. He previously worked at the University of Porto (Portugal) where he led the appraisal and optimisation of multimodal public transport networks in Lisbon and Porto. He has also advised Metro do Porto on demand forecasting, cost modelling, operational planning and network design issues relating to future system extensions. Prior to entering academia, Pedro worked for MVA Consultancy where he took part in pteg's Rail in the City Regions project and the Department for Transport's Road Pricing Feasibility Study.

Geoff Dudley is a research fellow in the Centre for Transport & Society at the University of the West of England, Bristol. He is a political scientist by discipline, and has also worked at the universities of Oxford, Essex, Warwick, Staffordshire and Strathclyde. He has a particular interest in the analysis of change processes, and has been Director or Co-Director of four Economic and Social Research Council projects that examine the dynamics of organisational and policy change. He also has a special interest in transport history, and has recently completed the official history of the government car service.

Phil Goodwin is Professor of Transport Policy at the Centre for Transport & Society at the University of the West of England, Bristol and Emeritus Professor at University College London (UCL). He was formerly Director of the Transport Studies Unit at the University of Oxford and UCL, and a transport planner at the Greater London Council. He was chair of the advisory panel helping to write the 1998 White Paper *A new deal for transport*. Phil has been a member of the Standing Advisory Committee on Trunk Road Assessment, a non-executive director of the Port of Dover, and adviser to parliamentary committees, UK government departments, local government, transport companies, the European Commission and foreign governments. His published research has included key references on demand analysis, traffic forecasts, elasticities and transport policy.

Brian Graham is Professor of Human Geography at the University of Ulster. He is a Chartered Geographer of the Royal Geographical Society (with the Institute of British Geographers) and was formerly chair of its Transport Geography Research Group. Brian is a member of the editorial boards of the *Journal of Transport Geography* and *Transport Reviews* and has published widely on many aspects of air transport. His present research interests focus on the interconnections between air transport, economic development and the environment. He is the author of *Geography and air transport* (Wiley, 1995), has acted as an adviser on aviation matters to government departments in Northern Ireland and is a director of Air Route Development (NI) Ltd.

Richard D. Knowles is Professor of Transport Geography at the University of Salford and a member of the Research Institute for the Built and Human Environment. He is editor of the *Journal of Transport Geography* and co-editor of Ashgate's *Transport and mobility* monographs. His research focuses on the effects of transport policy changes, including bus deregulation and rail privatisation, and the impacts of new transport infrastructure. Richard's books include *Transport geographies: Mobilities, flows and spaces* (Blackwell, 2008), *Modern transport geography* (Belhaven 1992; Wiley, 1998) and *Scandinavia* (Paul Chapman, 1991). In 2004 he received the Ullman Award in Transportation Geography from the Association of American Geographers.

Danny MacKinnon is Senior Lecturer in Geography at the University of Aberdeen. He is an economic and political geographer with interests in regional economic development, devolution and transport policy. He has recently completed a study of devolution and transport policy in the UK with Jon Shaw and Iain Docherty, the results of which are published in *Diverging mobilities: Devolution, transport and policy innovation* (Elsevier, 2008). Another recent project focused on the geography of employment relations in the privatised rail industry in Britain.

Graham Parkhurst is Reader in Sustainable Mobility in the Centre for Transport & Society at the University of the West of England, Bristol, where he leads the MSc in Transport Planning and teaches transport policy, economics and appraisal.

Graham's academic background is in psychology, anthropology and geography and he has conducted research on transport policy and planning since 1991, covering a range of economic and environmental transport problems in both rural and urban study contexts. His current interests include regional transport strategies, the climate change implications of in-vehicle comfort needs, the mobility needs of the ageing population and the promotion of walking and cycling.

David Pinder is Emeritus Professor of Geography at the University of Plymouth. Since the early 1980s his research and publications have centred on the closely related themes of ports, shipping, energy and coastal environmental degradation. In 2003 he was elected a Foreign Fellow of the Royal Netherlands Academy of Arts and Sciences in recognition of his work in these fields. Since 1991 he has also chaired the Devon and Cornwall Rail Partnership, which aims to maximise rural railways' economic, social and environmental benefits for local communities.

John Preston is Professor of Rail Transport at the Transportation Research Group at the University of Southampton and is the Director of Southampton Railway Systems Research. He was previously director of the Transport Studies Unit at the University of Oxford. He has held over 100 research grants and contracts and has published over 160 articles, book chapters, conference and working papers. His research in transport covers demand and cost modelling, regulatory studies and land-use and environment interactions, with a particular emphasis on rail. He has been an adviser to the railway industry's Passenger Demand Forecasting Executive and is currently expert adviser on rail to the House of Commons Transport Committee and the National Audit Office (NAO).

Tom Rye is Professor of Transport Policy and Mobility Management at Napier University, where his research activities cover mobility management, parking management, travel plans, concessionary fares, public transport scheme development and evaluation, and the development of local and regional transport policy. He has also carried out work on cross-national comparisons of transport policy implementation. During much of his time at Napier he has been seconded part time to the transport consultancy Colin Buchanan, and to the City of Edinburgh Council, and he maintains close links with government and industry. Tom is also Chair of the US Transportation Research Board's Parking Management Sub-committee, and a member of the European Platform on Mobility Management's Task Force on mobility management in Europe.

Rodney Tolley taught for over 30 years at Staffordshire University, where he published widely in the field of non-motorised transport planning. He edited three editions of *The greening of urban transport: Planning for walking and cycling in western cities* (Belhaven, 1990; Wiley 1997; Woodhead, 2003), which has been described as the 'bible' of green mode planning, and he served as specialist technical adviser to the UK government inquiry into walking in 2001. Rodney is now Director of Walk21, a non-governmental organisation that raises international awareness of walking issues and supports professionals in the delivery of best practice. As an independent consultant, his focus is primarily on walkability, accessibility, wayfinding and pedestrian amenity in public spaces, streets and arterial roads.

Geoff Vigar is Director of the Global Urban Research Unit and Senior Lecturer in the School of Architecture, Planning and Landscape at the University of Newcastle upon Tyne. His research focuses on governance with an emphasis on the construction and salience of environmental and social issues, and policy process concerns. These issues are typically explored through analyses of spatial planning practice and infrastructure development. He is the author of *Planning, governance and spatial strategy in Britain* (Macmillan, 2000) and *The politics of mobility: Transport, the environment and public policy* (Spon, 2002).

Peter White is Professor of Public Transport Systems at the University of Westminster. He is the author of the textbook *Public transport: Its planning, management and operation* (first edition 1976, fifth edition to be published by Taylor & Francis/Routledge in 2008) and many published papers. He is a co-author of *The demand for public transport: A practical guide* (Transport Research Laboratory, 2004). His research in recent years has focused on the effects of privatisation and deregulation in the coach and local bus industries, and the impacts of rail privatisation in Britain. He has a particular interest in quality of service factors affecting public transport demand in addition to well-established variables such as fare and service frequency. Peter has acted as specialist adviser to parliamentary committees in respect of the rail industry, rural bus services, the bus industry and education transport.

Christian Wolmar is a writer and broadcaster specialising in transport. He has spent nearly all of his working life as a journalist, and was at *The Independent* from 1989 to 1997, mostly as transport correspondent. Although he mainly concentrates on transport matters, he covers other social policy issues and has written on a wide range of subjects from cricket to the Private Finance Initiative. His books include *Stagecoach* (Orion, 1999), an account of the firm that rose from nothing to the FTSE 100 in 20 years; *On the wrong line* (Aurum, 2005), the story of British rail privatisation first published as *Broken rails* in 2001; *The subterranean railway* (Atlantic, 2004), a celebration of the London Underground's pioneers; and *Fire and steam* (Atlantic, 2007), the highly acclaimed history of railways in Britain.

Note

[1] The opinions expressed in this book are those of the authors and do not represent the official view of the Agency.

Part One
Policy and politics

ONE

New deal or no new deal? A decade of 'sustainable' transport in the UK

Jon Shaw and Iain Docherty

The Blair government's *New deal for transport* (DETR, 1998a) was born in a wave of optimism in the 1990s. The New Deal moniker was in fact employed by New Labour across a range of policy areas to demonstrate the return of proactive state intervention and social conscience to politics after 17 years of neoliberal-inspired marketisation under the Conservatives (Giddens, 2000). It was not exactly Keynesian in character, however, emphasising the virtues of a 'Third Way' arguably closer to Milton Friedman than either Keynes or J. K. Galbraith, Friedman's celebrated intellectual opponents. Indeed, although the New Deal programmes were – like Franklin Delano Roosevelt's original in depression-era America – billed as a radical departure from previous practice, in reality much of this departure was rhetorical in that many of the market-based elements of previous Conservative Party policies were retained. One defining characteristic of the New Deal for Transport, though, was its overt emphasis on sustainability, in the broadest sense. Motorised transport has been the bearer of huge economic and social benefit. It has literally driven the generation of wealth and provided countless opportunities for people to improve their life chances. It has also long been known that there are drawbacks with the way in which transport systems have developed: people are injured and killed in road traffic accidents, the air along busy streets does not smell very nice, waiting in traffic jams can be rather tiresome, and so on. But it is only within the relatively recent past that the scale of transport's *real* impacts has been anything like properly appreciated (and we are still learning); we now realise that the ways in which and how much we travel are capable of causing appreciable harm to entire populations. They can constrain economic development because congestion is not just irritating but also extremely expensive to businesses and individuals (Eddington, 2006); they can kill people not just by running them over but also by making them fat and unhealthy (Sloman, 2006); and they are not just bad for local air quality, they are also major contributors to global warming (Chapman, 2007).

The Stern Review (Stern, 2006) makes clear that the costs of global warming to the world economy could be catastrophic if nothing is done to arrest increasing carbon emissions, and perhaps its most significant contribution is laying to rest the idea that societies can only be 'rich and dirty' or 'green and poor'. Interestingly, though, while calling for some speedy action on transport, especially with regard to pricing, the review notes that emissions from the other sectors of the economy and society – energy supply, housing, industry and services – might be better tackled first on the grounds that it is cheaper and easier to secure 'quick wins' this way. This may be true, but it is, to some extent at least, unfortunate. Transport is responsible for around a quarter to a third of carbon emissions in most developed economies and is often the only major sector whose share of emissions is increasing (see Anable and Shaw, 2007); moreover, while all transport sectors are experiencing growth, those witnessing the most growth tend to be the most polluting (Chapman, 2007).

The extent of transport's impact on the environment, not to mention its negative side-effects on the economy and society, moved a small collection of policy wonks and opposition politicians to publish in 1996 a *Consensus for change* (Labour Party, 1996), which articulated a new direction for transport policy to make more sustainable the amount and manner in which we travel. Sadly, however, even after a landslide election victory in 1997, the envisaged shift towards what might reasonably be regarded as a more sustainable transport policy has never really taken place. Twelve years after *Consensus for change* (Labour Party, 1996) and a decade since *A new deal for transport* (DETR, 1998a), the ministerial successors to this visionary group will regard Stern's remarks on transport – which, incidentally, are not without thoughtful caveats – as a welcome 'get out of jail free' card. The transport analyst Stephen Glaister suggested that, following Stern – who prices a tonne of carbon dioxide (CO_2) emissions at £190 (as opposed to the Department of Food, Environment and Rural Affairs (Defra), which prices it at £4.80) – the CO_2 element of the tax levied on a litre of petrol would need only to be 14 pence (David Hume Institute, 2007). At the time of writing, fuel duty is already around 50 pence (DfT, 2007a) – partly a result of a 'Fuel Tax Escalator' introduced in the 1990s by the Conservatives and abandoned by Labour in 2000 (Lyons and Chatterjee, 2002) – and VAT accounts for another 13 to 14 pence, so this leaves the government with plenty of wriggle room with regard to how it responds in relation to CO_2 emissions. Certainly, it is unlikely that petrol tax as a proportion of the cost at the pump will increase much any time soon: Labour is experiencing its first consistent period of opinion poll deficit and the price of oil has reached a historic high, so sidestepping the issue of fuel tax increases absolves Gordon Brown's administration of appearing meaner to motorists than it already does. How long this will be a tenable position is unclear, for, notwithstanding the cost of oil it may be that the question moves from one concerning the theoretical price of carbon across all sectors to one of how much the price of petrol and diesel needs manipulating to prevent carbon reduction targets being undermined by continuing increases in car use.[1] Evidence shows that sustained price rises can reduce traffic growth (Goodwin et al, 2004; Graham and Glaister, 2004).

Looking back over the last decade, though, it is not as if Labour has been particularly disposed to doing all that much even when its opinion poll leads seemed unassailable and the Party sat on parliamentary majorities in excess of 150 (Docherty and Shaw, 2003). Aside from personal success in rescuing High

Speed 1 (HS1), the UK's first railway with a European standard line speed of 300 kilometres per hour, John Prescott, New Labour's first Transport Secretary, must regard progress in what he had earmarked as Labour's transport decade – *Transport 2010: The 10-year plan* (DETR, 2000a) followed *A new deal for transport* – as something of a disappointment, a litany of missed opportunities and political cowardice that has amounted in general terms to the managed decline of an already substandard transport system. The advent of devolution brought with it the hope of 'local solutions to local problems' (Tomaney, 2000; Adams and Schmuecker, 2005), but with the welcome exception of some modest rail schemes and a tramway in Scotland, it is debatable how much more the Labour-led administrations in Edinburgh and Cardiff achieved than their counterpart in Westminster in the years to 2007.[2] Only in London, also devolved but with far fewer powers than the Celtic nations, have circumstances coincided to produce real change of the kind that Prescott originally had in mind. Labour's response was to try and distance itself from the Mayor's most radical initiative of congestion charging (MacKinnon et al, 2008).

This book critically analyses transport developments in the UK in the 10 years following the publication of *A new deal for transport* (DETR, 1998a). After this general introduction and a discussion of how devolution has impacted on the formulation and implementation of UK transport policy, the chapters assess developments across each mode before switching tack to deal with some comparative issues, which bring the book to a conclusion. All have been written by experienced transport academics adhering to rigorous standards of evidence gathering, and the authors – as is to be expected – have been detailed and scholarly in arriving at the views they express. We asked the same of colleagues contributing to the precursor to this book (Docherty and Shaw, 2003), written after Labour's first term in office from 1997-2001. In that volume the mood was one of optimistic critique, recognising the difficulty of mobilising quickly what was in transport terms a cutting-edge agenda. This time, however, there is discernable frustration in the tenor of the contributions; while there has been progress in some areas, after 10 years and several high-profile statements of intent the Westminster government should by now have achieved a considerable amount more than it has, given ministers' initial optimism and strategic policy intentions. It is perhaps more difficult to judge the devolved administrations, as there is an extent to which they have been 'finding their feet' in a new political environment, although the first Mayor of London, albeit with the political experience of running the erstwhile Greater London Council and serving three terms as a Member of Parliament (MP), showed that it is possible to hit the ground running. By way of setting the scene for the discussions that follow, the remainder of this chapter sets out the relationship between transport and sustainability, and describes the general trajectory of Labour's 'sustainable' transport policy over the past decade. We also consider reasons why ministers have not promoted in office the New Deal for Transport to which they were apparently committed in opposition.

Sustainable transport as a political issue in the UK

It is possible to critique the concepts of sustainability and sustainable development on a number of levels, not least for their vagueness and openness to interpretation according to context and vested interests (Redclift, 1987; Pezzoli, 1997; Williams and Millington, 2004). The frequently cited definition advanced by *Our common future* (World Commission on Environment and Development, 1987, p 8) – development that 'meets the needs of the present without compromising the ability of future generations to meet their own needs' – is undoubtedly well intentioned, but can be picked apart relatively straightforwardly. In relation to transport matters, for example, Black (1998, p 337) makes the point that 'there is no limit placed on "future generations" and nothing is sustainable forever'. We would add that present needs for transport are unknown: we might well be aware as a society what it is that we consume, but this hardly equates with need (see also Turner, 1993; Farrington and Farrington, 2005). Despite such criticisms, so long as the terms of reference used in interpreting sustainability are clearly stated and the general limitations of such wide-ranging concepts are understood and accepted, we regard it as providing both a useful framework for analysing existing policies and a set of guiding principles for future development. For our purposes in this book, we subscribe to a conception of sustainability that emphasises the roughly equal significance of economic, social and environmental considerations. Rather like Stern, neither we nor our co-contributors take the line that economic development need be constrained to any significant degree by environmental policies and vice versa; nor do we think that 'social' policies need to be overlooked in the quest for economic or environmental benefit. In this context, then, promoting more sustainable transport is about crafting a suite of policies capable of influencing travel behaviour to appreciably reduce the environmental impact of transport systems, while still ensuring that they are capable of supporting economic growth and social inclusion.

Goodwin (1993) first advanced the notion of a 'green–gold coalition' to explore the assertion that transport policies introduced for environmental reasons could simultaneously benefit the economy. In the UK context, recent developments in London since the recreation of city-wide governance (Chapter Two) in 2000 offer support to his largely hypothetical discussion. Extremely heavy traffic in the centre of London had reduced the average speed of motorised journeys to those of the horse and cart (Newbery, 1990), emissions were high and public transport was unreliable and in need of heavy investment (Newman and Thornley, 1997; May and Gardner, 1999; Glaister and Travers, 2001). The would-be Mayor of London, Ken Livingstone, identified transport as the key priority in his election campaign, and on gaining office produced *The Mayor's transport strategy* (GLA, 2001). The document proposed a number of policies that would work together to address London's traffic problems: most famously, as we have already mentioned, Livingstone introduced a congestion charge in the centre of the city, but also of note were major improvements to bus services and a push to encourage the active modes of walking and cycling. Several years on, congestion and pollution have decreased, public transport has improved and people make more non-mechanised journeys (Chapter Nine; see also Santos and Shaffer, 2004; Prud'homme and Bocarejo, 2005; Transport for London, 2005, 2006; Leape, 2006). In other words, transport better serves the economy because journey times are more reliable; it better serves society and the economy because there is higher-quality public transport and people will receive the health benefits of being more active; and it better serves the environment because pollution is being actively tackled.

Livingstone is no doubt proud – and rightly so – of what he achieved, and, we suspect, would readily admit that he had plenty more to do when he lost the 2008 mayoral election to Boris Johnson. But London is atypical of both the UK's transport activity and its governance. It is a genuine (perhaps the leading – see MacKinnon and Cumbers, 2007; *The Independent*, 2007) World City, with a high population density and which already has (at least in spatial terms) a well-developed public transport network. Policy-wise, the Mayor not only has a wider range of transport powers at his disposal than any other UK conurbation, but also has geography in his favour: few Londoners have been negatively affected by the congestion charge because most do not drive into Central London during its operation periods, whereas many people from across the city have benefited from improved public transport. This is in stark contrast to much of the rest of the country where many people, especially in non-metropolitan areas, think they will be adversely affected by charging because they rely more on their cars in the absence of high-quality public transport systems (Anable and Shaw, 2007).[3] Indeed, in a spectacular public relations disaster for the government, over 1.7 million people signed a petition on the Prime Minister's website against national road-user charging, despite there having been no commitment to implement it (BBC, 2007). In this conundrum we can identify a key reason why, apart from in a small number of places and situations, sustainable transport remains talked about rather than acted upon. Attempting to change people's travel habits – from the largest provincial conurbation to the smallest town in which it is worth bothering to try – is a formidable endeavour that requires political bravery, risk taking and long-term planning, whose costs appear immediate but whose benefits will fall in a different electoral cycle; in short, politicians perceive it could cost them an election. This has always appeared odd to us because transport in the UK is never that much of an issue on which General Elections are fought, compared with, say, the Health Service, the economy and, latterly, immigration.

This said, the very fact that sustainable transport is talked about as much as it is and in such a wide range of forums is both encouraging and, in some ways, remarkable, because it has only really been on the political radar screen for around 20 years. Docherty (2003) notes the irony that the discourse surrounding UK transport policy was to change shortly after the publication of the most ambitious road-building programme advanced by the 1979-97 Conservative administrations. *Roads for prosperity* (DoT, 1989), containing proposals for 494 road schemes in its 'active programme', was a reaction to forecasts predicting enormous increases in road use that the existing network would have no hope of accommodating; Transport Secretary Paul Channon, bound by an intellectual straitjacket equating car ownership with freedom and economic development, announced that 'our main efforts to provide additional transport capacity in support of growth and prosperity must be directed towards widening existing roads and building new ones, and that a step change in the programme is essential' (*Hansard*, 1989, cols 483–4).

But serious challenges to this approach of 'predict and provide' were quick to arise. One issue was the environment. Two years after the publication of *Our common future* (World Commission on Environment and Development, 1987), which outlined the potential for an impending environmental crisis if current development trends were to continue, a meeting of the European Conference of Ministers of Transport (ECMT) received a number of papers arguing that transport was a large (and growing) part of the problem because of the sector's greenhouse gas emissions (ECMT, 1989). Of significance in undermining *Roads for prosperity* (DoT, 1989) was the point that the majority of these came from private road transport. At the same time, academic work was also exposing predict and provide as logically flawed and in so doing demonstrated the extent to which it was destined to fail even in its own terms. In essence, because of a range of factors including 'induced traffic' – the observation that building new roads generates more trips (SACTRA, 1994) – it would simply not be possible to build enough road capacity to cater for future demand in the way Channon envisaged: no matter how many roads the government could realistically build, congestion would still increase, especially since the demand for transport – and hence congestion – is geographically and temporally concentrated. This argument, initially advanced as the 'new realism' (Goodwin et al, 1991), invited policy makers to confront the uncomfortable reality that the only foreseeable outcome of the strategy they had deployed to make things better would in fact make them worse, not just environmentally, but also socially and economically.

In social terms, more attention was being paid to emerging concerns about the human and financial costs of transport-related pollution (which were estimated at around £17 billion per year) and the adverse health effects – principally linked to lack of exercise – of relying too much on private transport (RCEP, 1994; Hamer, 1996; Tolley, 2003; Sloman, 2006). Transport-related social exclusion, often a result of limited access to a car, was under renewed scrutiny in the light of fares increases and the contraction of public transport services in fragile communities after privatisation and deregulation (see Moseley, 1979; Lucas, 2004; Hine, 2008). With regard to economic matters, the Conservatives had become aware that continuing to pursue a policy of large-scale road-building was extremely costly – not least because of a series of well-coordinated environmental protests – and that cutting back its scope would realise savings for the Exchequer in a time of recession (Shaw and Walton, 2001). In a line that Goodwin could have written himself, the Department of Transport admitted that 'we cannot deal with the problems of increasing traffic simply by road building', noting in addition the need to 'strike the right balance between securing economic development, protecting the environment and sustaining future quality of life' (DoT, 1994, p 1). What this balance might consist of in policy terms was not expounded, but the fact that John Major's government had recognised that a change of approach would be necessary was significant. What, after all, would be the point of investing eye-watering amounts in new road space if the problem of congestion would continue to represent an equally eye-watering cost to the economy? The Confederation of British Industry famously calculated that congestion in the late 1990s was costing British business £15 billion annually, a figure that, although contestable, appeared in the early pages of *A new deal for transport* (DETR, 1998a) as partial justification for a strategic change of policy direction.

Against this background, the central point of the 'new realism' that transport conditions would continue to deteriorate unless policy makers embraced a suite of policy measures capable of promoting both modal shift and some form of demand *management* – as opposed to encouragement – becomes compelling. The new realist approach also requires better integration between transport modes (to allow more seamless non-car journeys) and between transport and other policy sectors (especially land-use planning to tackle sprawl and other decentralisation, which significantly increase the demand for travel, but also health, social security and so on), and to a greater or lesser extent these themes ran through both the Conservative government's *Transport: The way forward* Green Paper (DoT, 1996) and Labour's *Consensus for Change* document (Labour Party, 1996). The *Way forward* paper was stillborn in that, barring unimaginable scandal or other such 'events', the Conservatives were always going to be voted out of office at the end of their disastrous fourth term and in this sense it was only really *Consensus for change* that mattered. Mounting their vision for a more sustainable transport future on the back of a swingeing critique of Conservative policy, the document's authors argued that there was now agreement across a wide range of interests, including representatives of the roads lobby, that current trends in car usage were unsustainable. As such, in order to 'keep the country moving and breathing', transport policy would need to move 'beyond "predict and provide"' (Labour Party, 1996, pp 2, 18) towards the kind of ideas advanced by the new realism. A key plank of public transport strategy was to be support for a publicly owned and publicly accountable railway – as opposed to the privatised one the Conservatives had just introduced – promised by Tony Blair himself at the Labour Party conference (*The Independent*, 1995), although this particular pledge was dropped from Labour's 1997 manifesto and never actively pursued in office (Chapter Four). A commitment to undertake a wide-ranging review of the trunk road-building programme was, however, included (Labour Party, 1997).

Shortly after taking office in the spring of 1997, John Prescott, no doubt buoyed by the momentum of change that was ostensibly sweeping through the British political establishment, placed considerable faith in the new government's ability to deliver by proclaiming his now infamous hostage to fortune that 'I will have failed if in five years' time there are not many more people using public transport and far fewer journeys by car. It is a tall order but I urge you to hold me to it' (quoted in Friends of the Earth, 2000, p 1). He also appointed Phil Goodwin, principal architect of the new realism, as chair of the panel offering the new government expert advice on the preparation of *A new deal for transport*. There is little doubt either that Prescott was speaking with the best of intentions or that his commitment to the sustainability agenda was genuine (Docherty, 2003; see also Begg, 2007), but especially in hindsight his words, as noted by numerous commentators in mid-2002, were at best unduly precipitant and at worst rather misjudged. For, within weeks of his heady optimism, Prescott was being forced to realise just how tall an order bringing about change in people's transport behaviour was going to be.

From radicalism to pragmatism: 10 years of a 'sustainable' transport policy

It would be unfair to suggest anything other than that *A new deal for transport* contained a sound and well-contextualised analysis of the transport problems facing the UK in the late 1990s: incessant traffic growth and increasing congestion were linked with (for example) deteriorating air quality, climate change, social exclusion and rural sustainability. It would also, however, be incorrect to suggest that it advocated adopting some of the more radical solutions implied (and in some cases made explicit) by Labour's earlier statements. Potentially significant interventions such as motorway tolling and retail car parking charges were dropped from the final document following media displeasure and concerted lobbying by particular business groups such as the major supermarkets (Docherty, 2003). In the absence of powerful 'sticks' to force motorists out of their cars, emphasis was placed on 'carrots' designed to entice them out: key among these were proposed improvements to public – and especially bus – transport (increased service frequencies, extended hours of operation, higher-quality vehicles, enhanced integration, accessible real-time information), support for walking and cycling, integrated land-use policy and attempts to influence people's overall attitude to travel. Indeed, with its relatively modest policy measures, some critics argued that it fell short of the promised radicalism and vision and even that it was 'a poorly focused and indecisive document' (Glaister, 2001, p 3; see also Docherty and Hall, 1999).

Also of note was a subtle but significant shift in semantics towards the notion of 'integrated' rather than 'sustainable' transport. This need not necessarily have been problematic, but ministers failed to articulate what they actually meant by integration. Was it improved physical integration between buses and trains to make public transport more attractive? Was it integration between the car and public transport through policies such as park and ride? Or was it more general integration between transport and other policy areas to improve strategic linkages across the public sector?[4] This semantic shift was actually a manifestation of the often-claimed division between John Prescott and others, led by the then Prime

Minister Tony Blair, who had come to regard as dangerous the pursuit of what could be perceived by 'Middle England' – the sizeable constituency that both had brought Labour to power and by dint of lifestyle and income was likely to be most affected by policies to reduce car use – as a radical transport agenda. By the middle of 1998, Blair's desire to present his Party as business- and voter-friendly based on ephemeral ideas such as 'integration' and the 'Third Way' between market provision and state regulation was in the ascendancy (Docherty, 2003) and, judging by the content of subsequent transport documents, dropping the tag 'sustainable' was a mechanism employed to distance the government from measures that could be regarded as too overtly anti-car. The need to deliver progress on transport without alienating a powerful motoring lobby had become very apparent (Begg and Gray, 2004); integration, in its many forms, is the rhetorical device around which a politically more pragmatic approach to transport policy has been crafted (Shaw et al, 2006).

Following devolution in 1999, newly elected governments in Northern Ireland, Scotland and Wales became largely responsible for their own transport strategies (see below and Chapter Two), but ministers' plans for England were forthcoming in *Transport 2010: The 10-year plan for transport* (DETR, 2000a). The overall purpose of the strategy was to 'tackle congestion and pollution by improving all types of transport – rail and road, public and private – in ways that increase choice' (DETR, 2000a, p 1). A headline figure of £180 billion – around £150 billion in cash terms (Glaister, 2001), a fair proportion of which was to come from the private sector – was to underpin a decade-long programme of investment in road, rail and local transport initiatives. A great benefit of the 10-year plan was the length of its planning horizon, but a further retreat into the obfuscation of integration was very much in evidence (Docherty, 2001, 2003). Demand management would take second place to capacity enhancement and, as a corollary, the tackling of pollution would need to rely on a 'technological fix' rather than on policies capable of achieving more efficient infrastructure use or an absolute reduction in traffic levels, such as national road-user charging. Responsibility for this was passed off to local authorities, although precious little in the way of national-level support has ever been provided. *Transport 2010* offered the scenario that up to 20 towns and cities will have introduced some form of charging scheme by the end of the decade, although this was always optimistic given the lack of ministerial leadership and 'air cover' on offer for local authorities. To date only one authority – Durham – has adopted a charging scheme outside of London (Edinburgh tried but lost a referendum it did not actually need to have on the issue – see Gaunt et al, 2007). One recent development – the Transport Innovation Fund (TIF) – ties central government investment in local transport infrastructure to the requirement for local authorities to adopt some kind of charging scheme. The 10 authorities of Greater Manchester have submitted admissible proposals and some smaller towns and cities have also shown interest (*Transport Times*, 2007), although given the government's ongoing lukewarm attitude to national road pricing – the most recent transport discussion paper *Towards a sustainable transport system* described it as 'a decision for the future' (DfT, 2007b, p 13) – there is a strong sense in which the TIF can be interpreted as a bribe bolted onto pre-existing policy.

The absence of any meaningful demand management strategy in *Transport 2010* meant that the government had boxed itself into a corner: the only way out of congestion would be to build more infrastructure. Future congestion arising from induced traffic would of course be somebody else's problem, but at least some major investment in roads and railways would be required in current budget cycles. Significant problems in the rail industry, partly of the government's own making (Chapter Four), have meant that most new money spent on trains and track has been to bring the quality of the system up to an acceptable standard rather than to increase capacity (Shaw and Farrington, 2003; Wolmar, 2005). On the other hand, the road-building programme, although recently checked by rampant project cost inflation, became more adventurous (Chapter Three). While the number of roads in the 'Targeted Programme for Improvements' (TPI) – that is, those schemes which ministers decide to see through to completion – had started at around 40 in 1997, this rose quickly to the equivalent of 210 by 2000 (Shaw and Walton, 2001). *Transport 2010* committed the government to the delivery of around 41 schemes in the TPI, 30 more trunk road schemes to be decided as a result of a programme of multimodal studies (see below) and 360 miles of motorway widening. This somewhat undermined previous claims that road building was being relegated to a 'measure of the last resort', and in the absence of any significant road pricing scheme also left the government with a bill considerably larger than it might have been expecting: dropping charging meant that ministers had deprived themselves of a stream of revenue that could have been used to fund infrastructure improvements at the same time as 'locking in the benefits' by discouraging induced traffic. Work for the Commission for Integrated Transport (CfIT) (2002) estimated that congestion would fall by around 40% if a national charging scheme were introduced as drivers thought twice before using their cars to make a journey for which they would have to pay an additional charge.

The re-emergence of road building so soon into Labour's first term of office was arguably additionally surprising given that part of its original commitment to an integrated transport policy was the introduction of a New Approach To Appraisal (NATA) in England to address the longstanding bias in favour of road building at the appraisal stage of transport infrastructure development (Hanley and Spash, 1993; SACTRA, 1994; Mackie and Preston, 1998; see also Chapter Three). An equivalent, the Scottish Transport Appraisal Guidance (STAG), has been adopted north of the Border and the Welsh Transport Planning and Appraisal Guidance (WelTAG) now pertains to Wales. Under NATA, traffic congestion would be seen as a transport problem as opposed to simply a roads problem, and in the search for 'solutions' a range of modal options would be considered on an equal footing. In addition, two new appraisal criteria, those of accessibility and integration, were introduced alongside the existing three of economy, safety and environment. Accessibility was to be concerned with 'the "ease of reaching" opportunities (jobs, shops, leisure activities) or the "ease of being reached" by contacts' (DETR, 1998b, para 2.15), whereas integration was, as we have noted, far less tightly defined.

An excellent opportunity to demonstrate the utility of NATA was the programme of multimodal studies, which was to form an important component of Labour's integrated transport policy. This series of 22 studies commenced in 1999 to investigate potential solutions to traffic congestion problems on England's transport network (Marsden, 2005). They varied in their geographical scope, from large area-based studies such as London to south Wales and the south west of England to much smaller investigations focused on specific transport corridors such as the A453 from the M1 to Nottingham. Consistent with the spirit of NATA, the studies were to avoid focusing on road-based solutions and instead 'look at the contribution that all modes of transport and traffic management might make – including road, rail, bus and light rail, as well as walking and cycling' (DETR, 2000b, para 4.3). Road-user charging was also to be considered. The government's instruction was that, with the possible exception of the small-scale studies where fully worked-up multimodal solutions may not be appropriate, 'there should be a strong presumption against [providing more roads] unless all other options can be clearly shown to be impractical' (DETR, 1999, p 30). The consultants undertaking the studies advanced genuinely multimodal proposals, which involved a split in overall expenditure (which was around £30 billion) of around two-thirds for public transport and one-third for new roads (Shaw et al, 2006). Within each package, individual schemes had usually been taken by the consultants to be mutually reinforcing. The reverse, where the credibility of a package could be undermined by the loss of one or more constituent elements, was also generally true.

The ambitious size of the total investment package – in reality vastly in excess of anything that was likely to be funded – was largely due to Labour's failure to specify a budget for the process, and the 2002-06 Secretary of State for Transport, Alistair Darling, was later to rue that 'the studies did not have at the front of their mind the question of affordability and deliverability. I think if we were doing this again [affordability] most definitely would be [a criterion]' (House of Commons, 2003, p 50). Nevertheless, at this point Darling still had a number of options open to him. He might, for example, have decided to regard the studies as useful but impracticable and recommission them to more tightly specified criteria; he might have implemented some packages in full at the expense of others. Instead, in contradiction with both the consultants' recommendations and, worse, his own Department's previously stated intentions, he ignored most of the studies' public transport elements and sanctioned many of their road schemes. Despite the rejection (not just by Darling) of two road proposals in the Hastings area and other major schemes including the Stourbridge and Wolverhampton bypass, around 400 miles worth of road proposals were cherrypicked from the studies to be added to the TPI either immediately or following some additional development work (Shaw et al, 2006). No major rail schemes were taken forward and the only public transport package of note – which has since been dropped – was around £1 billion worth of investment in the West Midlands. The outcome of the Scottish equivalent of the multimodal studies – the Central Scotland Transport Corridor Studies – was somewhat more balanced, with the two recommended motorway projects amounting to 55-78% of the total budgeted spend, depending on how the figures are interpreted (Shaw, 2004).

Appraising transport investment

Darling's decisions obviously made something of a nonsense of the multimodal studies programme, but also serve to illustrate a broader point about Labour's attitude to appraisal: there appears to be inconsistency and a lack of transparency in government decisions – at UK and devolved levels – with regard to both the way in which appraisal techniques are employed and the extent to which their findings are taken account of in decisions over which policies or schemes should be taken forward.[5] Consider first the difference in approach taken in the approval of heavy rail schemes in London and the concessionary fares scheme for bus travel in England. New Labour ministers took around a decade to commit to part-fund Crossrail and the Thameslink Upgrade schemes – both to the tune of around 30% of their total cost – which they inherited from the Conservatives (who had done nothing with them).[6] Neither has a spectacular benefit-cost ratio (BCR) – 1.6 and 2.1 respectively[7] – but then the sums of money under consideration in the 'benefit' column are vast and London is in urgent need of such prestige schemes which promote the kind of connectivity increasingly expected within world and/or 'creative' cities (Florida, 2002; Docherty et al, 2004). The government now estimates that it will be spending around £7 billion on these projects, compared with their total cost of £21.5 billion.[8]

Investment on this scale is clearly not to be undertaken lightly since it represents a significant tranche of public funds, but such detailed deliberation seems not to have troubled the decision-making process employed to grant free bus travel to the over sixties and disabled people. The concessionary fares scheme was introduced across England in 2006 after similar schemes had proved popular in the devolved administrations (a longstanding scheme had been operating in London). It was first proposed in Gordon Brown's pre-election budget of March 2005 (HM Treasury, 2005) and was in operation the very next year (Chapter Five). A BCR has not been published, but we can guess that there are rather limited economic benefits and, because it is universal, such social benefits that do exist are poorly targeted. Whether or not inducing transport demand among pensioners counts as an environmental and/or a safety benefit remains to be seen. What is certain, however, is that the cost of the scheme is vast: currently it is around £1 billion per year, but this will rise quickly if experience in the devolved nations is a reliable barometer (Scottish Government, 2007; Welsh Assembly Government, 2007). On this basis, by the time Crossrail and the Thameslink Upgrade have been completed (2015 and 2017 respectively), ministers will have spent *at least* £5 billion more

– while spending about one-fortieth of the time thinking about it – on providing free bus travel for pensioners and working men aged 60-64 whether or not they actually need it, than on flagship infrastructure schemes for the capital.

Cynical observers might be tempted to reach two conclusions from all of this: first, that the government never really wanted to pay for the rail upgrades and kept finding excuses until pressure from the City could no longer be ignored; and second, that ministers could not resist a quick political win by trying to buy the 'grey' vote. Perhaps it would be better spending £1 billion per year making bus (and train) travel more appealing to all users given how the cost of using public transport has risen in real terms since Labour came to power, unlike the cost of motoring, which actually has fallen (Figure 1.1). Especially at a time when the importance of price signals in influencing transport behaviour is recognised as fundamental (Stern, 2006; DfT, 2007b), the fact that Labour has allowed this to happen as part of a so-called 'integrated' transport policy seems extraordinary.

In situations where consistent appraisal information for a range of competing schemes *is* known and publicly available, the question is not one of whether to use appraisal methodologies but how to interpret their results when choosing between schemes. Experience in Scotland is worth considering in this regard. In recent years the Scottish Executive/Government has quite overtly privileged economic growth as the most important aspect of transport infrastructure development (Docherty et al, 2007), and in something of a change in emphasis from the early days of devolution an ambitious collection of both road and rail projects is being pursued. Table 1.1 summarises the benefit-cost performance of the first set of road projects analysed by the 1999-2003 administration (under the central forecast traffic growth scenario), with schemes ranked from highest to lowest BCR. Those schemes adopted by the Executive are shown in bold. The schemes in italics

Figure 1.1: Real costs of road and public transport fares, 1997-2006

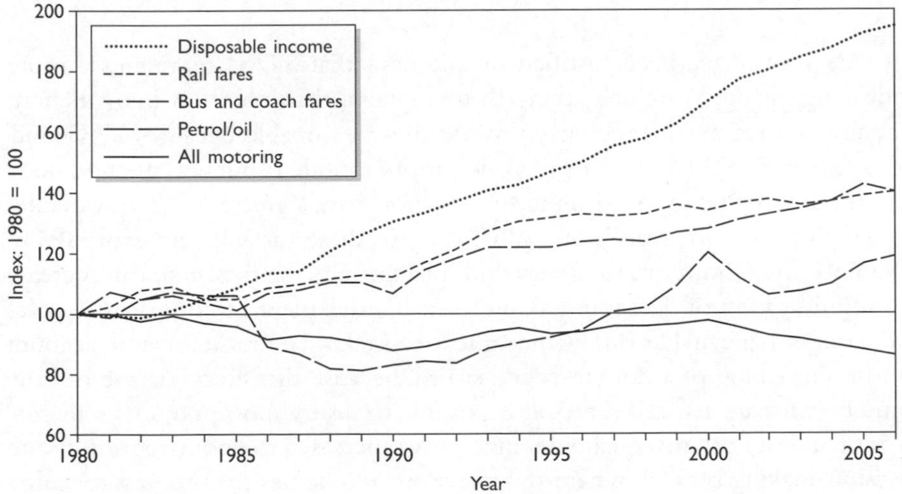

Source: DfT (2007c)

are those for which the Executive decided that local authorities should assume development responsibility. It is clear that no relationship existed between the relative BCR performance of the schemes and their success in retaining a place in the Executive's first roads programme – indeed, more recent decisions have added projects in the lower, rather than the upper, part of the table.

Table 1.1: Benefit-cost ratios of Scottish Executive road schemes

Scheme	BCR
A8000 Forth Road Bridge link motorway upgrade	24.49
M74 Northern Extension	16.69
A78 Three Towns Bypass	12.6
M8 Baillieston – Newhouse	8.26
A96 Fochabers Bypass	5.90
A92 Fife expressway	5.69
M80 Stepps – Haggs	5.16
A985 Rosyth Bypass	4.47
M77 Fenwick – Malletsheugh	4.18
New Kincardine Bridge and associated links	4.05
M8/M6 Fastlink	3.26
A90 Balmedie – Tipperty	2.48
A1 Haddington – Dunbar expressway	2.34
A68 Dalkeith Bypass	2.25
A830 Arisaig – Kinsadel	1.40
A9 Helmsdale	1.01
A96 Keith Bypass	0.78

Source: Scottish Executive (1999)

Such decisions have been justified on the basis that STAG represents a more wide-ranging, open-minded approach to appraisal than traditional cost-benefit techniques. To an extent, of course, this is entirely reasonable: because STAG (and, for that matter, NATA and WelTAG) is a more rounded appraisal methodology than the approach it replaced, policy makers now have a greater range of variables on which to base their decisions. What is more, these variables are expressed in different ways – both quantitatively and qualitatively – and as such can increase the sophistication of decision making, even if an element of comparing 'apples and oranges' is inevitable. But by the same token, taking more factors into account can be something of a double-edged sword, because the 'fuzzy' nature of how some benefits are assessed means it is possible to justify most potential schemes. In Scotland, at least, this quality seems to have increased the politicisation of the decision-making process, where the selection of schemes for progression came to depend as much on the ability of interest groups to articulate their demands, and to align them with the political cycle, as on the intrinsic economic value of the projects concerned. The Borders railway line – which under the DfT's BCR criteria would be at best described as 'low value for money' (National Assembly for Wales, 2006, p 7) – and the controversial Aberdeen Western Peripheral Route, which both impact heavily on high-profile marginal constituencies, are good examples.

Obviously the prioritisation of major infrastructure schemes – and, for that matter, many other investment decisions – is political, and we do not argue that this is wrong; in a democracy, strategic decisions over the allocation of public funds should be made by elected politicians. But there is also an obligation on ministers to be clear about what they are doing in order to avoid accusations of manipulating appraisal techniques and skewing their results for their own political ends. In Scotland, Labour and Liberal Democrat coalition ministers justified a series of schemes that did not align at all well with their stated primary aim of underpinning economic development, leading to a clear 'strategy gap' between stated policy intentions and actual policy implementation decisions (Shaw et al, 2005). Whether or not this will change under the new minority administration and following a 'refresh' of STAG remains to be seen. In England, the privileging of road building rather than (for example) expanding rail capacity has undermined the broader aim of pursuing an integrated transport policy, and in both countries concessionary bus fares were introduced with seemingly more adherence to political rather than transport – or indeed wider economic, social or environmental – logic (MacKinnon et al, 2008). And all this at the same time as hundreds of smaller, local and distinctly unglamorous transport improvements with compelling economic cases remain unfunded, as Eddington (2006) was keen to stress.

What future for transport under Labour?

By coincidence, we completed the typescript for *A new deal for transport? The UK's struggle with the sustainable transport agenda* (Docherty and Shaw, 2003), the precursor to this book, 20 years to the day after the BBC first aired 'A Bed of Nails', the episode of *Yes, Minister* in which the development of an integrated transport policy was added to the list of government initiatives that the Rt Hon Jim Hacker, Minister of State for Administrative Affairs, tried and failed to deliver. At first buoyed by the challenge – set by none other than the Prime Minister – Hacker's optimism was ground down after discussions with representatives of several transport sectors (each of whom argued that only their mode could deliver what the country required) and other truculent stakeholders. Hacker nevertheless devised and pressed ahead with his plans to rationalise Britain's transport system by eliminating duplication of effort and achieving important efficiencies, only to find himself in significant political trouble since this would entail unpopular changes in the Prime Minister's own constituency. Hacker's talent for political survival led him to a depressing but all-too-familiar conclusion: rather than try to implement an integrated transport policy, it was better to do nothing and avoid antagonising politicians and their electorates who were highly resistant to change, especially change driven by public policy imperatives.

A key theme running through *Yes, Minister* is the power of 'vested interests' intent on retaining the status quo to ensure 'good government'. Indeed, during the course of Hacker's efforts, Bernard Woolley, his Principal Private Secretary, explains that each section of the civil service exists to protect its own interests, and those of the stakeholders operating in relevant allied sectors. Although Hacker and his Department were fictitious, it has long been acknowledged that *Yes, Minister* was an incisive and not wholly inaccurate – albeit highly influenced by public choice theory (see Buchanan et al, 1978) – portrayal of affairs in government and the nature and influence of vested interests is worth considering in assessing Labour's record in transport. Why have ministers not pursued in government the kind of sustainable transport policy they had outlined in opposition? What influences and interests have militated against radical change? How might politicians begin to take on these interests to deliver better, more sustainable transport?'[9] The allegory of the traffic jam we have employed to title this book is not only that it summarises the daily battle between individual liberty and the wider common good in which neither wins,[10] but also that, in the words of James Taylor's song of the same name (now over 30 years old), continuing to do nothing about the negative externalities of transport is to drive (slowly) 'down the road to ruin'. The unfettered perpetuation of current transport trends will contribute more and more towards the unpleasant side-effects of a world development trajectory predicated upon the lavish consumption of fossil fuels. As we have tried to show in this chapter, it is not that ministers have not recognised this, it is just that they have not done all that much about it.

The usual empirical explanations, of course, are that transport's long-term nature does not align with electoral cycles and that the government has been scared of being seen as overtly anti-car. Considering the matter in more theoretical terms might lead to the conclusion that transport – or, indeed, sustainability more generally – is insufficiently important to constitute a 'state strategy' in which to invest significant resources/political capital in persuading people to alter their travel behaviour (see Jessop, 1990), or that with the exception of the London example there is not enough 'strategic capacity' (Jones and MacLeod, 1999; Sweeting, 2002) in government to make the case for *and* deliver significant change. A book of this nature is not the forum to develop such conceptual ideas (although see MacKinnon et al, 2008), but we have attempted in Table 1.2 to extend our empirical understanding by bringing together, using the standard PESTEL approach (which focuses on political, economic, social, technological, environmental and legal factors), a range of the pressures that act as forces counteracting change in the formulation of UK transport policy with the effect of 'jamming up' the system.

Table 1.2: PESTEL analysis of influences and constraints on transport policy making

Political	Economic	Social	Technological	Environmental	Legal
Lack of political will for radical change, ostrich mentality	Globalisation of world economy	Car-owning democracy/ consumerist attitudes to transport	No 'technological fix' yet apparent	Carbon emissions and climate change policy agenda	Response to climate change from European and global institutions
Short-termist, incremental political culture	Treasury attitude to value of infrastructure and capital rationing	Individualism and the 'right to mobility' (eg the freedom to fly)	Appraisal and modelling techniques limited and can be manipulated	Impact of climate change on transport infrastructure	Constitutional issues: devolution, potential independence, etc
Civil service risk aversion	Ideological fixation with competition	Feminisation and increasing complexity of transport demand	Reliance on expertise of consultancies and financial sector who have their own agenda	Uncertain impact of emissions trading	Developing law in areas pertaining to transport, ie regulation
Attitudes and electoral importance of 'Middle England'	Increasing costs of congestion	Evolving lifestyle trends	Project complexity	Local area air quality issues	Impacts of health and safety and disability discrimination legislation on procurement costs

Table 1.2: PESTEL analysis of influences and constraints on transport policy making (continued)

Political	Economic	Social	Technological	Environmental	Legal
Terrorism/security environment	$150 per barrel of crude oil and further price increases possible (*Transport 2010* assumed it would fall to $16 by 2005!)	Social exclusion and polarisation	Internet and information and communication technology changing patterns of physical mobility	Links between transport, activity patterns and public health	Human rights legislation and resulting new obligations on government and transport providers
Power and influence of transport and other vested interest groups	Overcrowding in the south east; lack of coherent central government regional policy	Fear of crime/antisocial behaviour	Quality and attractiveness of car industry products, and persuasiveness of their marketing	Continuing urban sprawl as a response to demographic and lifestyle change	Land use planning legislation
Complicated and fragmented governance structures	Renewed prosperity of major provincial cities	NIMBYism	Car efficiency gains lost through purchase of bigger/more powerful vehicles		
Politicians overawed by private sector and hold dim view of public sector's ability to deliver					

The table is by no means exhaustive (the technique itself having obvious limitations – there is no ranking of the importance of each individual factor given that they overlap with one another, for example) – but even using only those factors we identify it is clear that ministers face a challenge of considerable complexity and that the forces acting on transport policy come from all possible directions. Faced with this reality, it is tempting to suggest that developing a sustainable transport policy is an immensely difficult task, perhaps even a 'wicked problem' (Rittel and Webber, 1973; Conklin, 2006). But this would surely hold true for a variety of public policy areas – consider the sheer scope of the possible corresponding analyses of health policy, for example – and, in any case, serves to highlight rather than diminish the importance of the government doing something positive about the situation rather than burying its head in the sand. Perhaps the gamut of forces we identify really can be reduced to the issues of timescale and political timidity in taking on vested interests. Either way, in the final analysis it is difficult to avoid the conclusion that New Labour's ministers have just not been interested enough in promoting more sustainable transport to invest sufficient thought and take the political risk (such as it actually is) necessary to push for major change in both the amount and the manner in which we travel. None of this would surprise Wackernagel and Rees (1995, p 64) who, writing about sustainability more generally, note that the 'deliberate vagueness' associated with the concept is 'a reflection of power politics and political bargaining, not a manifestation of insurmountable intellectual difficulty'.

In many decades to come it might be that the political recognition of transport's external problems in the 1990s is seen as the start of a process which, although faltering at first, ultimately led to radical change in the way in which and how much we travel. Glenn Lyons has compared the position of sustainable transport now with that of anti-smoking campaigners in the 1950s: who would have thought then that an activity positively encouraged in polite society would attain almost pariah status half a century later, with smoking bans now in effect across the UK and in a good many other jurisdictions.[11] History suggests that, although one single event might constitute the 'tipping point' (Gladwell, 2002), radical ideas often take time to locate themselves in public and political consciousness especially when the veracity of evidence produced in support of change is doubted by those with an interest in maintaining the status quo. Certainly in the last decade the Labour government has moved away from the worst excesses of predict and provide. Writing four years after Labour came to power, Shaw and Walton (2001) advanced the argument that the Party's approach to transport could be characterised as 'pragmatic multimodalism', where a partial return to road building is pursued alongside increased public transport investment in a policy compromise based on what it is politically realistic to deliver. This assessment, it seems to us, retains purchase today and given the track record ministers have developed in the last 10 years it is unlikely that anything genuinely radical will be attempted in terms of sustainable transport before significant political upheaval. Whatever the White Papers might say, nothing fundamental will change; the government has considered its hand and, for a variety of reasons, chosen to fold.

In closing this introductory chapter, we lay our own cards on the table. Undoubtedly there is some merit in a pragmatic approach, but politics should not obscure properly informed debate. Too often, the British approach to policy formulation – across all sectors – has been affectionately described as 'muddling through' (although 'muddling along' might be a better metaphor given the systemic and cultural preference to avoid setting meaningful outcome-focused objectives – rather than spurious targets – for government intervention). In policy terms, to *some* extent we agree with Banks et al (2007) who bemoan Labour's muddling and in so doing argue for more road building since there will always be particular nodes and corridors that justify such investment no matter what the (realistic) cost of carbon becomes. We also concur with the report's substantial caveat that some form of charging regime should be put in place to 'lock in' the benefits of new road capacity, although as geographers we are keen to ensure that the form of charging adopted does not simply encourage the diversion of trips and provide renewed momentum to the decentralisation and deconcentration of population and economic activity. At the same time, our sympathy with policy measures capable of capturing transport's true external costs stems from our attraction to the elegance of many of the ideas contained within the new realism (Goodwin et al, 1991). Indeed, we do not see a necessary contradiction between calls for new road building on the one hand, and arguments for demand restraint on the other.

We believe first and foremost in good transport – good for the economy, society and the environment, but also good for the user. As such we reject the view that new infrastructure (including roads) is unnecessary on the grounds that a high-quality transport service depends on high-quality infrastructure, be that motorways, urban metros, buses, cycle paths or the public realm for pedestrians. We do not think it outrageous to suggest that a good journey experience is the right of the traveller. But we are also aware that with rights come responsibilities, and as such we would argue in favour of genuinely radical demand management and a concerted effort to reduce the need to travel; much contemporary mobility – at least in the way it is currently expressed – is fundamentally superfluous (see Lyons and Loo, 2008). In our view, people should pay the true external costs of their travel choices (and in some cases, such as bus journeys, these may well be lower than at present), policy should reduce the need for mobility through active planning and management, and government should ensure that regulation and concerted investment produces excellent infrastructure and service provision. In other words, we should not travel – other than by walking and cycling – when we do not need to, but when we do, and we pay the true external costs for the privilege, the experience should be first class. We do not believe this is in any way inconsistent with the idea of a 'green–gold coalition' (Goodwin, 1993), but it does move away from predict and provide, the new realism and pragmatic multimodalism. It is instead a kind of 'progressive realism', inherently positive in outlook and fully cognisant of the economic, environmental and social dimensions of sustainability.

Notes

[1] This point was raised by Phil Goodwin at a round table discussion on UK transport policy on 5 December 2007, involving most of the authors contributing to this book.

[2] Transport developments in Northern Ireland have taken place against a backdrop of on-and-off devolution stemming from local political squabbles between unionists and nationalists.

[3] There are also concerns about 'big brother' satellite tracking. This is curious since the near ubiquity of mobile phones, which consistently transmit their location to their host network, means that most of the population are already volunteering detailed information about their journey-making habits.

[4] This last form of integration – attempting to tackle the 'silo' mentality often associated with large organisations and institutions, especially governments (Jessop, 2000; Newman, 2005) – is notoriously difficult and seems to stretch the limits of policy endeavour.

[5] Fittingly, modern appraisal techniques, founded on the longstanding process of benefit-cost ratio (BCR) analysis, first emerged as a means of prioritising projects in Roosevelt's New Deal: see Adler and Posner (2001).

[6] The idea for Crossrail can be traced back to Isambard Kingdom Brunel, although more recently a version was formally proposed in the 1970s and the current incarnation is associated with a recommendation in the Central London Rail Study of 1989.

[7] Others, estimating greater agglomeration benefits, have estimated 3.0 and 2.6 respectively: see Chapter Four.

[8] These delays significantly increased the overall cost of the projects – their 1991 total combined price tag in current prices was astonishingly modest, at £3 billion (Buchanan and Volterra Consulting, 2007; HM Treasury, 2007; Hughes, 2007). Even assuming a very sizeable cost overrun (see Flyvbjerg et al, 2003) by doubling the Treasury's 100% 'optimism bias', the overall cost would still only have been £9 billion in today's money.

[9] We acknowledge here the insights of another *Yes, Minister* afficionado, John Preston, who developed this analysis at the first authors' round table convened prior to the writing of this book. Interestingly, Sloman (2006, p 140) places considerable store in the analysis that elements of the civil service are holding back change, not least because they are unrepresentative of the population as a whole and do not share their transport experiences. As such, she argues, they 'simply do not see the wider problems of our car-dependent culture'.

[10] Versions of this statement have appeared in the writings of various authors but, so far as we are aware, the general sentiment can be traced back to Reuben Smeed and John Wardrop in the 1960s.

[11] This was in discussion with Jon over lunch at the 2008 Universities' Transport Studies Group conference.

References

Adams, J. and Schmuecker, K. (2005) 'Introduction and overview', in J. Adams and K. Schmueker (eds) *Devolution in practice 2006: Public policy differences within the UK*, Newcastle upon Tyne: Institute for Public Policy Research, pp 3-9.

Adler, M. and Posner, E. (2001) *Cost-benefit analysis: Economic, philosophical, and legal perspectives*, Chicago IL: University of Chicago Press.

Anable, J. and Shaw, J. (2007) 'Priorities, policies and (time)scales: the delivery of emissions reductions in the UK transport sector', *Area*, 39, pp 443-57.

Banks, N., Bayliss, D. and Glaister, S. (2007) *Motoring towards 2050: Roads and reality*, London: RAC Foundation.

BBC (2007) *Q&A: Road pricing*, http:// news.bbc.co.uk/1/hi/uk/6382211.stm (accessed 20 March 2007).

Begg, D. (2007) 'John Prescott: a politician ahead of his time', *Transport Times*, November, p 13.

Begg, D. and Gray, D. (2004) 'Transport policy and vehicle emission objectives in the UK: is the marriage between transport and environment policy over?', *Environmental Policy and Science*, 7, pp 155-63.

Black, W. (1998) 'Sustainability of transport', in B. Hoyle and R. Knowles (eds) *Modern transport geography* (2nd edition), Chichester: Wiley, pp 337-51.

Buchanan, J., Rowley, V., Breton, A., Wiseman, J., Frey, B., Peacock, A., Grimond, J., Johnson, N., Judgem, K., Legage, H., Grant, R., Whitely, P., Niskanen, W. and Ricketts, M. (1978) *The economics of politics*, London: Institute of Economic Affairs.

Buchanan, P. and Volterra Consulting (2007) *Crossrail – costs of delay*, London: Colin Buchanan and Partners.

CfIT (Commission for Integrated Transport) (2002) *Paying for road use*, London: CfIT, www.cfit.gov.uk/docs/2002/pfru/index.htm (accessed 14 January 2008).

Chapman, L. (2007) 'Transport and climate change: a review', *Journal of Transport Geography*, 15, pp 354-67.

Conklin, E. (2006) *Dialogue mapping: Building shared understanding of wicked problems*, Chichester: Wiley.

David Hume Institute (2007) *Transport strategy – with or without road pricing*, www.davidhumeinstitute.com/.../events%202007/transport%20seminar%20commentary.pdf (accessed 10 January 2008).

DETR (Department of the Environment, Transport and the Regions) (1998a) *A new deal for transport: Better for everyone*, Cm 3950, London: The Stationery Office.

DETR (1998b) *Guidance on the new approach to appraisal*, London: The Stationery Office.

DETR (1999) *Breaking the logjam: The government's response to the consultation*, London: The Stationery Office.

DETR (2000a) *Transport 2010: The 10-year plan for transport*, London: DETR.

DETR (2000b) *Guidance on the methodology for multi-modal studies*, volumes 1 and 2, London: DETR.

DfT (2007a) *Transport statistics Great Britain*, London: DfT.

DfT (2007b) *Towards a sustainable transport system*, Cm7226, London: DfT.

DfT (2007c) *Transport trends: 2007 edition*, London: DfT, www.dft.gov.uk/162259/162469/221412/190425/220778/trends2007a.pdf (accessed 14 January 2008).

Docherty, I. (2001) 'Interrogating the ten-year transport plan', *Area*, 33, pp 321-8.

Docherty, I. (2003) 'Policy, politics and sustainable transport: the nature of Labour's dilemma', in I. Docherty and J. Shaw (eds) *A new deal for transport? The UK's struggle with the sustainable transport agenda*, Oxford: Blackwell.

Docherty, I. and Hall, D. (1999) 'Which travel choices for Scotland?', *Scottish Geographical Journal*, 115, pp 193-209.

Docherty, I. and Shaw, J. (2003) *A new deal for transport? The UK's struggle with the sustainable transport agenda*, Oxford: Blackwell.

Docherty, I., Gulliver, S. and Drake, P. (2004) 'Exploring the potential benefits of city collaboration', *Regional Studies*, 38, pp 445-56.

DoT (Department of Transport) (1989) *Roads for prosperity*, London: HMSO.

DoT (1994) *Trunk roads in England: 1994 review*, London: HMSO.

DoT (1996) *Transport: The way forward*, London: DfT.

ECMT (European Conference of Ministers of Transport) (1989) *Transport policy and the environment*, Paris: OECD.

Eddington, R. (2006) *The Eddington transport study: The case for change: Sir Rod Eddington's advice to the government*, London: HM Treasury.

Farrington, J. and Farrington, C. (2005) 'Rural accessibility, social inclusion and social justice: towards conceptualisation', *Journal of Transport Geography*, 13, pp 1-12.

Florida, R. (2002) *The rise of the creative class ... and how it's transforming work, leisure, community and everyday life*, New York: Basic Books.

Flyvbjerg, B., Bruzelius, N. and Rothengatter, W. (2003) *Megaprojects and risk: An anatomy of ambition*, Cambridge: Cambridge University Press.

Friends of the Earth (2000) 'Paved with good intentions? Government transport plans', Press Release, 20 July.

Gaunt, M., Rye, T. and Allen, S. (2007) 'Public acceptability of road user charging: the case of Edinburgh and the 2005 referendum', *Transport Reviews*, 27, pp 85-102.

Giddens, A. (2000) *The third way and its critics*, Cambridge: Polity.

GLA (Greater London Authority) (2001) *The Mayor's transport strategy*, London: GLA.

Gladwell, M. (2002) *The tipping point: How little things can make a big difference*, Grand Rapids, MI: Abacus.

Glaister, S. (2001) 'UK transport policy 1997-2001', Address to the British Association for the Advancement of Science, Glasgow, 1 September.

Glaister, S. and Travers, T. (2001) 'Crossing London: overcoming the obstacles to Crossrail', *Public Money and Management*, 21, pp 11-18.

Goodwin, P. (1993) 'Efficiency and the environment: possibilities of a green–gold coalition', in D. Banister and K. Button (eds) *Transport, the environment and sustainable development*, London: Spon.

Goodwin, P., Dargay, J. and Hanly, M. (2004) 'Elasticities of road traffic and fuel consumption with respect to price and income: a review', *Transport Reviews*, 24, pp 275-92.

Goodwin, P., Hallett, S., Kenny, P. and Stokes, G. (1991) *Transport: The new realism*, Oxford: Transport Studies Unit, University of Oxford.

Graham, D. and Glaister, S. (2004) 'Road traffic demand elasticity estimates: a review', *Transport Reviews*, 24, pp 261-74.

Hamer, M. (1996) 'Clean air strategy fails to tackle traffic', *New Scientist*, 6 August.

Hanley, N. and Spash, C. (1993) *Cost benefit analysis and the environment*, Cheltenham: Edward Elgar.

Hansard (1989) Volume 153, 18 May, cols 483-4.

Hine, J. (2008) 'Transport and social justice', in R. Knowles, J. Shaw and I. Docherty (eds) *Transport geographies: Mobilities, flows and spaces*, Oxford: Blackwell.

HM Treasury (2005) *Budget Press Notice No 1: Investing for our future: Fairness and opportunity for Britain's hard-working families*, www.hm-treasury.gov.uk/budget/budget_05/press_notices/bud_bud05_press01.cfm (accessed 10 January 2008).

HM Treasury (2007) *GDP deflators: Latest figures*, www.hm-treasury.gov.uk./economic_data_and_tools/gdp_deflators/data_gdp_fig.cfm (accessed 14 January 2008).

House of Commons (2003) *Jam tomorrow? The multi modal studies investment plans: Third report of the Transport Committee. Session 2002-2003*, London: The Stationery Office.

Hughes, M. (2007) 'Cross-London projects languish on the back burner', *Railway Gazette International*, February.

Jessop, B. (1990) *State theory: Putting capitalist states in their place*, Oxford: Blackwell.

Jessop, B. (2000) 'Governance failure', in G. Stoker (ed) *The new politics of British urban governance*, Basingstoke: Macmillan.

Jones, M. and MacLeod, G. (1999) 'Towards a regional renaissance? Reconfiguring and rescaling England's economic governance', *Transactions of the Institute of British Geographers*, pp 295-313.

Labour Party (1996) *Consensus for change: Labour's transport strategy for the 21st century*, London: Labour Party.

Labour Party (1997) *New Labour: Because Britain deserves better*, www.psr.keele.ac.uk/area/uk/man/lab97.htm (accessed 10 January 2008).

Leape, J. (2006) 'The London congestion charge', *Journal of Economic Perspectives*, 20, pp 157-76.

Lucas, K. (2004) *Running on empty: Transport, social exclusion and environmental justice*, Bristol: The Policy Press.

Lyons, G. and Chatterjee, K. (eds) (2002) *Transport lessons from the fuel tax protests of 2000*, Aldershot: Ashgate.

Lyons, G. and Loo, B. (2008) 'Transport directions to the future', in R. Knowles, J. Shaw and I. Docherty (eds) *Transport geographies: Mobilities, flows and spaces*, Oxford: Blackwell, pp 215-26.

Mackie, P. and Preston, J. (1998) 'Twenty-one sources of error and bias in transport project appraisal', *Transport Policy*, 5, pp 1-7.

MacKinnon, D. and Cumbers, A. (2007) *An introduction to economic geography: Globalization, uneven development and place*, Harlow: Pearson.

MacKinnon, D., Shaw, J. and Docherty, I. (2008) *Diverging mobilities? Devolution, transport and policy innovation*, Oxford: Elsevier.

Marsden, G. (2005) 'The multi modal study transport investment plans', *Proceedings of Institution of Civil Engineers: Transport*, 158, pp 75-87.

May, A. and Gardner, K. (1999) 'Transport policy for London in 2001: the case for an integrated approach', *Transportation*, 16, pp 257-77.

Moseley, M. (1979) *Accessibility: The rural challenge*, London: Methuen.

National Assembly for Wales (2006) *Rail Infrastructure and Improved Passenger Services Committee – Memorandum from the Department for Transport (DfT)*, Cardiff: NAW.

Newbery, D. (1990) 'Pricing and congestion: economic principles relevant to pricing roads', *Oxford Review of Economic Policy*, 6, pp 22-38.

Newman, J. (2005) 'Bending bureaucracy: leadership and multi-level governance', in P. du Gay (ed) *The values of bureaucracy*, Oxford: Oxford University Press.

Newman, P. and Thornley, A. (1997) 'Fragmentation and centralisation in the governance of London: influencing the urban policy and planning agenda', *Urban Studies*, 34, pp 967-88.

Pezzoli, K. (1997) 'Sustainable development: a transdisciplinary review of the literature', *Journal of Environmental Planning and Management*, 40, pp 549-74.

Prud'homme, R. and Bocarejo, J.-P. (2005) 'The London congestion charge: a tentative economic appraisal', *Transport Policy*, 12, pp 279-87.

RCEP (Royal Commission on Environmental Pollution) (1994) *Eighteenth report: Transport and the environment*, London: HMSO.

Redclift, D. (1987) *Sustainable development: Exploring the contradictions*, London: Methuen.

Rittel, H. and Webber, M. (1973) 'Dilemmas in a general theory of planning', *Policy Sciences*, 4, pp 155-69.

SACTRA (Standing Advisory Committee on Trunk Road Assessment) (1994) *Trunk roads and the generation of traffic*, London: HMSO.

Santos, G. and Shaffer, B. (2004) 'Preliminary results of the London congestion charging scheme', *Public Works Management & Policy*, 9, pp 164-81.

Scottish Executive (1999) *Travel choices for Scotland: Strategic roads review*, Edinburgh: Scottish Executive.

Scottish Government (2007) *Scottish Budget Spending Review 2007*, Edinburgh: Scottish Government.

Shaw, J. (2004) 'Transport choices? The Central Scotland transport corridor studies', *Scottish Geographical Journal*, 120, pp 289-310.

Shaw, J. and Farrington, J. (2003) 'A railway renaissance?', in I. Docherty and J. Shaw (eds) *A new deal for transport? The UK's struggle with the sustainable transport agenda*, Oxford: Blackwell.

Shaw, J. and Walton, W. (2001) 'Labour's new trunk-roads policy for England: an emerging pragmatic multimodalism', *Environment & Planning A*, 33, pp 1131-56.

Shaw, J., Hunter, C. and Gray, D. (2006) 'Disintegrated transport policy: the multi modal studies process in England', *Environment and Planning C: Government and Policy*, 24, pp 575-96.

Shaw, J., Docherty, I., Begg, D. and Gray, D. (2005) *Building better transport? A critical overview of Scottish transport strategy*, Policy Paper Series 11, Aberdeen: Centre for Transport Policy.

Sloman, L. (2006) *Car sick: Solutions for our car-addicted culture*, Totnes: Green Books.

Stern, N. (2006) *Stern review on the economics of climate change*, London: HM Treasury, www.hm-treasury.gov.uk/independent_reviews/stern_review_economics_climate_change/sternreview_index.cfm (accessed 14 January 2008).

Sweeting, D. (2002) 'Leadership in urban governance: the Mayor of London', *Local Government Studies*, 28, pp 3-20.

The Independent (1995) 'Blair on defensive over rail', 16 January, http://findarticles.com/p/articles/mi_qn4158/is_19950116/ai_n14871782 (accessed 8 January 2008).

The Independent (2007) 'London: capital of the world', 22 December, p 1.

Tolley, R. (2003) 'Ubiquitous, everyday walking and cycling: the acid test of a sustainable transport policy', in I. Docherty and J. Shaw (2003) *A new deal for transport? The UK's struggle with the sustainable transport agenda*, Oxford: Blackwell, pp 178-97.

Tomaney, J. (2000) 'End of the empire state? New Labour and devolution in the United Kingdom', *International Journal of Urban and Regional Research*, 24, pp 675-88.

Transport for London (2005) *Central London congestion charging scheme impacts monitoring*, London:TfL, www.tfl.gov.uk/tfl/downloads/pdf/cclondon/impacts-monitoring-report-january-2005.pdf (accessed 16 April 2008).

Transport for London (2006) *Impacts monitoring programme: Fourth annual report*. TfL, London. www.tfl.gov.uk/tfl/cclondon/pdfs/FourthAnnualReportFinal.pdf (accessed 16 April 2008).

Transport Times (2007) 'Manchester marches ahead in TIF bid', December, pp 4-5.

Turner, R. K. (1993) 'Sustainability: principles and practice, in R. Turner (ed) *Sustainable environmental economics and management: Principles and practice*, London: Belhaven, pp 1-36.

Wackernagel, M. and Rees, W. (1995) *One ecological footprint: Reducing human impact on the earth*, Gabricola, Canada: New Society Publishers.

Welsh Assembly Government (2007) *Press release: Economy & transport budget will deliver One Wales*, Cardiff:WAG, 6 November, http://newydd.cymru.gov.uk/news/ThirdAssembly/Business/2007/1867149/?lang=en

Williams, C. and Millington, A. (2004) 'The diverse and contested meanings of sustainable development', *The Geographical Journal*, 170, pp 99-104.

Wolmar, C. (2005) *On the wrong line: How ideology and incompetence wrecked Britain's railways*, London: Aurum Press.

World Commission on Environment and Development (1987) *Our common inheritance*, Oxford: Oxford University Press.

TWO

Devolution and the UK's new transport policy landscape

Danny MacKinnon and Geoff Vigar

Transport policy making has become increasingly complex in recent years as various 'intermediate' levels of governance between local authorities and central government have acquired a new prominence. In particular, the introduction of devolution has created new elected administrations in Scotland, Wales and Northern Ireland, and the English regions have also become more important as administrative units. Such transfers of power have not entirely satisfied arguments for reforming transport governance, however, as we demonstrate in this chapter. The emergence of new governing bodies raises important questions about the extent to which policies diverge and/or converge between jurisdictions, since there can be substantially different interpretations of what sustainable transport actually means in different places. Devolution granted the new Scottish Parliament and Welsh and Northern Irish Assemblies considerable latitude to determine their own policy priorities – indeed, one of its key underlying rationales is to foster distinctive 'local solutions' to 'local problems' (Adams and Schmuecker, 2005) – although in practice this tends to be balanced by pressures to ensure that devolved policies do not contradict those pursued by the central state (Smyth, 2003). MacKinnon et al (2008) note that the impact of devolution has received less attention in transport studies compared to neighbouring fields of enquiry such as economic development or health, although some research has considered the effects of institutional arrangements on transport policy implementation (Rye et al, 2003; Cole, 2005; Marsden and May, 2006; Docherty et al, 2007; MacKinnon et al, 2008).

This chapter examines the relationship between changing spaces of governance and transport policy across the UK. We begin by introducing the notion of geographical scale and considering its significance in the context of UK transport policy. This is followed by a discussion of policy divergence and convergence. We then provide a substantive examination of transport policy across the different spaces of governance in the UK. This is structured into two main parts. First, we outline the development of transport policy at the national scale, focusing particularly on the devolved jurisdictions of Scotland, Wales and Northern Ireland. Second, we assess developments at the subnational scale, highlighting the emergence of a stronger regional dimension, primarily in England, but also in

Scotland and Wales. A concluding section draws out the key points of the chapter and considers their implications.

'Rescaling' transport governance

Scale refers to the different *territorial levels* of governance – national, regional, local and so on. The process of 'rescaling' is therefore concerned with the redefinition and reallocation of rights and responsibilities between levels of governance, which in the UK as in much of Europe has resulted in greater prominence for both substate nations and regions and supranational organisations such as the European Union (EU) (Keating, 1998; Peck, 2001). The organisation of state powers at any particular scale is structured by contrasting processes of 'hollowing out', which refers to a loss of powers and responsibilities at the level of the state, and 'filling in', which involves the establishment of new organisational structures and policy priorities (Goodwin et al, 2005; Peck, 2001). UK transport governance has been subject to two main forms of rescaling over the past decade, each involving some decentralisation of power in conjunction with a certain consolidation or integration of existing governmental responsibilities.

The first of these concerns the devolution of responsibilities from the UK government to Scotland, Wales and Northern Ireland (and in a slightly different sense, to London) in 1999-2000 (Hazell, 2000; Keating, 2002). UK devolution was and remains essentially a political project associated with constitutional issues of identity and representation, but it was also informed by the idea – especially from the perspective of New Labour – of stimulating greater policy innovation and integration, not least to overcome the extremely centralised nature of the UK state and the 'silo mentality' evident in Whitehall (Cabinet Office, 1999; Jeffery, 2002). Despite its complex and asymmetrical nature, with different territories granted different powers and institutional arrangements,[1] devolution (outside of Northern Ireland) was implemented in a relatively smooth fashion underpinned by common Labour Party control of Westminster and the first devolved administrations, and increases in public expenditure. This extended first phase of devolution ended in 2007, however, with the entry of nationalist parties into government in Scotland, Wales and Northern Ireland, the political travails of the UK Labour government under the new Prime Minister, Gordon Brown, and the introduction of much tighter budget settlements.

The second key process concerns the renewed focus on cities and city-regions across the UK as the principal drivers of economic growth in a post-industrial, 'knowledge' economy (Jonas and Ward, 2007). This has focused attention on the perceived need for metropolitan-area, or city-region, management in order to promote a larger area for competitiveness purposes. At the same time, the metropolitan scale is also being mobilised to help integrate policies and deal with the externalities of growth and the tendency for 'free-riding' behaviour of smaller municipalities surrounding major cities (Buitelaar et al, 2007). Transport issues are often very much to the fore here (Grant Thornton, 2008) due to the complex nature of contemporary mobility patterns and a desire on the part of central government to maximise the impact of investment – especially in infrastructure – and avoid wasteful inter-authority competition for resources. This is partly driven by a business agenda of fast, congestion-free links to and from city cores, but also reflects the slow (and partial) adoption by policy makers of the compact city agenda, which advocates making best use of existing infrastructure and views regeneration as a means of moderating sprawl and the overall demand for transport (Guy and Marvin, 1999; Giuliano, 2004).

Policy divergence and convergence

The issue of policy divergence and convergence is concerned with how policy changes between geographical units or jurisdictions. Arguments for local decentralisation and devolution have emphasised the potential for this to foster innovation in policy making. Transport, in common with other devolved policy areas such as education, social services and local government, is characterised by autonomy in policy making in terms of the capacities of the devolved administrations to make different choices from Westminster (in its role as the domestic government for England) (Keating, 2002). At the same time, however, transport policy making is subject to a rather complex division of devolved and reserved powers.[2] Substantial policy autonomy under devolution also encourages direct policy comparisons to be made between jurisdictions, fostering policy competition and potentially leading to policy imitation and transfer, particularly in relation to popular measures that offer benefits to key sections of the population, such as concessionary fares (see below, and Chapters One and Five).

The unique blend of social, environmental and economic conditions within each territory is an obvious force favouring policy divergence. For example, deep rural issues and interests are relatively more prominent in Scotland, Wales and Northern Ireland than they are in England, creating greater pressures against policies that aim to reduce car use on which rural areas remain more dependent and to which there are fewer realistic alternatives (Smyth, 2003). The relative peripherality of such regions, coupled with historically lower levels of prosperity, results in a greater emphasis being placed on the importance of economic development and social inclusion compared to the south of England where prosperity and population density have fostered a preoccupation with congestion and quality of life concerns. At the subnational level too, economic and social conditions vary between different regions, with the transport needs of the Scottish Highlands and Islands or North Wales distinct from those of the Central Belt or the M4 corridor.

Policy dynamics are also influenced by the funding mechanisms that provide the finance to support different choices and outcomes. Here, the provision of block grant funding by Westminster allows the devolved administrations the flexibility to allocate funds according to local policy priorities, encouraging divergence. At the same time, however, the fact that such grants are raised on a common UK tax base may also encourage convergence since any decisions to provide more generous entitlements will spark protest from the rest of the UK, as was the case when the Scottish Executive chose to press ahead with free personal care for older people (Keating, 2002; MacKinnon et al, 2008). The level of the devolved block grants is a function of the so-called 'Barnett Formula', which awards Scotland, Wales and Northern Ireland a population-based share of increases in public expenditure awarded to England (Bell and Christie, 2001). The devolved administrations' general lack of revenue-raising powers means that macro-level decisions taken by Westminster can alter the context for transport policy making in the devolved jurisdictions. For example, if HM Treasury were to raise the taxes on aviation significantly, the promotion of low-cost air travel to Scotland or Northern Ireland in pursuit of economic development objectives might be seriously undermined. Equally, the devolved administrations are unable to introduce a number of potential policy interventions, such as differential rates of fuel tax or Vehicle Excise Duty (VED), payroll taxes to direct towards infrastructure funds, or tax relief on public transport season tickets, as is common across much of Europe (Smyth, 2003). Local and regional authorities are even more dependent on central funding, which accounts for approximately 75% of local government funding in England (ODPM, 2004), imposing greater limits on policy divergence.

'National' transport policies

The generally asymmetrical and shifting nature of UK devolution is reflected in the distribution of transport powers between Westminster and the four devolved jurisdictions. The introduction of devolution codified and confirmed a clear distinction between those transport powers deemed part of 'domestic' (and hence devolved) competence, and those judged to be closely linked with the UK economy and common market, and hence reserved to Westminster (Table 2.1). Thus, the main transport responsibilities of each devolved territory are the construction and maintenance of road infrastructure (having been administered by the three nations prior to devolution), and other generally local issues such as bus policy and concessionary fares. Those functions retained at the UK level focused on regulatory powers – such as transport safety, vehicle and driver licensing and so on – and those responsibilities governed by international treaty, especially aviation and shipping.

Table 2.1: Devolved and reserved functions in transport

	Scotland	Wales	Northern Ireland	London
Road	Totally	Limited	Totally	Total
Rail	Substantial	Limited	Totally	Limited
Bus	Totally	Limited	Totally	Total
Air	Limited	None	None	N/A
Sea (ferry)	Substantial	None	None	N/A

Source: MacKinnon et al (2008), adapted from Smyth (2003)

The railways fell between these two stools, being largely 'domestic' in nature, but subject to a strong regulatory regime. For Scotland, a compromise – the so-called 'McLeish Settlement' – was devised during the passage of the 1998 Scotland Act, giving Scottish ministers a limited advisory role with regard to the rail network, enhanced by the movement of financial responsibility for the ScotRail franchise payments from Whitehall in 2001. This was followed by 'the most significant transfer of powers since devolution' (Scottish Executive, 2005, unpaginated) when responsibility for funding rail infrastructure and specifying services was transferred to the Scottish Executive by the 2005 Railways Act. The Act also made the National Assembly for Wales a co-signatory of the Wales and Borders franchise. Exempt from privatisation in the 1990s reforms, the railways in Northern Ireland have remained in public control throughout.

The Scottish Parliament, Northern Ireland Assembly and National Assembly for Wales therefore have different formal competencies over transport and related policy areas (Table 2.1). Scotland enjoys full legislative power over roads policy and, since 2005, over the railways, but the Parliament has very little direct power with respect to shipping or aviation, which remain reserved to Westminster, despite these being a critical part of the transport system, especially in the Highlands and Islands.[3] Although it also gained additional powers over rail services in 2005, the Welsh Assembly still has limited influence over transport policy, since primary legislative competence for all functions remains at Westminster. Northern Ireland is the most devolved jurisdiction, with the Assembly having full control over all surface transport modes in the province.

Turning to national transport strategies, the publication of *A new deal for transport* (DETR, 1998) was accompanied by comparable 'sister' documents in Scotland and Wales (Scottish Office, 1998; Welsh Office, 1998). The pre-devolution publication of *A new deal for transport* acted as a 'binding agent' for policy across the UK (Smyth, 2003), especially in Scotland and Wales where Labour was the majority coalition partner and substantial policy shifts might be interpreted as 'splits' in government (Laffin and Shaw, 2007). This arguably involved the importation of a 'London-centric' analysis of transport issues in that the UK White Paper was written by metropolitan civil servants and their advisers for whom sustainable transport was primarily defined by the need to reduce congestion, whereas transport needs in the more rural Celtic nations were (and are) different in many respects (Smyth, 2003). Table 2.2 demonstrates that expenditure on transport has risen substantially in all three jurisdictions as well as in England, both in absolute terms and relative to overall budgets, which rose by around 40% between 2001/02 and 2006/07. Overall budget increases meant that increased transport expenditure did not have to be matched by cuts in other areas within the devolved administrations' block grants.

We have noted that the asymmetrical nature of UK devolution means that the UK government exercises control over English domestic policy, including transport. The Department for Transport (DfT) has extended its direct control over railways in England following the abolition of the Strategic Rail Authority.

Table 2.2: Identifiable capital and current expenditure on transport in England and the devolved jurisdictions (£ million), 2001/02 to 2006/07

Year	England	Scotland[1]	Wales[2]	Northern Ireland
2001/02	8,432	1,020	629	259
2002/03	10,214	1,249	722	304
2003/04	13,453	1,669	749	332
2004/05	13,350	1,616	842	341
2005/06	13,716	1,983	889	353
2006/07	15,471	2,499	920	392
% increase 2001/02-2006/07	83.5	145	46.3	51.4

Notes: [1] Includes subsidy payments for the ScotRail franchise transferred from Westminster in 2001/02, and in 2006/07 an additional £360 million, which accompanied the transfer of additional rail powers to Scottish ministers. Removing this £360 million gives an overall (and more accurate) increase in transport spending of 109%.

[2] Includes Wales and Borders franchise subsidy payments from Westminster.

Source: MacKinnon et al (2008)

In policy terms, the Labour government has retreated somewhat from the ideas of sustainable transport and traffic reduction to emphasise the rather more ambiguous notion of integration (Chapter One). Responsibility for urban congestion charging has been devolved to local authorities and the government has shied away from any commitment to national road pricing, conveniently described as 'a decision for the future', in the wake of the Downing Street petition of 2007 (DfT, 2007, p 13). The DfT's recent strategic discussion document cites the Stern Review (Stern, 2006) in support of the belief that the two key goals of maximising economic competitiveness and addressing climate change can be made compatible. Instead of major new investment in 'grand schemes' such as high-speed rail (HSR), the favoured approach, recommended by Eddington (2006), is focused on improving the most congested and crowded parts of the network, emphasising existing infrastructure projects (for example, London Crossrail and Birmingham New Street station redevelopment) and local public and sustainable transport schemes alongside targeted road development (DfT, 2007).

In Scotland, the 2001 Transport (Scotland) Act contained a range of measures focusing on better integration but which were, like their Westminster parallels, rather loosely defined and advocated. The Act followed the approach taken in England by providing local authorities with the legal powers to introduce congestion charging within their own areas, but falling short of committing the Executive to the introduction of a national scheme. A headline commitment has been to prioritise public transport through a 70:30 split in favour of public transport in overall transport expenditure.[4] One identifiable aspect of transport strategy formulation is a certain 'objective fatigue' (Docherty et al, 2007) in large part resulting from the rapid turnover of ministers. The arrival of each new transport minister seems to have brought a new document containing a differently worded set of strategic objectives. As such, civil servants have become extremely adept at drafting bland 'motherhood and apple pie' statements to introduce the latest minister's 'glossy' strategy. Whereas *Travel choices for Scotland* (Scottish Office, 1998) made clear the need to 'address excessive and inappropriate car use', such clarity had largely disappeared in *Scotland's transport future* (Scottish Executive, 2004). The collection of associated objectives was rather vague and had no obvious prioritisation, suggesting that everything could get better, everywhere (Docherty et al, 2007). *Scotland's national transport strategy* (Scottish Executive, 2006), published only two years later by replacement transport minister Tavish Scott, contains a similarly banal statement of purpose, which is a pity since its analysis and three reasonably specific headline objectives of improving journey times, reducing emissions and improving quality, accessibility and affordability, are generally robust.

In Wales, the Welsh Office's (1998) pre-devolution document *Transporting Wales into the future* was followed up by the *Transport framework for Wales* (Welsh Assembly Government, 2001), but the full Welsh transport strategy – the requirement for which was stipulated in the 2006 Transport (Wales) Act– remains 'in preparation' at the time of writing. In common with Scotland, the emphasis has been on integration, with the *Framework* identifying the need to 'develop a better coordinated and sustainable transport system to support local communities and the creation of a prosperous economy' (Welsh Assembly Government, 2001, p 1). The document makes clear that the Assembly saw the improvement of public transport as a high priority, although the need to improve strategic roads to tackle congestion is also emphasised and the concept of a national target for traffic reduction is deemed 'inappropriate'. Devolution has also encouraged transport to be viewed as an important means of nation-building, particularly by developing improved north–south road and air links.

In Northern Ireland, efforts to devise a transport strategy were concentrated into the period up until the suspension of the Assembly in late 2002. The recognition that transport needed to be considered as part of a broader regional development agenda was reflected in the development of *Shaping our future: Regional development strategy for Northern Ireland* from the mid-1990s (DRDNI, 2002a). A 'daughter' *Regional transportation strategy for Northern Ireland 2002-2012* (DRDNI, 2002b) was adopted by the Northern Ireland Assembly in 2002. The Strategy begins by restating the long-term vision for transport contained within the Regional Development Strategy: 'to have a modern, sustainable, safe transportation system which benefits society, the economy, and the environment and which actively contributes to social inclusion and everyone's quality of life' (DRDNI, 2002b, 1). Roughly 35% of the total expenditure is planned to be on public transport whereas roads take up 63% of the proposed budget (although much of this is directed at making good a maintenance backlog).

The new phase of devolution associated with the entry of nationalist parties into government in May 2007 has led to some reappraisal of transport strategies in the different devolved jurisdictions. The minority SNP government in Scotland signalled its opposition to two major east of Scotland transport schemes – the Edinburgh Airport Rail Link (EARL) and the Edinburgh Tram project – ultimately abandoning EARL, but allowing the trams to proceed within existing budget limits following a parliamentary defeat on these issues. A high-profile election commitment to abolish bridge tolls has also been implemented, and detailed plans for a new road bridge across the Firth of Forth have been approved. Under the new coalition arrangements in Wales, the Plaid Cymru leader and Deputy First Minister, Ieuan Wyn Jones, is responsible for the economy and transport, emphasising the importance of transport to achieving the new government's vision of a prosperous and vibrant nation (Welsh Labour Party/Plaid Cymru, 2007). Interestingly, the emphasis on nation-building has increased, with the Deputy First Minister prioritising the improvement of north–south links (National Assembly for Wales, 2007). The new Programme for Government agreed between the Democratic Unionist Party (DUP) and Sinn Fein in Northern Ireland identified economic growth as the top priority, supported by investment in infrastructure, particularly roads.

In general, all the national strategies represent a shift away from the 'predict and provide' approach that characterised UK transport policy in the 1980s and early 1990s (Chapter One). The foundations for this shift were laid by *A new deal for transport* (DETR, 1998) and its sister documents prior to devolution, but it is significant that none of the jurisdictions sought an immediate return to a predominantly roads-based transport strategy despite the bulk of their institutional expertise being in this area. In Scotland (particularly) and Wales the approach to transport has moved from initially stressing environmental considerations to emphasising the links between transport and the economy,[5] although this has not resulted in divergence from England because ministers in the UK government were also refocusing their general approach away from ambitions to reduce individual car use (Chapter One). At the level of strategic policy direction, then, the picture is one of convergence in the 1999-2007 period, followed by more recent uncertainty in the aftermath of the 2007 elections.

In addition to these national strategies, four specific policies are worthy of comment: roads and road-user charging, additional rail investment, concessionary fares and air route development funds (RDFs). Table 2.3 summarises the 'headline' instances of divergence and convergence between the devolved jurisdictions and England in relation to these policies. Here, the picture is largely one of marked divergence between the devolved administrations themselves and England. Although the possibility of road-user charging is mentioned in the draft transport strategy for Wales (Welsh Assembly Government, 2006), there has been little interest in the policy in Northern Ireland and in Scotland it was left to City of Edinburgh Council to promote a London-style scheme (Chapter One). The failure of this scheme (Gaunt et al, 2007) means that London remains the only part of the UK where a significant road–user charging scheme has been introduced. Scotland has led the way on additional rail investment, introducing the largest programme of reopenings and new line construction and more recently announcing significant electrification, in stark contrast to England where resisting a move away from diesel as part of a wider objective to reduce the amount spent on the railways seems a more pressing priority. All three of the devolved administrations introduced concessionary fares schemes, with England following suit in 2006. Finally, the devolved administrations also established RDFs – utilising their economic development powers to intervene in this ostensibly reserved area – to provide financial support for new air services, although RDFs are now to be abolished in all three jurisdictions.

Table 2.3: 'Headline' divergence and convergence between policies adopted by the devolved administrations and those pursued in England

	Scotland	Wales	Northern Ireland	London
Road building	C	C	C	D
Road-user charging	C	C	C	D
Additional rail investment	D	D	D	D
Concessionary fares	C	C	C	C
Regional transport governance	D	D	C	C
Air route development funds	D (C)	D (C)	D (C)	C

Notes: D = divergence from England, C = convergence with England.

Source: MacKinnon et al (2008)

Subnational transport planning

There has also been considerable change in subnational transport governance since Labour's election to power in 1997. In England a complicated pattern emerges with considerable churn in the institutional infrastructure (Table 2.4). The absence of a national spatial strategy makes England distinct from the other cases (see below), and indeed a national transport strategy only exists in the sense that one can be implied from the growing collection of White Papers emanating from the DfT. This is likely to be consolidated through National Policy Statements on infrastructure promoted by a new Infrastructure Planning Commission. Below the national level, outside of London, nine regions exist to deliver transport policy (Figure 2.1), reflecting the efforts of the Labour government to mobilise the regional level as a scale of policy integration (Cabinet Office, 1999). Here, Regional Spatial Strategies (RSSs) are prepared, which incorporate Regional Transport Strategies (RTSs) in an attempt to join up transport and other policy areas, particularly land-use issues.[6] The creation of the RTS within an RSS has made regional transport policy more visible than previously. Such regional strategies are potentially equivalent to the national strategies of the devolved territories as the English regions have populations of a broadly comparable size. Government Offices for the Regions (GORs) track work carried out on RSSs, supported by the Regional Coordination Unit within central government, and are ultimately responsible for issuing revisions. One potentially important innovation at the regional scale in England is the increasing joint working between regions, especially the north west, Yorkshire and Humber and the north east, which together form 'The Northern Way'. Increasingly vocal on issues of transport policy, The Northern Way has published both a transport priorities report, and research advocating the construction of a north–south high speed rail line (Steer Davies Gleave, 2007; The Northern Way, 2007).

Table 2.4: Transport policy structures in England

	Transport (institution)	Transport (strategy)
REGIONAL	• Regional Assemblies • Some 'meta-regional' activity, eg Northern Way	• Regional Spatial Strategy (incorporating a Regional Transport Strategy)
LOCAL (one and two tier)	• Passenger transport authorities/executives exist in 6 'city-regions' • Mostly unitary districts; some areas have two-tier county and district councils	• Local Transport Plans (prepared individually or between local authorities)

RSSs provide a vehicle for the expression of regional transport policies and priorities, but this is hampered by the lack of an elected tier of government at this level to take what are often difficult decisions over priorities – a key task allocated to them by Westminster in recent years. This lack of elected authority and a continuing dependence on central government funding means that regional strategies across England tend to be very uniform. Another important constraint is the limited number of specialists available to staff transport planning units in councils and regional organisations (Vigar, 2006), especially given the lure of London (MacKinnon et al, 2008).

London differs significantly from other English 'regions' both in terms of institutions and policy direction (Chapter Nine). It was granted devolution in recognition of the unique problems of governing a major world city following the abolition of the Greater London Council (GLC) in 1986 (Syrett and Baldock, 2003). The executive model of devolution in London is unique within the UK, with the Greater London Authority (GLA), comprised of the elected Mayor and Greater London Assembly, holding specified powers over planning and transport investment (Sweeting, 2002). These powers include the preparation of *The London*

Figure 2.1: English regions

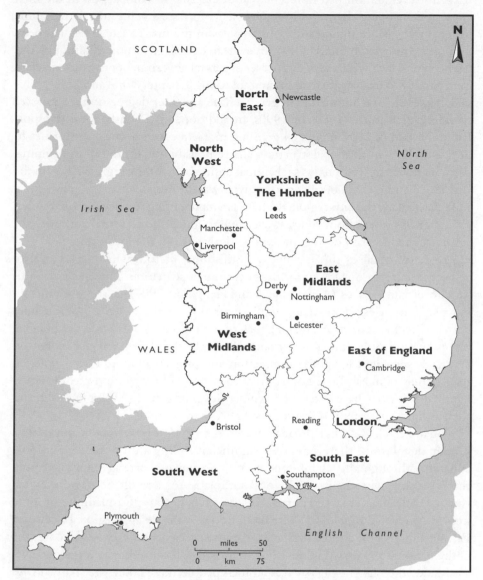

Plan and the preparation and delivery of a transport strategy, with Transport for London (TfL) – an executive agency of the Mayor – responsible for delivery. In terms of policy direction, it is London that has probably come closest to fulfilling the objectives of the 1998 UK transport White Paper by implementing congestion charging and by directing significant investment into public transport and cycling, reflecting the elected authority of, and strategic political leadership provided by, the Mayor, supported by key officers within TfL (MacKinnon et al, 2008).

Local Transport Plans (LTPs) are the vehicles for local transport investment in England outside of London (see Chapter Nine). Levels of funding for LTPs have, however, diminished in recent years, especially in comparison to the high costs of developing them (with requirements for assessments and consultation, for example). More significant in urban areas in the mid to late 2000s has been Transport Innovation Fund (TIF) money from central government, although this has been provided with a very distinct set of central government priorities attached to it, namely to investigate road pricing solutions (Chapters One and Three). This said, however, local authorities in general have a greater degree of freedom over spending than in the 1980s or 1990s. In addition, an (English) local transport Bill published in 2007 suggested granting more freedom to local authorities to decide on local institutional structures and responsibilities for transport planning, particularly in city-regions. As such, initial enthusiasm for the regional level in the late 1990s and early 2000s has partly given way to initiatives at the subregional scale, particularly the city-region. Rather than representing real devolution through a transfer of powers from central government, much of the actual authority for action at the level of city-regions will be derived from the local scale.

The result of all of this is a messy institutional picture with a great deal of activity occurring outside of formal government structures. This move towards 'soft governance spaces' (Allmendinger and Haughton, 2007) has some advantages but also some clear democratic implications such as the absence of clear lines between decisions made in and on behalf of such spaces and structures of political representation. Subnational governance in England also remains dependent on central government for political direction and project funding. Thus, while we may criticise English local government for often failing to innovate, changing national priorities have often undermined local efforts at developing solutions such as light rail systems (Chapter Five).

Scotland has had a single formal elected tier of local government since 1996. Under devolution, there has been significant 'filling in' of the institutional apparatus through the establishment of 'intermediate' arrangements between the Scottish Government and 32 local authorities. As a result, Scotland now has two parallel subnational territorial structures where transport planning of some kind is conducted (Table 2.5). The first of these is the seven Regional Transport Partnerships (RTPs) created by the 2004 Transport (Scotland) Act, which cover the entire national territory (Figure 2.2). Comprised of local authority representatives alongside other stakeholders such as business people, these bodies are charged with developing priorities for investment through the development of an RTS.

RTPs were designed to overcome problems with executing transport planning in very small local authorities, involving a limited transport skills base in many cases and problems of cross-boundary competition (Docherty and Begg, 2003). In the event, the creation of RTPs disappointed supporters of the concept due to the limited nature of their powers and the low levels of funding available to them. Their long-term future is already in doubt, the SNP government's first budget having removed their dedicated funding streams, leaving them dependent on local authorities for project finance. Thus, while there appears to be a double process of devolution occurring as transport powers cascade from the UK government

Table 2.5: Transport policy structures in Scotland

	Transport (institution)	Transport (strategy)
REGIONAL/CITY-REGIONAL	• 7 Regional Transport Partnerships cover the entire territory • City-region committees in 4 areas	• Regional Transport Strategy • Strategic Development Plans (in 4 city-regions)
LOCAL	• 32 local authorities	• Development Plans/Local Transport Strategies

Figure 2.2: Scottish Regional Transport Partnerships

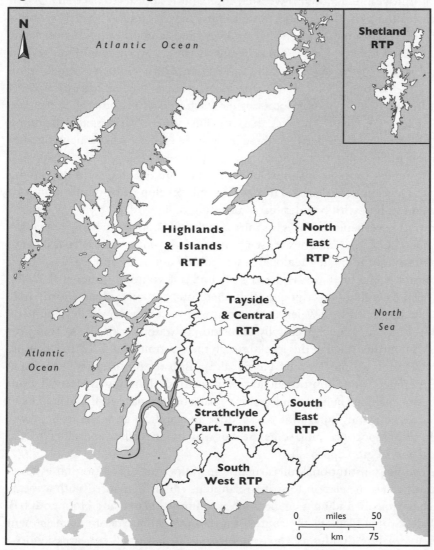

Source: Adapted from Scottish Executive (2006)

to the Scottish Parliament and then to RTPs, in reality a new form of 'centrism' has concentrated regulatory (through power of approval) and investment power at the Scottish national level. The latter was evident in the parallel establishment of Transport Scotland as a national transport agency, arguably creating further 'clutter' in the institutional landscape and increasing the policy coordination challenge (Pangbourne, 2007), especially given that Local Transport Strategies (LTSs) remain in place despite being highly variable in their focus and outlook.

Second, development plans are also expected to make a statement of transport policies, providing a vehicle for integrating infrastructure questions with land-use planning concerns and the demands of other policy sectors. Traditionally, the UK planning system has not performed well in this regard compared with those of European neighbours (Webster, 2005). Little appears to have changed in Scottish planning on the ground, even under a new regime of 'spatial planning' (Vigar, 2007), although this may change over time as mindsets and governance cultures shift. Of particular relevance here is the new government's draft revised *National planning framework* (Scottish Government, 2008), which is much more of a genuine national plan than its predecessor, given its explicit identification of nationally important economic locations and the transport and other infrastructure required to serve them. The fact that coordination between spatial planning and transport (as well as between these areas and health boards) is demanded in legislation in Scotland may also reinvigorate planning, as might the creation of four city-region strategic planning bodies, which are charged with developing Strategic Development Plans (SDPs), which will develop priorities for transport investment in line with broader spatial planning objectives.

Transport governance in Wales has mirrored that of Scotland in many respects. A single tier of local government was established in both countries in 1996 following the abolition of the higher 'regional' level (county councils) and there has been a significant 'filling in' of the 'regional' scale under devolution (Jones et al, 2005). The Welsh Assembly Government established four regional offices (north, mid, south east and south west Wales) dealing primarily with economic development, transport and education. Specifically in relation to transport, the 2006 Transport (Wales) Act further filled in this level through the creation of an RTP mechanism. Regional plans are prepared by Regional Transport Consortia (RTCs), made up of members from constituent local authorities.[7] Funding is derived from constituent member budgets and regional plans may replace individual LTPs in many areas to avoid duplication and reduce preparation costs. As in Scotland, then, local transport planning still exists but may be gradually superseded by the regional/city-region approach.

The evolving institutional infrastructure in Wales post devolution raises some important issues in relation to spatial planning, which is charged with a meta-governance role in guiding strategies such as transport (Harris and Hooper, 2004). The Wales Spatial Plan sets the context for transport infrastructure management and delivery but divides the nation into six 'functional' sub-areas whose boundaries are not coterminous with the four RTC regions. The new system is not without operational difficulties either. In similar fashion to Scotland, these were compounded by the devolved elections in 2007 and subsequent changes to the composition of the devolved governments. The first concerned uncertainty over funding levels, which impinged on the ability of RTCs to initiate project appraisals to bid for monies. Second, while RTPs are both guided by and ultimately feed into the Wales Transport Strategy, there have been significant delays in the production of the latter, creating great uncertainty for the RTCs. While difficulties in the meshing of strategies in time is somewhat inevitable, the newness of the key organisations, in Wales and Scotland alike, caused particular problems in terms of a lack of experience and established procedures to draw on.

Governance generally, and transport planning in particular, has historically been highly centralised in Northern Ireland. As discussed above, the policy context for the province is set by the Department for Regional Development Northern Ireland (DRDNI). At the local scale, infrastructure development depends on close links to the planning system and area development plans are prepared by the Planning Service of the Department of the Environment. In this way, local plans have been centrally controlled. These governance arrangements suggest that optimising the effectiveness of transport governance in Northern Ireland rests heavily on cooperation between central government departments. In reality, however,

> 'There is a very strong silo mentality here amongst civil servants both within departments and between departments … and the overarching strategies that have been developed … they inevitably end up being housed in a particular department and then become ghettoised as a result. There are major fault lines between departments that really should be working closely together.' (Interview with civil servant, 2006)

Local government has played a limited role in transport policy making. It has been in effect a consultee with a useful role in integrating transport and land-use proposals on the ground but very limited powers. This may change with the reform of local government in Northern Ireland, granting local authorities the capacity to administer decisions related to issues such as local roads and planning.

Nationally, Northern Ireland was the first devolved territory to develop a (award-winning) spatial strategy to guide future territorial direction. And, in common with the rest of the UK and much of Europe (Buitelaar et al, 2007; Salet and Thornley, 2007), in the Belfast metropolitan area we see efforts to make policy at the city-region scale. Beyond Belfast, however, it is the one 'nation' in which there have not been substantial efforts to 'fill in' a subnational tier between the devolved administration and local authorities. This reflects the small size of the province and will be reinforced by local government reform with the move to larger unitary councils mirroring changes elsewhere in the UK.

Conclusions

Transport governance is bound up in wider processes of 'rescaling'. Changing patterns of local–central relations and local government reorganisation in the 1980s and the 1990s stripped away many formal tiers of subnational government with a broad move in the UK towards unitary local authorities. What the subsequent period demonstrates, however, is a filling back of these levels. This has resulted in the enhancement of city-regional, regional and national scales of governance with London, Scotland and Wales taking on greater powers alongside some more limited attempts to strengthen the English regions, sometimes by filling in with 'softer', often not directly accountable, institutions.

Turning to questions of policy divergence and convergence, the transport strategies of each of the devolved jurisdictions display general 'horizontal' convergence with *A new deal for transport* (DETR, 1998), mirroring the continuing shift in emphasis away from 'sustainable' transport towards the weaker notion of 'integration' seen at Westminster since 1997 (Chapter One). In both Scotland and Wales, movement from an early environmentalist orientation towards a renewed economic development emphasis is clearly discernible – particularly in the former case – where the new nationalist government's declaration of a 'national purpose' to increase economic growth involves a restating of the importance of major transport infrastructure (Scottish Government, 2007). Key policies such as additional rail investment in Scotland and air RDFs in the three Celtic territories demonstrate greater divergence between the devolved administrations and England than is apparent at the level of strategy. This form of policy divergence is less discernible at the subnational scale, reflecting the limited capacity of local authorities and regional partnerships in an uncertain political climate.

A key question arising from this chapter is: what institutional structures best promote sustainable transport policies? It is important to recognise that policy outcomes are a product of the interaction between institutional structures, broadly defined, and political agency rather than being determined directly by the existence of a particular set of institutional arrangements. The example of London highlights the importance of political commitment and leadership even when devolved powers, at least initially, were relatively weak (Chapter Nine). That said, there is substantial evidence internationally that the creation of city-regional authorities offers a promising way forward (Marsden and May, 2006; Anable and Shaw, 2007; Grant Thornton, 2008), not least because they provide the best match between the scale of policy intervention and that of individual travel behaviour. In addition to selecting the right scale of governance, better policy integration and greater sustainability would seem to require structural integration in the sense of city-regional authorities being granted effective powers over a broad suite of transport modes, allowing them to select the measures best suited to local circumstances. As we have seen, such integration is present in London and Northern Ireland, both of which avoided the travails of bus and rail privatisation in the 1980s and 1990s, although this is associated with rather different travel outcomes in the two territories. The rest of the UK still falls some way short, however, and the focus on regions has thus far largely resulted in greater institutional complexity and 'clutter', raising questions of policy responsibility and democratic accountability (Pierre, 2000). In order to really promote effective delivery, the strengthening of subnational authorities must be accompanied by a rethinking of the existing institutional landscape, including some genuine 'double devolution' of powers away from both the UK government and the devolved administrations.

Notes

[1] Devolution involved the establishment of an elected Parliament for Scotland, an elected power-sharing Assembly in Northern Ireland, a weaker Assembly without legislative powers for Wales and an elected Mayor and Assembly for London. The English regions outside London, by contrast, were subject to more limited administrative reform.

[2] Reserved powers are those that affect the devolved jurisdictions but remain the responsibility of the UK government.

[3] This situation is further complicated by the fact that planning powers are devolved, with the Scottish Parliament therefore capable of blocking reserved decisions such as airport development through this mechanism.

[4] A large proportion of this 70% was to cover revenue support for rail, bus and ferry services.

[5] It is far more difficult to assess the trajectory of the transport strategy in Northern Ireland under devolution because of the suspension of the Assembly between October 2002 and May 2007.

[6] RSSs, previously prepared by Regional Assemblies, are to be integrated with Regional Economic Strategies from 2008 with responsibility for their preparation shifting to Regional Development Agencies.

[7] RTCs pre-existed the 2006 Act, having been established by local authorities themselves following the 1996 reforms.

Acknowledgements
Geoff Vigar's work for this chapter was funded by ESRC grant number RES-000-23-0756. The diagrams are Crown Copyright material reproduced with the permission of HMSO and the Queen's Printer for Scotland (licence number CO2W002008). Other research on which the chapter is based was funded by the Carnegie Trust for the Universities of Scotland and the Royal Geographical Society.

References
Adams, J. and Schmuecker, K. (2005) 'Introduction and overview', in J. Adams and K. Schmuecker (eds) *Devolution in practice 2006: Public policy differences within the UK*, Newcastle upon Tyne: Institute for Public Policy Research, pp 3–9.
Allmendinger, P. and Haughton, G. (2007) 'The fluid scales and scope of UK spatial planning', Environment and Planning A, 39, pp 1478–96.

Anable, J. and Shaw, J. (2007) 'Priorities, policies and (time)scales: the delivery of emissions reductions in the UK transport sector', *Area*, 39, pp 443-57.

Bell, D. and Christie, A. (2001) 'Finance – the Barnett formula: nobody's child?', in A. Trench (ed) *The state of the nations 2001: The second year of devolution in the United Kingdom*, Exeter: Imprint Academic, pp 135-52.

Buitelaar, E., Lagendijk, A. and Jacobs, W. (2007) 'A theory of institutional change: illustrated by Dutch city-provinces and Dutch land policy', *Environment and Planning A*, 39, pp 891-908.

Cabinet Office (1999) *Modernising government*, Cm 4310, London: The Stationery Office.

Cole, S. (2005) 'Devolved government and transport – relationships, process and policy', *Public Money and Management*, 25, pp 179-85.

DETR (Department of the Environment, Transport and the Regions) (1998) *A new deal for transport: Better for everyone*, www.dft.gov.uk/about/strategy/whitepapers/previous/anewdealfortransportbetterfo5695?page=1#a1000 (accessed 13 May 2008).

DfT (Department for Transport) (2007) *Towards a sustainable transport system: Supporting economic growth in low carbon world*, London: DfT.

Docherty, I. and Begg, D. (2003) 'Back to the city-region? The future of strategic transport planning in Scotland', *Scottish Affairs*, 45, pp 128-56.

Docherty, I., Shaw, J. and Gray, D. (2007) 'Transport strategy in Scotland since devolution', *Public Money and Management*, 27, pp 141-8.

DRDNI (Department for Regional Development Northern Ireland) (2002a) *Shaping our future: Regional development strategy for Northern Ireland 2025*, Belfast: DRDNI.

DRDNI (2002b) *Regional transportation strategy for Northern Ireland 2002-2012*, Belfast: DRDNI.

Eddington, R. (2006) *The Eddington transport study: The case for action: Sir Rod Eddington's advice to the government*, London: HM Treasury.

Gaunt, M., Rye, T. and Allen, S. (2007) 'Public acceptability of road user charging: the case of Edinburgh and the 2005 referendum', *Transport Reviews*, 27, pp 85-102.

Giuliano, G. (2004) 'The land use impacts of transportation investments: highway and transit', in S. Hanson and G. Giuliano (eds) *The geography of urban transportation* (3rd edition), New York: Guilford Press.

Goodwin, M., Jones, M. and Jones, P. (2005) 'Devolution, constitutional change and economic development: explaining and understanding the new institutional geographies of the British state', *Regional Studies*, 39, pp 421-36.

Grant Thornton (2008) *Connecting for competitiveness: The future of transport in the UK city regions*, London: Grant Thornton LLP.

Guy, S. and Marvin, S. (1999) 'Understanding sustainable cities: competing urban futures', *European Urban and Regional Studies*, 6, pp 268-75.

Harris, N. and Hooper, A. (2004) 'Rediscovering the spatial in public policy and planning: an examination of the spatial content of sectoral policy documents', *Planning Theory and Practice*, 52, pp 147-69.

Hazell, R. (2000) 'Introduction: the first year of devolution', in R. Hazell (ed) *The state and the nations: The first year of devolution in the United Kingdom*, Exeter: Imprint Academic, pp 1-12.

Jeffery, C. (2002) 'Uniformity and diversity in policy provision: insights from the US, Germany and Canada', in J. Adams and P. Robinson (eds) *Devolution in practice: Public policy differences within the UK*, London: Institute for Public Policy Research and the Economic and Social Research Council, pp 176-97.

Jonas, A. and Ward, K. (2007) 'Introduction to a debate on city-regions: new geographies of governance, democracy and social reproduction', *International Journal of Urban and Regional Research*, 31, pp 169-78.

Jones, R., Goodwin, M., Jones, M. and Pett, K. (2005) '"Filling in" the state: economic governance and the evolution of devolution in Wales', *Environment and Planning C: Government and Policy*, 23, pp 337-60.

Keating, M. (1998) *The new regionalism in western Europe*, Cheltenham: Edward Elgar.

Keating, M. (2002) 'Devolution and public policy in the United Kingdom: divergence or convergence?', in J. Adams and P. Robinson (eds) *Devolution in practice: Public policy differences within the UK*, London: Institute for Public Policy Research and the Economic and Social Research Council, pp 3-21.

Laffin, M. and Shaw, E. (2007) 'British devolution and the Labour Party: how a national party adapts to devolution', *British Journal of Politics and International Relations*, 9, pp 55-72.

MacKinnon, D., Shaw, J. and Docherty, I. (2008) *Diverging mobilities? Devolution, transport and policy innovation*, Oxford: Elsevier Science.

Marsden, M. and May, A. (2006) 'Do institutional arrangements make a difference to transport policy and implementation? Lessons for Britain', *Environment and Planning C: Government and Policy*, 24, pp 771-89.

National Assembly for Wales (2007) *Official report*, 2 October.

ODPM (Office of the Deputy Prime Minister) (2004) *Balance of funding review – report*, London: The Stationery Office.

Pangbourne, K. (2007) 'The changing geography of Scottish transport governance – over-stuffed and under-powered?', *Conference Proceedings of the Regional Studies Association Winter Conference*, November, pp 102-3.

Peck, J. (2001) 'Neoliberalising states: thin policies/hard outcomes', *Progress in Human Geography*, 25, pp 445-55.

Pierre, J. (2000) 'Introduction: understanding governance', in J. Pierre (ed) *Debating governance: Authority, steering and democracy*, Oxford: Oxford University Press.

Rye, T., Ison, S. and Santos, G. (2003) 'Political acceptability of road pricing: will London confirm the theory?', Proceedings of 2003 European Transport Conference, Strasbourg, 8-10 October.

Salet, W. and Thornley, A. (2007) 'Institutional influences on the integration of multilevel governance and spatial policy in European city-regions', *Journal of Planning Education and Research*, 27, pp 188-98.

Scottish Executive (2004) *Scotland's transport future: The transport White Paper*, Edinburgh: Scottish Executive, www.scotland.gov.uk/library5/transport/stfwp-01.asp (accessed 14 May 2007).

Scottish Executive (2005) 'Transfer of rail power to executive', Press Release, 17 October, www.scotland.gov.uk/News/Releases/2005/10/17110722 (accessed 27 October 2006).

Scottish Executive (2006) *Scotland's national transport strategy*, Edinburgh: Scottish Executive, www.scotland.gov.uk/Publications/2006/12/04104414/0 (accessed 25 June 2007).

Scottish Government (2007) *Scottish budget spending review*, Edinburgh: Scottish Government.

Scottish Government (2008) *National planning framework for Scotland 2: Discussion draft*, Edinburgh: Scottish Government, www.scotland.gov.uk/Resource/Doc/208174/0055210.pdf (accessed 13 May 2008).

Scottish Office (1998) *Travel choices for Scotland: The Scottish integrated transport White Paper*, Edinburgh: Scottish Office.

Smyth, A. (2003) 'Devolution and sustainable transport', in I. Docherty and J. Shaw (eds) *A new deal for transport? The UK's struggle with the sustainable transport agenda*, Oxford: Blackwell, pp 229-44.

Steer Davies Gleave (2007) *Northern Way: North–south connections: Report*, London: SDG, www.thenorthernway.co.uk/downloaddoc.asp?id=319&page=66&skin=0 (accessed 13 May 2008).

Stern, N. (2006) *Stern review on the economics of climate change*, London: HM Treasury.

Sweeting, D. (2002) 'Leadership in urban governance: the Mayor of London', *Local Government Studies*, 28, pp 3-20.

Syrett, S. and Baldock, R. (2003) 'Reshaping London's economic governance: the role of the London Development Agency', *European Urban and Regional Studies*, 10, pp 69-86.

The Northern Way (2007) *Moving forward: The Northern Way, short, medium and long term transport priorities*, Newcastle-upon-Tyne: The Northern Way Secretariat, www.thenorthernway.co.uk/downloaddoc.asp?id=320&page=325&skin=0 (accessed 13 May 2008).

Vigar, G. (2006) 'Participation, deliberation and learning in the development of regional strategies', *Planning Theory and Practice*, 7(3), pp 267-87.

Vigar, G. (2007) 'Towards an integrated spatial planning?', Unpublished working document, available from the author.

Webster, C. (2005) 'Diversifying the institutions of local planning', *Economic Affairs*, December, pp 4-10.

Welsh Assembly Government (2001) *The transport framework for Wales*, Cardiff: Welsh Assembly Government.

Welsh Assembly Government (2006) *Wales transport strategy consultation document: Connecting Wales*, Cardiff: Welsh Assembly Government.

Welsh Labour Party/Plaid Cymru (2007) *One Wales: A progressive agenda for the government of Wales*, Agreement between Labour Plaid Cymru groups in the National Assembly, 27 June, Cardiff: National Assembly of Wales.

Welsh Office (1998) *Transporting Wales into the future*, London: Welsh Office.

Part Two
Progress in policy implementation

THREE

Roads and traffic: from 'predict and provide' to 'making best use'

Graham Parkhurst and Geoff Dudley

'Predict and provide' can be defined as calculating how much unconstrained demand for road travel exists and adopting policy measures and providing funding streams to deliver the required capacity. As a concept, it effectively summarises government policy towards roads for much of the second half of the 20th century, but is perhaps most closely associated with the Conservatives' White Paper *Roads for prosperity* (DoT, 1989) and subsequent roads expansion programme. Walton (2003) felt able to consign predict and provide to the bin of discredited policies, although he was less than complementary about what he saw as the 'pragmatic multimodalism' (Shaw and Walton, 2001) emerging in its place. Writing two years after the publication of *Transport 2010: The 10-year plan* (DETR, 2000), which specified the policy approach enshrined in *A new deal for transport: Better for everyone* (DETR, 1998a), Walton's position was that the Plan was sufficiently slippery to demand further detailed critique, but within a year the government had substituted the expected 'third annual progress report' with a new White Paper *The future of transport* (DfT, 2004a). This, while not officially replacing the Plan, abandoned its targets, themselves much criticised for timidity, but now nonetheless unachievable in the face of obstacles including a crisis of delivery on the railways and the introduction of only one noteworthy road-user charging scheme, in London (Chapters One, Four and Nine).

In this chapter we assess Labour's roads and traffic policies in the decade since 1998. Following a brief contextual discussion, we turn to define the principles of a 'sustainable' roads and traffic policy, taking into account broad sustainability objectives and the recommendations of two special policy reviews, both inspired by the Treasury rather than the Department for Transport (DfT) and published in autumn 2006: the Eddington Review on transport, productivity and competitiveness and the Stern Review on climate change (Eddington, 2006; Stern, 2006). We then consider the extent to which ministers have embraced a sustainable roads policy in practice, examining some of the key quantitative indicators and the debate and rhetoric that surround them. Such a policy emerges as much harder to construct than predict and provide, requiring much higher levels of coordination between government departments, levels of government, delivery structures and funding lines. We also identify some of the gaps between where policy 'is' and where it 'needs to be' as being partly related to disconnects in the much-vaunted process of integration in transport policy; importantly, the failure of the government to embrace a national system of road-user charging in any meaningful sense emerges as a key failure of policy, which is paralysing delivery against high-level sustainability principles, despite these being endorsed as strategic objectives across government. We conclude by contrasting the current approach of 'management at the margins', in which current trends are allowed broadly to continue against the hope that technology will eventually deliver 'easy' solutions, with that of 'radical leadership', which might result in response to external shocks such as a permanent and significant increase in crude oil prices.

Breaking the addiction to roads? Policy 1997-2003

New Labour's roads policy can only be understood in the context of the degree to which predict and provide had already been severely undermined during the latter days of the preceding Conservative government. This shift was all the more remarkable given that, at the end of the 1980s and beginning of the 1990s, predict and provide appeared dominant in trunk roads policy. *Roads for prosperity* (DoT, 1989) had explicitly stated that the only way of dealing with growing and forecast inter-urban congestion was by widening existing roads and building new ones in a greatly expanded roads programme. An expanded programme of over £6 billion was identified (over £10 billion at 2006/07 prices), including a doubling of the trunk roads programme. As the 1990s progressed, however, a variety of factors – including cost escalations, a heightened sense of environmentalism and the emergence of 'new realism' in transport thinking (Goodwin et al, 1991) – combined to place sustainable development and mobility ideas at the heart of trunk roads policy (Chapter One). By 1997, a political consensus had emerged around the principles of 'new realism' and the new government took office with a pledge to implement a sustainable transport policy. This included a review of the whole trunk roads programme, which sought to question the actual basis of road-building decisions. The new approach was set out in *A new deal for transport* (DETR, 1998a), which stated explicitly that the days of predict and provide were over, and instead the top priority would be improving the maintenance and management of existing roads. In addition, charging for motorway and trunk road use was to be considered.

Significantly, it was also intended that the priorities for trunk roads would complement improvements to rail in particular, as part of an 'integrated' transport approach. New technology was to be used extensively in network control and traffic management, including through new Regional Traffic Control Centres. Carefully targeted capacity improvements were envisaged, but at the same time it was intended that some roads would be 'detrunked' and handed over to local authorities where it was decided that these roads served mainly local and regional traffic. The strategy envisaged the Highways Agency evolving as a 'network operator' rather than a road builder, with the Agency exploring sustainable transport options with local authorities and public transport operators. The trunk roads review, *A new deal for trunk roads in England* (DETR, 1998b), detailed the principles set out in the White Paper. Labour had inherited a trunk roads programme of 147 schemes. Of these, it was decided that 67 required an early decision. From this list, 37 schemes were placed in the targeted programme, costing £1.4 billion. It was intended to start these schemes within the subsequent seven years, subject to the completion of statutory processes. On the other hand, 36 schemes were withdrawn from the programme, although these included 19 schemes on roads to be detrunked, placing the decisions in the hands of local authorities (DETR, 1998b, p 10).

A new deal for transport was followed in 2000 by *Transport 2010: The ten-year plan* (DETR, 2000), a document designed to outline the scale of resources available and specify the interventions required to put an integrated transport policy into practice. It was envisaged that all modes of transport would benefit from greatly increased public and private funding totalling £180 billion (£150 billion in real terms) over the decade from 2001-02 to 2010-11. Of this, spending on rail would total £60 billion, and spending on local and national roads would total £59 billion. *Transport 2010* estimated that demand for travel on the strategic road network would grow by 29% over the decade, and acknowledged that, without new measures, congestion would increase. The response to this was rather contradictory. On the one hand, the government continued to argue that simply building more, bigger roads was not the answer, and that a more strategic approach was needed. For example, it was estimated that the large-scale expansion in rail passenger and freight traffic would cut road congestion by at least 3%. On the other hand, though, it was clear that ministers were by now extremely concerned about the political costs of being perceived as 'anti-motorist', with the result that *Transport 2010* envisaged significant increases in roads expenditure. Although few major new roads were proposed, government now intended to widen around 5% of the strategic network, some 360 miles, with associated junction improvements. In addition, the Plan envisaged 30 trunk road bypasses, together with 80 'major schemes' (that is, costing over £5 million each) tackling bottlenecks at junctions. Overall, the highly ambitious aim was to reduce congestion on inter-urban trunk roads to 5% below then existing levels, compared with a forecast growth of 28% by 2010. In terms of public and private annual expenditure on strategic roads at out-turn prices, the figure was due to increase from £1.4 billion in 2000-01 to £3.1 billion in 2010-11.

There was, of course, no guarantee that all the schemes described in *Transport 2010* would be implemented: as successive governments had discovered, economic constraints and environmental protests can frustrate the best-laid plans. The emphasis on road widening and dealing with bottlenecks was also on a significantly smaller scale than the predict and provide new road building of earlier decades. Shaw and Walton (2001) labelled the middle course that government transport policy sought to steer at this point as 'pragmatic multimodalism', which describes well the intention to satisfy the needs and interests of both the public transport and car-using constituencies; the government had been forced to retreat from, if not abandon, the 'idealist' position of opposing new road building in the light of the remorseless growth in traffic volumes. In the event, however, the political pressures on ministers not to be seen as 'anti-car' greatly intensified shortly after publication of *Transport 2010*, in the form of fuel protests in September 2000 – protests that briefly seemed to threaten the very survival of the administration. This scare no doubt further concentrated the minds of ministers on the dangers of overlooking the interests of private vehicle users.

By December 2002, then Transport Secretary Alistair Darling conceded that the government would not meet its *Transport 2010* targets for reducing congestion by 2010. One of the reasons for this failure was said to be that ministers had been far too optimistic about the numbers of councils willing to introduce congestion-charging schemes. It was assumed that eight councils would introduce congestion-charging schemes and 12 others would introduce parking levies. In the event, the only congestion-charging scheme in the pipeline was the one to be introduced in London in February 2003, with no workplace parking levy schemes in the offing. It appeared that once the government acknowledged the over-optimism of its *Transport 2010* targets, including the great difficulties in introducing demand management and the miserable failure to move anywhere near the promised investment in 25 light rail schemes (Chapter Five), then it was only a short step to falling back on plans to expand road space.

The government's acknowledgement of its inability to reduce congestion meant that the revised programme was, by definition, not in strict terms a return to predict and provide. Indeed, Darling accompanied his new roads programme with two announcements of arguably even greater long-term significance for roads policy. First, with regard to network management, a pilot project would allow vehicles on a section of the M42 to use the hard shoulder at peak times, with the possibility that the scheme could be extended to other motorways (this indeed was confirmed in April 2008). There was no doubt about the logic of official thinking here: if the widening programme faltered, then using the hard shoulder offered a *relatively* cheap and painless alternative to new 'full-time' capacity. Second, concerning demand management, Darling announced a feasibility study into a nationwide road-charging scheme, which seemed at the time to suggest that ministers were beginning to grasp the nettle and consider the possibility of road pricing as an alternative to road building.

Towards a more sustainable roads policy?

The title of the 2004 White Paper *The future of transport: A network for 2030* (DfT, 2004a) sought to emphasise the long-term nature of challenges in the transport sector; following the failure of *Transport 2010* it would have been injudicious to propose another high-profile, medium-term strategy with specific targets relating to traffic and congestion levels. Instead, the broad goal was described of a road network that 'provides a more reliable and freer-flowing system for motorists, other road users and businesses, where travellers can make informed choices about how and when they travel, and so minimise the adverse impact of road traffic on the environment and other people' (DfT, 2004a, p 34). As well as taking a managerial 'quality of service' approach, *The future of transport* emphasises investment and resource allocation. The Prime Ministerial foreword mentions the possibility of road pricing after 2014 as a means to cut congestion and carbon emissions, but environmental sustainability objectives scarcely receive a mention in the three key themes identified: *sustained investment, improvement in transport management* and *planning ahead*.

The White Paper's strategy was later broadly endorsed by the Eddington Review, in which the key recommendation was that '[t]o meet the changing needs of the UK economy, government should focus policy and sustained investment on improving the performance of *existing* transport networks, in those places that are important for the UK's economic success' (Eddington, 2006, p 7, emphasis added). A key difference, however, between 2004 national policy and the 2006 review was the importance placed on road pricing, with the latter arguing that '[p]olicy should get the prices right (especially congestion pricing on the roads and environmental pricing across all modes)'. UK policy on road pricing is considered in more detail later in this chapter. Implicit support for the approach outlined in *The future of transport* may also be identified – although only up to a point – in the Stern Review. Stern provided trajectories that foresee the peaking of climate-change emissions between 2015 and 2030 and also acknowledged that the transport sector faced particular difficulties in the short term and might contribute relatively late in the overall process of decarbonisation. The Stern strategy was endorsed by ministers a year later by the introduction of a Bill to enshrine the national target of a 60% reduction in carbon dioxide (CO_2)-equivalent emissions by 2050.

It is important to note, though, that the later the transport sector makes its contribution, the higher will be the total emissions level from which it needs to reduce (Co-operative Bank/Friends of the Earth, 2006), and the more important its reduction will be, as by that stage early-contributing sectors will have less remaining potential for further reductions. The sector will also become more dependent on effective technical fixes emerging in time to assist the transformation. While a number of promising alternative technologies have been identified, mainly based around fuel cells and renewable electricity as power sources, there is uncertainty as to whether they will be commercially deployable by 2030, in time to make a difference. There is also an international dimension to be considered, because there is enormous potential for transport-related emissions to rise in developing countries over the coming decades, symbolised well by the January 2008 launch in India of the £1,300 Tata Nano 'people's car', half the price of its nearest rival and designed to bring car ownership within the financial reach of the expanding middle classes. Some growth is perhaps unavoidable, but a share may be averted if developed countries provide technical and political leadership in decarbonising the transport sector in an effective way.

It is much harder, however, to construct an effective sustainable roads policy than it is to apply predict and provide. At least five key areas of overall strategy are important. First is infrastructure supply and management policy, which requires careful coordination across modes and, as discussed above, appears hard to achieve in practice, especially where political sensitivities are involved. A second important area is environmental taxation – in the UK led by HM Treasury – intended to encourage the use of efficient, clean vehicles. Treasury agreement would also be essential for any future national road-pricing system. Third is the regulation of vehicle emissions, an area of policy now dominated by agreements and directives at the European level, and likely to be increasingly influenced by global-level politics in the future. A fourth consideration is achieving a roads system that results in fewer injuries and fatalities. Finally, while reducing the need to travel by car is largely within the remit of the DfT, reducing the need to travel per se is arguably mainly influenced by other government departments, notably those determining the location of development that influences travel demand, particularly hospitals, schools and new homes.

A further complexity in achieving a coherent approach to sustainable transport delivery across the UK has been the establishment of devolved governments in Scotland, Wales and Northern Ireland (MacKinnon et al, 2008). The Scottish Parliament and Welsh and Northern Irish Assemblies have complete authority over roads within their jurisdictions, and *The future of transport* (DfT, 2004a) reflects its status as the first transport White Paper since devolution by focusing predominantly on English matters.

Road infrastructure supply policies

Although lower profile and less specific than the targets in *Transport 2010* (DETR, 2000), the Westminster government has overall targets relevant to sustainability objectives, such as the Public Service Agreement (PSA) targets for transport. All the targets (Table 3.1) are influenced by strategic roads and traffic policy to some extent, while the achievability of targets 1, 4, 5, 6 and 7 derives directly from roads policy (although the last target is jointly held with other government departments). Evidence presented in the Progress Report published in autumn 2006 (DfT, 2006) suggests that PSA1 and PSA4 were unlikely to be met. PSA1 requires that the most-delayed 10% of journeys on each of 87 routes show an aggregate reduction in journey time, but in practice the 58 for which reliable data were returned showed a 2.9% increase in delays (to 3.9 minutes per 10 miles travelled).

While the principle of predict and provide requires that infrastructure supply keeps pace with growth in traffic, decisions not to build particular roads do not necessarily indicate a turn towards sustainable mobility. Even in the absence of further road construction, the existing network could become much more carbon intensive. Some increases in capacity may be justified on sustainability grounds as a means of delivering prosperity, enabling vehicles to operate efficiently (traffic emits less CO_2 when free-flowing at modest speed than when congested), or tackling poor environmental conditions near homes (for example through new

Table 3.1: Transport PSA targets from April 2005

PSA	Summary definition
1	By 2007-08, make journeys on strategic roads more reliable (against specific metric)
2	Improve punctuality/reliability of rail services to >85% by 2006, with further improvements by 2008
3	By 2010, increase use of bus and light rail in England by >12% over 2000 (with identifiable growth occurring in every region)
4	By 2010-11, 10 largest urban areas to meet congestion targets in Local Transport Plans (LTPs) (against specific metric)
5	By 2010, reduce deaths and serious injuries from road accidents in Great Britain by 40% on the average observed between 1994-98 (50% for children; particular focus on disadvantaged groups)
6	Meet Air Quality Strategy targets for seven specific air pollutants
7	Reduce greenhouse gas emissions by 12.5% below 1990 levels and move towards 20% by 2010

Source: DfT (2006)

bypasses – Banks et al, 2007). Nonetheless, the level of road construction remains an indicator of overall policy balance in practice, particularly when considered against the investment in other modes. Figure 3.1 indicates Labour's record to date in terms of new strategic road network starts and completions. The first period of administration to 2001 in fact shows a high level of completions, but these were mainly roads that had starts confirmed by the Conservatives. The self-imposed moratorium on new starts is evident in 1997-98. An increase in the lane-kilometres of new starts per year is evident through the last decade, but only in the last two years does the rate of starts exceed that of completions in any significant way.

Statistics for trunk and principal motorways (DfT, 2007a) indicate that the network grew by 258 route-kilometres in the decade 1996-2006, equivalent to 8%, while urban principal road length grew by 811 kilometres, also 8%. Despite the reduced rate and type of delivery, it is evident that expansion of the network is ongoing. Hence, supply-led policies still have a strong base of support and road building does not emerge as the 'option of last resort' it was promised to become.

Traffic growth in the same period was much higher than the increase in strategic capacity, at 15% overall in Great Britain and 27% on motorways (Figure 3.2), with growth in most years ranging from 1.4% to 2.1%. While detailed knowledge of the distribution of trips on the network in time and space is required in order to relate road capacity with overall demand, it is clear from the rise in observed congestion that change in demand has outstripped change in supply. The road traffic forecasts for 2015 and 2025 in England suggest that a further 19% and

Figure 3.1: Motorway and trunk road starts and completions, 1996/97-2006/07

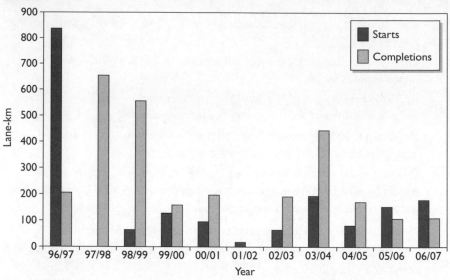

Source: DfT (2007a)

27% growth respectively could occur on 2006 traffic levels, but congestion is in fact quite localised: just 8% of UK traffic experiences very congested conditions (Eddington, 2006, p 28), although the focus of this congestion on trunk roads and in the major urban centres underlines the economic importance of delays.

In autumn 2006 the targeted programme contained around £12 billion worth of schemes at various stages of planning but to be delivered by 2016–17. To be

Figure 3.2: Motor vehicle traffic by road class

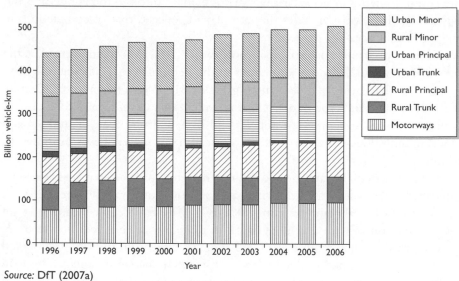

Source: DfT (2007a)

achieved, the rate of investment will need to rise from £0.3 billion per annum in the seven years from April 1999 to April 2006 by more than a factor of three to around £1 billion per annum, and also achieve a peak of £1.6 billion per annum early in the next decade. Moreover, for expenditure at those levels to deliver the intended number of schemes, costs will need to be brought under control. In July 2006 the Secretary of State ordered a review into cost increases of 25% in the previous 18 months, with specific schemes in the targeted programme showing up to 300% increases since entry, with most additional costs being incurred at the pre-construction phase. The Department for Business, Enterprise and Regulatory Reform (BERR) road construction price index shows 51% inflation in road costs since Labour took power (DfT, 2007a). One inflation pressure is that much additional strategic capacity is delivered through widening existing routes rather than building new ones, as this entails high costs due to working on a 'live' road, with complex temporary traffic management, overnight working and the need to adapt every junction and relocate roadside infrastructure to make space for the new lanes. If the inevitable protest is overcome, however, there may be greater pressure to return to building new routes in the future. It has been argued that the motorway system has very little network redundancy and new parallel routes would provide some insurance against the loss of critical infrastructure links through crisis events such as major accidents, extreme weather or even terrorist attack (Boin and Smith, 2006).

Considering the devolved jurisdictions, MacKinnon et al (2008) identify a shift in emphasis away from car restraint between the Scottish Office's (1998) *Travel choices for Scotland* 'sister document' accompanying the 1998 White Paper and *Scotland's transport future* (Scottish Executive, 2004): while the priority of public transport is clear in the objectives, they are neutral in respect of roads provision and traffic levels. Interestingly, the target to reduce road traffic to 2001 levels by 2021 has been retained, although this is largely understood to be an aspirational objective. In Wales, following the 2006 Transport (Wales) Act, a full transport strategy to replace the 2001 *Transport framework for Wales* (Welsh Assembly Government, 2001) was still evolving at the time of writing, although signs of a more definite underlying change in civil service culture away from road building towards public transport priorities can be detected. This is not to deny, however, that established policy supports strategic road construction as a means of reducing congestion, and the Framework stops short of seeking Welsh road traffic reduction targets. Northern Ireland roads policy emerges from a context in which transport planning in the province has been strongly roads oriented, and hence the high profile given to public transport in the *Regional transportation strategy for Northern Ireland 2002-2012* (DRDNI, 2002) is particularly significant.

In Scotland in particular transport decision making has been criticised for departing from the traditions of rational and objective prioritisation in respect of roads. For example, the 1999 Strategic Roads Review did not approve the two schemes with comfortably the strongest benefit-cost ratios (Chapter One). In Wales, the road construction aspirations have perhaps been most ambitious, with more than 30 priority trunk schemes identified. Whereas the most significant of these schemes in terms of cost and scale would increase east–west capacity in the A55 and M4 cross-border routes with England, there is also evidence of 'nation-building': the A470 is a largely 'unimproved' north–south route, which is included despite not attracting significant strategic flows. In Northern Ireland, around two-thirds of planned spending in the strategy is for roads, including for maintenance, but with around a fifth of all funds for strategic roads. Hence, none of the devolved administrations can be regarded as having moved further or faster than the UK government in implementing a more sustainable roads policy.

Policies to reduce emissions and casualties related to road transport

Road and vehicle taxation and safety policies were not affected by the 1999 devolution settlements and UK initiatives in these areas are largely the responsibility of Westminster. There are a number of different taxes paid by motorists that impact on the relative price of motoring. With regard to fuel prices, of which tax forms a significant part (Figure 3.3), stabilisation in the global crude oil price after 2000 and cuts in fuel duty following the protests of the same year resulted initially in a fall in real-terms road fuel prices, although subsequently – despite further (real-terms) cuts in fuel duty in most budgets to 2006 – the price at the pump has risen sharply due to a resurgence in the crude oil price. The price of new cars has shown a progressive fall since New Labour has been in power, and this is one factor behind a 22% increase in the number of private cars registered in that

Figure 3.3: Fuel product and tax shares of unleaded petrol pump prices, as at April each year (2006 prices)

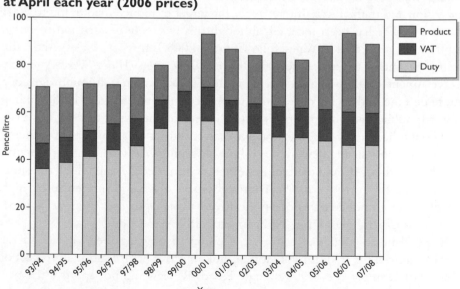

Source: DfT (various years) *Transport statistics Great Britain*

period (DfT, 2007a), with forecasts suggesting that the fleet will grow by a further 13% to 2015 and 19% before 2025. The light goods vehicle fleet has grown twice as fast as this, and is forecast to grow by a further 61% by 2025.

The fuel efficiency of new cars (both petrol and diesel) as tested by official procedures has improved by 11% since Labour took office (DfT, 2007a). Although this improvement reflects technological change promoted by European Union (EU)-level agreements with manufacturers signed prior to New Labour taking office, the change has been supported by UK fiscal measures introduced in the last decade, notably the variation of Vehicle Excise Duty (VED) and company car tax liabilities according to emissions. In the case of the graduated VED the regime was progressively adjusted after being introduced in 2001, so that the maximum difference in liability had grown from £55 to £300 per annum by 2008 (Table 3.2).

Table 3.2: Growing range of CO$_2$-linked rates of VED for petrol cars (£)

CO$_2$ bands (g/km)	Effective date:					
	1 March 2001	1 May 2002	1 May 2003	1 April 2005	23 March 2006	22 March 2007
≤100	–	–	65	65	0	0
101-20	–	70	75	75	40	35
121-50	100	100	105	105	100	115
151-65	120	120	125	125	125	140
166-85	140	140	145	150	150	165
≥186	155	155	160	165	190	205
≥ 225[1]	–	–	–	–	210	300

Note: [1] Band applies to new vehicles registered after 23 March 2006 only.

Source: HM Treasury Budget reports, 2000-07

Europe-wide, however, the voluntary agreements with manufacturers have not been sufficiently effective to achieve the pledged 25% average CO$_2$ emissions improvement on 1995 for *new* cars sold, variously by 2008 and 2009. Instead the manufacturers had achieved only around a 17% reduction by 2008, leading the European Commission to propose that a further target for a 35% reduction by 2012 be enforced by regulation (Meyer and Peterse, 2007). Moreover, the specification of energy-intensive optional equipment has substantially offset even this modest improvement. Air conditioning was rare in cars in 1997, but by 2003 was fitted in 70% of new cars in the EU, and is hence estimated to be present in 70% of the cars in use by 2010 and 95% by 2015. The energy penalty for the use of air conditioning is typically 20-40%, but for small, efficient cars can rise to 50% and even higher for hybrid models (Farrington and Rugh, 2000). Leaks of refrigerants from air conditioning systems increase the carbon-related climate change implications by a factor of three (European Commission, 2003). Considering this and other factors, estimates of CO_2 emissions from private cars in the national environmental accounts suggest that they fell by just 2.6% between 1997 and 2005 as a net result of growth in car ownership and use, and more efficient vehicles entering the fleet.

The reduction in emissions of noxious pollution from road transport vehicles is a more notable area of positive change over the last two decades. Table 3.3 indicates the absolute percentage reductions since 1997, as a result of four waves of EU-wide new-vehicle emissions standards, highlighting both the importance of the European institutions in the road transport sector and the power of regulation when technological solutions are potentially available and policy makers are determined to see change. UK government policies since 1997 have used tax incentives and grants to encourage the upgrading or purchase of cleaner technology vehicles, combined with stricter monitoring of emissions during their life. A significant air-quality problem and associated health implications nonetheless remain in the UK: exposure to particulates has been estimated to cause 8,100 premature deaths and 10,500 hospital admissions per year, while the morbidity associated with oxides of nitrogen NO_x is harder to estimate but believed to be greater than for particulates (Committee on the Medical Effects of Air Pollutants, 1998). Notably these are the two pollutants for which reductions have been smallest. The level of atmospheric concentration has resulted in 144 local authorities in England declaring one or more statutory Air Quality Management Areas (AQMA; as defined by the 1995 Environment Act). Nearly all AQMAs are due to the targets set for nitrogen dioxides (NO_2) and particulates (PM_{10}) being exceeded due to emissions from road transport. In the case of the Bristol city centre AQMA, for example, 97% of the (NO_x) emissions (which react to form NO_2) are due to road traffic (Bristol City Council, 2003). The limited effect of AQMAs to date means that PSA4 will not be achieved in many places. One reason is that, due to technological constraints and the longer vehicle replacement cycles, the improvement from large diesel vehicles has been much less than from smaller vehicles, and requires greater attention by policy makers in the future (Parkhurst, 2004). Consumers have also responded to improving fuel efficiency by buying larger and more powerful vehicles.

An area of considerable policy success has been the fall in overall mortality from road collisions. Deaths fell by 30% (DfT, 2007a) in the decade prior to New Labour entering power, as a result of improved vehicle safety during impacts combined with high-profile initiatives targeting speeding, driving under the influence of alcohol and the wearing of safety belts. Against this historic trend, it

Table 3.3: Reductions in noxious emissions from road transport, 1997-2005

Pollutant	% reduction
Carbon monoxide	69.3
NO_x	45.8
PM_{10}	29.0
Benzene	87.2
1,3-butadiene	73.2
Lead	99.7
Sulphur dioxide	79.3

Source: DfT (2007a)

would perhaps prove hard to achieve further dramatic reductions, particularly in the context of traffic growth, which other things being equal would be expected to increase the absolute incidence of mortality and morbidity. Furthermore, as the 'easy wins' might have been achieved in the 1990s, more policy resources might be necessary to maintain a downward trend. Figure 3.4 indicates that the level of deaths showed little change in the first seven years under New Labour, but there has been a noticeable reduction in the last three years of the series. An overall 12% reduction was achieved between 1997 and 2006 and reductions were recorded for all modes other than cycling. However, while more than half of all fatalities occur to occupants of motor vehicles, this is a function of their dominance in annual passenger-kilometres travelled, and the accident rates for walking, cycling and motorcycling remain significantly higher than those for motor vehicles with cabins. Given the advances in medical care for road casualties, the falling death rate has also been accompanied by a 33% fall in serious injuries and a 19% fall in slight injuries. The reductions in killed and seriously injured children have also been particularly notable, with 51% fewer child pedestrian victims, and 59% fewer child cyclist victims (DfT, 2007a), although concerns exist that this has in part been achieved as a result of lower participation in these activities rather than improved safety. Nonetheless, PSA5 relating to adults is unlikely to be achieved on current performance, although it is likely that the part of the target relating to children will be.

Notwithstanding this positive trend, roads policing has emerged as a key public debate over the decade. Although a cultural change is under way concerning the unacceptability of road casualty rates, and this has resulted in a general tightening of penalties for criminal motoring offences, some motorists have objected strongly

Figure 3.4: Annual deaths on British roads

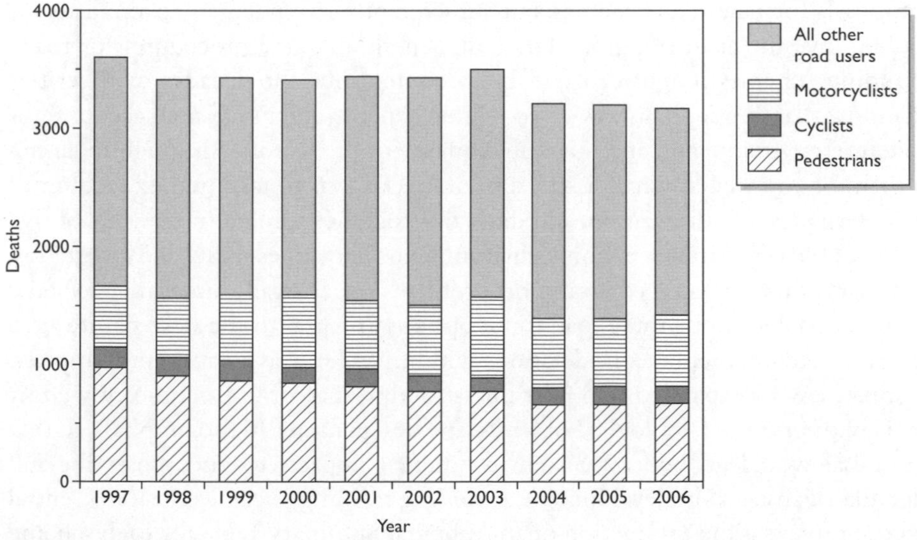

Source: DfT (2007a)

to the use of automatic speed monitoring equipment, which has substantially increased the incidence of speeding being detected. Arguments have emerged around the effectiveness of the equipment in improving safety, as separate from reducing speeding, and whether, as in the case of fuel duty increases, the key motivation for the authorities is raising revenue, rather than behaviour change. The government responded by issuing guidelines that speed cameras and signs warning of their presence be more obvious to motorists and the criteria for the location of cameras be more closely related to past accident sites. From the financial year 2007-08 funding is also delivered through the Local Transport Plan (LTP) (Chapter Two) process and all revenues returned to the Treasury, thus removing any financial incentive, at least at the local level, for camera provision.

Future prospects for 'modal neutrality'

That 89% of road delay is caused by congestion in urban areas (Eddington, 2006), where there is particularly limited potential to expand the road network, is one reason among many that confirms the importance of promoting alternatives to private motor vehicle use, including public transport, cycling, walking and reducing the need to travel altogether. Policies for these other modes are considered in detail in other chapters, but here we consider the extent to which appraisal tools and funding mechanisms that influence the allocation of transport resources remain biased towards road supply solutions.

The New Approach to Appraisal

The New Approach to Appraisal (NATA), discussed briefly in Chapter One, was first set out in *A new deal for transport* (DETR, 1998a), initially to be applied to proposals for new road schemes, but subsequently extended to cover all major public investment in transport. The cost-benefit appraisal procedures for road-building schemes it replaced had been contentious for decades, with critics claiming that the emphasis was on economic benefits, and insufficient account was taken of environmental and intangible quality of life factors. Although retaining a form of cost-benefit analysis, the aim of NATA was to take proper account of a wider range of information, and draw this together using a framework of five overarching objectives – economy, environment, safety, accessibility and integration – as part of the appraisal of a transport problem and, critically, alternative *solutions* to that problem, not simply road route options. Integral to the new significance given to environmental considerations within NATA, was a strong presumption against new or expanded transport infrastructure that would significantly affect sites with protected ecological or landscape designations. It also emphasised that appraisal would go wider than environmental impacts to encompass the full agenda of sustainable development, including tackling social exclusion. Central to the process is the production of an Appraisal Summary Table for each scheme option, intended to make the appraisal process between rival options and schemes more transparent and accessible to decision takers. The intention was that NATA would establish a 'level playing field' between the modes (DETR, 1998a).[1]

Hence, there was a clear implication that major road schemes would in future find it more difficult to find acceptance among the consideration of a range of alternative means of tackling a transport problem. Unfortunately, however, the institutional legacy of many years spent prioritising road building is significant, and has left the DfT and its agencies with a clear and relatively speedy delivery mechanism for roads-based solutions. By contrast, ongoing upheaval in the railway industry (Chapter Four) has significantly complicated delivery. Moreover, Marsden (2002) questions whether the rail schemes identified by the multimodal studies (Chapter One) were in accordance with strategic rail objectives, which focused on managing existing capacity shortfalls rather than attracting significant new patronage. Similarly, local bus and light rail solutions would require development through the local authority LTP process, often in partnership with an operator. In other words, Labour had failed to appreciate the extent and nature of barriers to the promotion of the alternatives to roads.

Given the limited success in moving policy on from predict and provide, a 2007 acknowledgement by the government that NATA needed a 'refresh' was timely. The announcement was made in the light of recommendations by the Eddington Review, and echoed in Scotland where a STAG refresh was also announced. Significantly, the DfT conceded that, although NATA had been devised as part of the non-car philosophy that shaped the 1998 White Paper, it still reflected its road schemes origin, and so the refresh would seek to make the guidance more consistent with 'mode neutrality' (DfT, 2007b).

Novel funding mechanisms

In this context, a 2005 decision to involve the regional institutions in providing prioritisation advice on Regional Funding Allocations (RFAs) to be spent on road and public transport projects was potentially a positive development, although the concept was limited by the exclusion of rail, at least for the first round of the process. Early in this first funding cycle it is not possible to identify definite outcomes as to the effects of the process, but there are some indications that it will be subject to a similar critique to that levelled at the multimodal studies (Chapter One). Parkhurst (2007) discusses the process in the south west. Since advice was to be provided within six months, in time for the 2006–07 financial year, only schemes at an advanced state of planning could be included for the first year (South West Regional Assembly/South West Regional Development Agency, 2006). Beyond this, the advice shows strong sequential priority for deliverable, planned and costed road schemes. Potential public transport schemes were at a later stage of planning and required joint working with the bus industry and integration with the LTP processes covering complex local government geographies (Chapter Two). Hence, only one public transport scheme was included in three initial years of 'firmly allocated' budgets, representing 19% of the allocated capital (Figure 3.5).

The main beneficiaries of future allocations are likely to be non-strategic rural and bypass roads, particularly if there are continued delays in the more complex public transport planning. Such issues have resulted in the advice being criticised for not supporting the key transport needs of the Regional Spatial Strategy (RSS; see Chapter Two), which emphasises infrastructure for the strategic urban areas.

Figure 3.5: South West Regional Funding Allocation: schemes with approval to proceed, 2006/07-2008/09

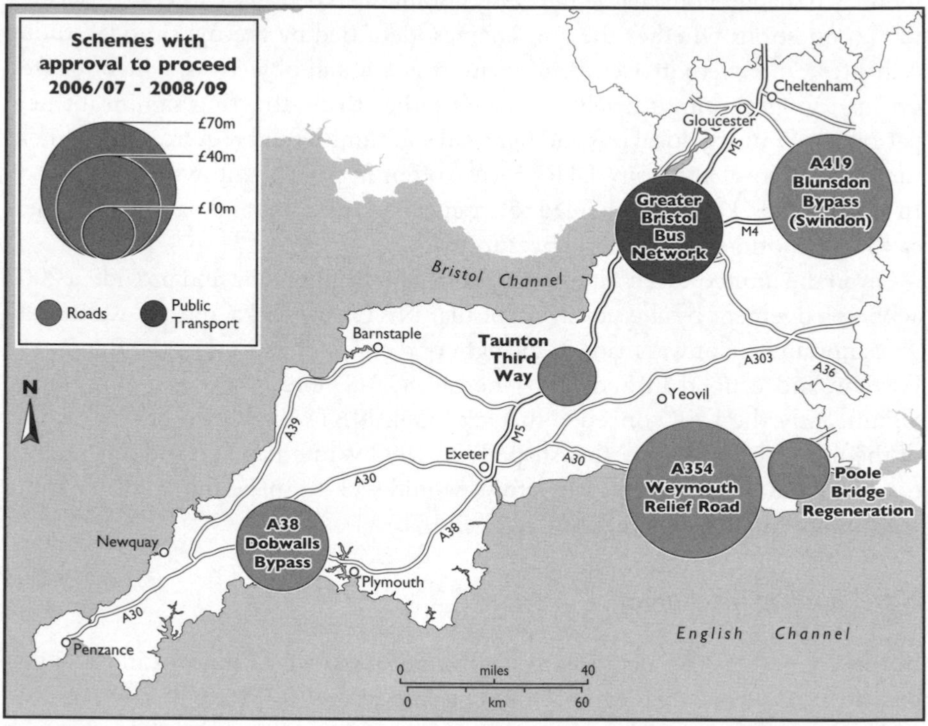

Source: South West Regional Assembly/South West Regional Development Agency (2006)

Another major delivery and funding initiative that emerged from *The future of transport* (DfT, 2004a) is the Transport Innovation Fund (TIF). Local authorities were able to bid for infrastructure investment funds from a budget of £1.4 billion for packages of schemes that overall will have a significant impact on road congestion or economic productivity. A number of authorities sought pump-priming funding to support work towards a bid to the fund, but at the time of writing only three authorities (or groups of authorities) were pursuing full bids: the 10 Greater Manchester councils, four authorities in the west of England area surrounding Bristol, and Cambridgeshire County Council.

Road-user charging

A key factor explaining the limited enthusiasm for TIF among local authorities was the realisation that, in practice, plans for a significant reduction in congestion would only be acceptable to government if they included road-user charging – a circumstance that at once highlights the importance of charging to achieving a more sustainable roads policy, but also underlines the lack of consensus among local politicians about whether it is the 'right' policy for their own areas to pioneer.

A new deal for transport (DETR, 1998a) had discussed the importance of undertaking a number of pilot road-pricing schemes in different places including urban areas and parts of the trunk road network. Road-user charging had also been considered in the multimodal studies process (and indeed was recommended by some studies), but the government had refused to countenance its introduction in this context. The 2000 Transport Act enabled local authorities to take the initiative in introducing schemes and *Transport 2010* – rather optimistically, since central government had effectively made clear that it would have nothing to do with introducing such schemes – estimated that £3 billion of public sector spending on transport would be available in the form of hypothecated revenues from *local* road user and workplace parking charges in the period 2004-05 to 2010-11. This was based on the assumption that 19 cities in addition to London would adopt charging schemes. In the event, when Ken Livingstone introduced the London congestion charge in February 2003, it was in the face of the active opposition of central government (despite a clear popular mandate provided by the London elections). Elsewhere, still the only user charge to have been introduced on the national trunk road network is on the M6 Toll motorway (agreed under the Conservatives), while the rejection of a proposed Edinburgh city cordon scheme at referendum markedly slowed the wider momentum behind charging (Chapter Two).

The fuel price protests of 2000 seemed to have had a fundamental influence on transport policy ambition in general and, in the long run, road-user charging in particular. Almost paradoxically, however, in the two years following the fuel protests, policy development in respect of strategic road pricing seemed to take a significant step forward, with the government proposing in the November 2000 pre-budget report to consult on a heavy goods vehicle (HGV)-only charge to replace part of the existing lorry taxation regime. One of the key grievances underpinning road hauliers' role in the fuel protests had been the belief that foreign operators were undercutting UK operators by fuelling in cheaper continental states while not paying UK VED. In applying to all lorries and offering rebates only to UK hauliers, the charge would have directly addressed such concerns and attracted broad support. Successful introduction of the charge would have also provided a piloting exercise for a general traffic charge and strengthened the case for 'efficient pricing' to be applied to all road trips. Similar charges for large vehicles were subsequently introduced in the central European 'transit' states of Switzerland, Austria and Germany, and in 2004 *The future of transport* confirmed that Labour was 'pressing ahead' with the delivery of a distance-based scheme by 2007-08 (DfT, 2004a, para 8.9). Suddenly, however, the lorry-only policy was abandoned in July 2005, despite procurement being at an advanced stage. McKinnon (2006) observes that the scheme was more complex than the German scheme – indeed over-complex – and it can also be argued that a congestion-oriented freight-charging scheme makes little sense in isolation from a general traffic scheme, given that car traffic dominates demand.

Although the practical focus hitherto for general traffic charging has been on local schemes, policy documents such as the *Feasibility study of road pricing in the UK* (DfT, 2004b) accept that it will ultimately be more effective to introduce a nationwide scheme than rely on a series of different local ones. A second likely shift in future charging practice is that – unlike the London charge, which, despite its name, is only crudely associated with the dynamic experience of congestion – the operation of future schemes will be closely related to congestion levels. The Commission for Integrated Transport (CfIT) (2002) predicted that a 44% reduction in congestion was possible with only a 5% reduction in traffic levels because motorists would change their routes and/or departure times as their dominant responses. Third, it is also likely that any new national scheme will be revenue neutral, which in practice would see any road-user charging scheme replacing some aspects of existing motoring taxes.

Given that the strategic context of road-user charging is in fact relatively clearly defined, and that the 'devil in the detail' requires strategy to be confirmed before it can be addressed, and in the context of a large House of Commons majority, the line taken in *The future of transport* (DfT, 2004a) may in years to come be viewed as both unacceptably and unnecessarily cautious, providing a prima facie case of 'failure of leadership'. The document in fact states the stark choice facing UK road users in language that is perhaps untypically clear for a strategic policy statement:

> Looking ahead, the key strategic choice for road users is between service levels which continually deteriorate (since we cannot build our way out of congestion) [and] new ways of paying for road use, which incentivise smarter individual choices about when and how we travel. (DfT, 2004a, para 3.22)

It is, then, striking that this statement is followed not by specific proposed policy actions, but instead the rather wanting assertion that the 'time has come *seriously to consider* the role that could be played by some form of road pricing policy' (DfT, 2004a, para 3.23, emphasis added); this ultimately supports the weak conclusion that the government would be 'leading the debate' on road pricing'. This ignores the urgency of a decision in principle and the allocation of commensurate resources necessary for the policy to become a reality in the relatively short period of a decade. In the context of the 2005 rejection of the Edinburgh scheme and over 1.7 million citizens signing an online petition against charging in early 2007

(BBC, 2007), simply waiting for public opinion to move is unlikely to be effective; the public's understanding of the technology remains limited, and suspicions about the non-transport implications such as the consequences for privacy and social justice are easy to exploit in a context of uncertainty.

The validity of the 'leadership' policy development path is in fact demonstrated by the case of the Netherlands. Notwithstanding that country having had its own 'on-off' relationship with charging in the last decade related to party political stances, in autumn 2007 the Dutch government agreed to introduce national charging from 2011 for freight vehicles and 2012 for private cars, with the full scheme implemented by 2016. Notably, given the spatial development pattern of the Netherlands has much in common with south east England, the strategic Dutch policy context is for a revenue-neutral, distance-related charge varied by congestion as well as by other environmental factors and delivered by satellite-based technology (*Transport Times*, 2007). By contrast, the UK experience of the last four years has continued to echo the schizophrenia of *The future of transport*, with technical studies confirming the necessity for and likely effects of different types of charging being met with political statements that move the earliest expected date for a national scheme again beyond a rolling 10-year horizon.

Conclusion

If predict and provide were still the underlying agenda, current rates of new road scheme starts and completions and future prospects for increasing those rates suggest that it would be a failing policy. Instead, the shift in discourse from journey-time savings to reliability describes a roads policy that is less focused on capacity expansion. To some extent this may only reflect historical progression towards a near-complete high-quality road network. Eddington (2006), for example, confirms that more than 45% of the UK's urban population is directly connected to the strategic road network and more than two-thirds of the largest towns and cities are directly connected to the motorway network. More than three-quarters of the UK's population can also be reached by a day-return lorry movement from the main logistics bases in the English Midlands. And while Eddington observes that transport efficiency is valuable for business, with a 5% reduction in travel time on the roads possibly worth £2.5 billion in cost savings, or 0.2% of Gross Domestic Product (GDP), there are arguably few areas of the UK in which, to follow Banister and Berechman (2000), the fundamental economic problems relate to accessibility rather than dynamism. In other words, there are few cases of regions well equipped in terms of the 'factors of production' such as development land, suitably skilled labour, and capital investment awaiting only investment in strategic transport capacity in order to have their prosperities transformed.

Moving on from predict and provide does not imply, of course, that the case for strategic road building will not still be argued and justified, at least on congestion grounds. Banks et al (2007) argue that in a demand management policy context including road-user charging, the case for road construction in fact grows, because tolls at 'acceptable' – that is, politically deliverable – levels will not remove all congestion, and where it persists, the benefits of construction will be high (as demonstrated by willingness to pay the tolls) and these benefits can also be 'locked in' by charging. And, more pragmatically, if motorists pay tolls intended to reduce congestion, creating a significant revenue stream as a result, they will expect some of the funds to be spent on new road construction in order to deliver that expected outcome.

Meanwhile, in a pre-charging context, other evidence confirms that the UK is a long way from achieving a sustainable roads policy. While Stern potentially offers some comfort to ministers in that the transport sector can be a 'late contributor' to national emissions reduction, government seems to be over-reliant on the hope that effective 'technical fixes' lie just over the policy horizon; a risky strategy not in accordance with the precautionary principle. Forecast trends indicate rising car ownership and use, and the more dependent on cars society is allowed to become, the harder it will be to reduce the carbon intensity of transport and achieve the wider sustainable community objectives. Of the seven transport PSA targets, road transport policy is central to delivering five and all have an 'achieve-by' date earlier than 2012. It is too late to achieve the two relating to congestion in the absence of road-user charging; that relating to air quality will also not be achieved, largely because affordable technical fixes have not been deliverable for large diesel vehicles; transport will also make little or no contribution to the climate-change emissions target. Only in the case of road safety is the PSA likely to be achieved in part, although for it to be achieved in full would require policy to target aggressively the minority groups of motorists who are responsible for the majority of deaths and injuries.

The government, having opposed the London congestion charge and considered but then shelved a national scheme for HGVs, at least now accepts implicitly within its TIF initiative that charging is essential to address congestion objectives. Yet the focus on this local instrument serves to reinforce the view that central government is seeking to pass the political risk of a potentially unpopular policy down to lower tiers of government rather than directly seek to lead public opinion on the issue. The TIF schemes, if implemented, will only address a few more specific locations, while the thrust of national policy on this topic again seeks to 'buy time', emphasising technical measures such as hard-shoulder running and better information provision for reasons of both political and financial expediency. These measures, however, only provide temporary or virtual capacity increases, achieving a measure of short-term congestion reduction but without addressing its fundamental causes.

In critiquing government policy for timidity, reactiveness and excess faith in future technologies, it must be acknowledged that the politics of road transport is not an 'easy' arena, compared perhaps with the utilities sector: people generally accept, for example, metered supply of water as a means of relating supply and demand, and changes in consumer behaviour to improve energy efficiency – to the benefit of both the consumer and the environment – can often be achieved with relatively little price adjustment. By contrast, the road transport 'consumer' may perceive that the roads have been 'paid for already' and that behavioural change, such as the use of different modes of transport, is a major step that is personally disadvantageous. Nonetheless, a cultural change has been achieved in London, and examples of leadership on this issue elsewhere have delivered road-freight charging in three European states and the prospect of the first universal charging scheme in another. While market pricing is most obviously a right-of-centre policy, a left-of-centre Mayor introduced the only major UK scheme to date, suggesting that policy entrepreneurship – an important feature of road transport policy in the past (Dudley and Richardson, 2000) – may be a vital, missing ingredient for paradigm shift at the UK national level (MacKinnon et al, 2008).

In the final analysis, however, the 'elephant in the room' may well be the global oil price. The $16-$18 per barrel long-run price assumption of *Transport 2010* (DETR, 2000) now seems a policy lifetime away, with $100 per barrel passed in December 2007 and prices approaching $150 in July 2008. Ultimately, it may be this increasingly uncontrollable, external factor that creates the space in the policy arena for 'radical leadership' and real policy change to emerge.

Note

[1] Scottish Transport Appraisal Guidance (STAG) and Welsh Transport Appraisal Guidance (WelTAG) operate on similar principles in Scotland and Wales respectively (Chapter One).

References

Banister, D. and Berechman, J. (2000) *Transport investment and economic development*, London: University College London Press.

Banks, N., Bayliss, T. and Glaister, S. (2007) *Motoring towards 2050: Roads and reality*, London: RAC Foundation.

BBC (British Broadcasting Corporation) (2007) *Q&A: Road pricing*, http://news.bbc.co.uk/1/hi/uk/6382211.stm (accessed 30 March 2008).

Boin, A. and Smith, D. (2006) 'Terrorism and critical infrastructures: implications for public–private crisis management', *Public Money and Management*, 26(5), pp 295-30.

Bristol City Council (2003) *Air Quality Action Plan Consultation*, Bristol: Bristol City Council.

CfIT (Commission for Integrated Transport) (2002) *Paying for road use*, London: CfIT, www.cfit.gov.uk/docs/2002/pfru/index.htm (accessed 14 January 2008).

Committee on the Medical Effects of Air Pollutants (1998) *The quantification of the effects of air pollution on health in the United Kingdom*, London: The Stationery Office.

Co-operative Bank/Friends of the Earth (2006) *The future starts here: The route to a low-carbon economy*, London: Friends of the Earth.

DETR (Department of the Environment, Transport and the Regions) (1998a) *A new deal for transport: Better for everyone*, Cm 3950, The government's White Paper on the future of transport, London: The Stationery Office.

DETR (1998b) *A new deal for trunk roads in England*, London: DETR.

DETR (2000) *Transport 2010: The ten-year plan*, London: DETR.

DfT (Department for Transport) (2004a) *The future of transport: A network for 2030*, Cm 6234, London: The Stationery Office.

DfT (2004b) *Feasibility study of road pricing in the UK*, London: DfT.

DfT (2006) *Autumn performance report 2006*, Cm 6976, London: DfT.

DfT (2007a) *Transport statistics Great Britain* (33rd edition), London: The Stationery Office.

DfT (2007b) *The NATA refresh: Reviewing the New Approach to Appraisal*, London: DfT.

DoT (Department of Transport) (1989) *Roads for prosperity*, Cm 693, London: HMSO.

DRDNI (Department for Regional Development Northern Ireland) (2002) *Regional transportation strategy for Northern Ireland 2002-2012*, Belfast: DRDNI.

Dudley, G. and Richardson, J. (2000) *Why does policy change? Lessons from British transport policy 1945-1999*, London: Routledge.

Eddington, R. (2006) *The Eddington transport study: The case for action: Sir Rod Eddington's advice to the government*, London: HM Treasury.

European Commission (2003) *Consultation paper: How to considerably reduce greenhouse gas emissions due to mobile air conditioners*, Brussels: EC.

Farrington, R. and Rugh, J. (2000) *Impact of vehicle air-conditioning on fuel economy, tailpipe emissions and electric vehicle range*, Paper to the Earth Technologies Forum, Washington DC, 31 October, Colorado: National Renewable Energy Laboratory.

Goodwin, P., Hallett, S., Kenny, F. and Stokes, G. (1991) *Transport: The new realism*, London: Rees Jeffreys Road Fund.

MacKinnon, D., Shaw, J. and Docherty, I. (2008) *Diverging mobilities: Devolution, transport and policy innovation*, Oxford: Elsevier.

Marsden, G. (2002) *The multi-modal studies: How they all add up*, London: Transport Planning Society.

McKinnon, A. (2006) 'Government plans for lorry road-user charging in the UK: a critique and an alternative', *Transport Policy*, 13, pp 204-16.

Meyer, K. and Peterse, A. (2007) *Regulating CO$_2$ emissions of new cars*, Background Briefing (October 2007 edition), Brussels: European Federation for Transport and Environment.

Parkhurst, G. (2004) 'Air quality and the environmental transport policy discourse in Oxford', *Transportation Research D: Transport and Environment*, 9(6), pp 419-36.

Parkhurst, G. (2007) 'Does the regionalisation of transport decision-making promote sustainability? The case of the English south west', Proceedings of Regional Studies Association Conference on Transport, Mobility and Regional Development, 23 November, RSA, Seaford.

Scottish Executive (2004) *Scotland's transport future: The transport White Paper*, Edinburgh: Scottish Executive, www.scotland.gov.uk/library5/transport/stfwp-01.asp (accessed 14 May 2007).

Scottish Office (1998) *Travel choices for Scotland: The Scottish integrated transport White Paper*, Edinburgh: Scottish Office.

Shaw, J. and Walton, W. (2001) 'Labour's new trunk-roads policy for England: an emerging pragmatic multimodalism?' *Environment and Planning A*, 33, pp 1031-56.

South West Regional Assembly/South West Regional Development Agency (2006) *South West Regional Funding Allocations – transport: Spreadsheets*, Bristol: GOSW, www.gosw.gov.uk/gosw/OurRegion/335990/?a=42496 (accessed 5 October 2007).

Stern, N. (2006) *Stern review of the economics of climate change*, London: HM Treasury.

Transport Times (2007) 'UK can learn from Dutch road pricing move', December, p 7.

Walton, W. (2003) 'Roads and traffic congestion policies: one step forward, two steps back', in I. Docherty and J. Shaw (eds) *A new deal for transport?*, Oxford: Blackwell, pp 75-107.

Welsh Assembly Government (2001) *The transport framework for Wales*, Cardiff: Welsh Assembly Government.

FOUR

Is Labour delivering a sustainable railway?

John Preston

On one level, the railways under New Labour seem a runaway success. In the 10 years since the administration took control, passenger kilometres carried by the national rail network have increased by over 40% and freight tonne kilometres have increased by more than 70% (ORR, 2007). Yet this does not seem consistent with the continual reforms to the industry that have been undertaken by the government. The 2000 Transport Act provided the legal basis for the establishment of the Strategic Rail Authority (SRA), while *Transport 2010: The 10-year plan* (DETR, 2000) established performance targets and investment levels for rail (see Shaw and Farrington, 2003). These reforms were undermined by a serious accident at Hatfield, north of London, in October 2000 and the subsequent deterioration of infrastructure performance, increases in rail costs and the failure of Railtrack and around one-half of the franchised passenger train operators. This led to a further period of introspection for the railways that has included two White Papers (2004 and 2007), a Railways Act (2005) and the abolition of the ill-fated SRA. At the end of this period the concept of sustainability has become more firmly entrenched in the rail industry's psyche, as epitomised by the title of the 2007 White Paper *Delivering a sustainable railway* (DfT, 2007a). I argue in this chapter, though, that the emphasis on sustainability largely reflects the government's desire to achieve financial stability and is less about achieving broader economic, social and environmental goals. As a result, the longstanding tensions between commercial and social objectives in the rail sector have not been explicitly recognised and these may provide the fault lines that will necessitate further change in years to come.

The railway under New Labour

As Wolmar (2007) has pointed out, the strained relationship between the railways and the state is almost as old as the railways themselves. The privatisation idealists of the early 1990s thought they might solve this problem by reducing the role of government, but in many ways the new regime that was established by the 1993 Railways Act actually increased the role of the state (Shaw, 2000). Although passenger train operations were to be privatised by franchising, the Office of Passenger Rail Franchising (OPRAF) would set minimum service levels, while almost half of all fares would be regulated and detailed arrangements were put in place for the provision of integrated ticketing, retailing and information provision. The regulation by government of punctuality, reliability and overcrowding would be tightened. The franchised operators would be protected from open access competition by the moderation of competition rules established by the Office of the Rail Regulator (ORR), who would also ensure that competition law applied to the passenger rail industry.[1] Infrastructure ownership was transferred to Railtrack in 1994, which was floated in 1996. A substantial degree of public control remained, however, with access charges and investment levels determined in conjunction with ORR through five-year control periods (commencing in 1994) and with the conditions that ORR could attach to Railtrack's network licence.

In opposition, (old) Labour vigorously opposed privatisation, but by the time of the May 1997 General Election privatisation was a done deal. New Labour's 1997 manifesto did not commit itself to the publicly owned, publicly accountable railway (*The Independent*, 1995; Chapter One), which John Prescott and others had called for before the election (and to which the trades unions[2] still aspire – see TSSA, 2007). Instead, immediately before the election, Labour stated: 'Our task will be to improve the situation as we find it, not as we would wish it to be' (Labour Party, 1997, unpaginated). The reasons were largely pragmatic: renationalisation would have been expensive and, perhaps more importantly, perceived as being anti-business, thus conflicting with New Labour's wider economic goals. Moreover, transport was not a real priority for the Blair government (Chapter One). Over time, however, there was a realisation that, although privatised, with the important exception of the freight sector the industry was *not deregulated*. There remained relatively tight public control and this would give ministers sufficient wriggle room to try and achieve their goals.

The first manifestation of this was the creation of the SRA and the more visionary use of franchises to achieve long-run investment through the late Sir Alistair Morton's championing of special purpose vehicles (SPVs), a form of public–private partnership. With the exception of the Chiltern and, to a lesser extent, Merseyrail franchises, this approach was blown out of the water by the recasting of rail economics precipitated by the Hatfield accident, as the SRA was forced to become a reactive rather than proactive body.

Indeed, the second manifestation was New Labour's response to the events triggered by the Hatfield accident (described in more detail in Preston, 2002). In terms of fatalities the Hatfield accident was relatively minor but it revealed that Railtrack had failed to maintain one of its principal assets – its track – to an appropriate standard and exposed the lack of engineering and managerial expertise to prevent and remedy this problem in a company by then fixated by its share price and property activities. The remedial measures required drastically weakened Railtrack's finances but the fatal mistake was probably for the company's senior managers (in particular John Robinson, the Chairman) to deal directly with the Secretary of State, Stephen Byers, rather than seek a regulatory review from the Rail Regulator, Tom Winsor. Byers saw his chance to bring Railtrack more firmly under public control and placed it in administration using powers that existed under the 1993 Railways Act (see also Wolmar, 2001). This would, at least in formal terms, fall short of renationalisation. Instead, a company limited by guarantee, Network Rail, governed by independent 'members' rather than shareholders, was eventually established in 2002. In a subsequent review of these arrangements, the National Audit Office (2004) highlighted weaknesses in this new organisational structure and the lack of appropriate incentives. Despite its unusual governance structure, under the leadership of its first Chief Executive, John Armitt, Network Rail proved quite effective in managing its engineering functions and has made substantial efficiency gains, although as we shall see there remains a question mark over the degree of cost control it has exhibited. Nonetheless, this structure probably means it will be vulnerable to future reform, particularly if there is a change in political control, or a repetition of the events of the 2007/08 New Year period, when severe overruns in several major engineering operations earned the company the moniker 'Network Failed' (*The Times*, 2008).

The third manifestation of more proactive regulation was New Labour's response to the failures of around half the franchised train operating companies (TOCs) following the increases in both capital and operating costs that followed the Hatfield accident. For reasons that were never fully articulated, the government had lost faith in the SRA, its own creation; in part this might have been due to a breakdown in relations between Richard Bowker, Alistair Morton's successor as head of the SRA, and ministers. But it was also due to ministers' desire to have firmer control over financial support and investment levels in the rail industry, and a recognition that persuasion and negotiation were no longer enough to solve the rail industry's problems. The desire to set rail in a multimodal context was also expressed (see, for example, DfT, 2004). The solution, implemented by the 2005 Railways Act, was to abolish the arm's-length SRA and bring its functions under more direct ministerial control as a division of the Department for Transport (DfT). At the same time, some regulatory functions of the ORR with respect to Network Rail's performance and capacity transferred to the DfT, although ORR retained responsibility for determining track access and charges and became responsible for safety regulation, a hot potato that had already been passed from Railtrack to the Health and Safety Executive.

One of the main upshots of these changes has been a new round of franchising, in which the service requirements are tightly specified by the government, revenue risks are shared between the government and the winning bidder through a 'cap-and-collar' regime,[3] and the DfT has committed itself to not negotiating with franchises that are in danger of defaulting (and has even put 'cross default' provisions in place for companies owning more than one franchise). Already, the Department has specified and let five franchises (East Coast, East Midlands, Cross Country, South Western and London Midland) and has overseen a further three that were initiated by the SRA (Thameslink/Great Northern,[4] Great Western and South Eastern Trains). Some lines formerly operated by Silverlink are also now administered by Transport for London (TfL). Of these nine franchises, all awarded in 2006 and 2007, only two have been won by the incumbent.

The East Coast franchise was particularly interesting as this had initially been awarded by the SRA to Great North Eastern Railway (GNER) in May 2005. The winning bidder was almost immediately hit by a series of unfortunate events that would wreck its financial plans. It had not anticipated the upsurge in fuel costs that occurred in 2005/06. In addition, its revenue was hit by the 7 July 2005 bombings in Central London. Moreover, entry by an open access operator, Grand Central, which was awarded a licence by the ORR for a proposed route between London and Sunderland, will abstract some revenue, particularly at York. To compound matters, GNER's parent company, Sea Containers, was also in financial difficulties. In December 2006, GNER entered into a management agreement with the DfT, although in this case GNER would receive no fee but instead an incentive if revenue growth exceeded an agreed target. Almost immediately, the process of reletting the franchise was begun. The bids for these were submitted in June 2007 and the new franchise awarded in August, to begin operations at the end of the year. GNER was made to cover the DfT's costs in reletting the franchise. Somewhat controversially, the existing GNER management team was permitted to join a bid from Stagecoach and Virgin but this was to no avail as the franchise was awarded to National Express. In this case, the government has just about been able to keep its promise not to renegotiate, but it is unlikely that the line could be held in the event of mass defaults of the like seen in 2001/02, or that would probably be inevitable in the case of any economic downturn. Moreover, the government was fortunate that GNER was a single-franchise business so the cross-default provisions were not applicable.

The other main upshot was the publication in July 2007 of the White Paper *Delivering a sustainable railway* (DfT, 2007a), which, like many of Labour's previous pronouncements examined elsewhere in the book, makes little attempt to deal explicitly with the concept of sustainability, except in the economic domain, for reasons that will become apparent later in the chapter. The White Paper speaks of the first plan for major growth since the Modernisation Plan of the 1950s – which seems rather to downplay the aspirations of *Transport 2010* (DETR, 2000) – and illustrates the government's continued penchant for setting targets while in actual fact muddling along with various short-lived, tactical policy interventions and institutional structures (Chapter One). Whereas previously the aim had been to increase passenger kilometres by 50% and freight kilometres by 80% in the decade from 2000, *Delivering a sustainable railway* specifies, for example, by 2014:

- a 3% reduction in the risk of death and injury to passengers and employees from rail accidents;
- an improvement in punctuality and reliability performance to 92.6% (from the then current 88%);
- a 25% reduction in the number of delays of over 30 minutes;
- an increase in capacity to accommodate a 22.5% growth in passenger demand.

In the absence of a suite of broader sustainable transport measures including road pricing and significant rail capacity increases, the last target represents something of a reality check after *Transport 2010*. The targets in that document were subsequently redefined as benchmarks and despite favourable economic conditions they are unlikely to be met: the seven-year growth from 1999/00 to 2006/07 was 25% for passengers and 21% for freight.

Delivering a sustainable railway is therefore partly about getting the basics right – about ensuring that reliability recovers from the downturn initiated by the Hatfield accident (Figure 4.1), that improvements in safety are continued (Figure 4.2), and that extra capacity is provided by running longer trains and removing pinch points on the network such as at Birmingham New Street and Reading and finally committing to the Thameslink upgrade and, subsequently, Crossrail projects. Perhaps most significantly, however, its main theme is about ensuring stable funding – in other words, achieving financial and economic sustainability – rather than a more strategic appraisal of rail's role as part of a wider sustainable transport policy taking into account environmental and social as well as economic needs.

Figure 4.1: Public performance measures

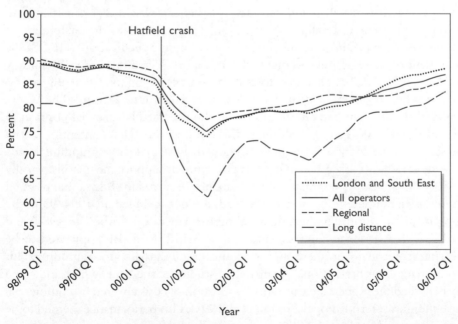

Note: For long-distance operators the percentage shown is that of trains arriving within 10 minutes of schedule at the final destination; for London and the south east and for regional operators it is within five minutes of this time. QI = Quarter One.

Source: DfT (2007a)

Figure 4.2: Safety performance

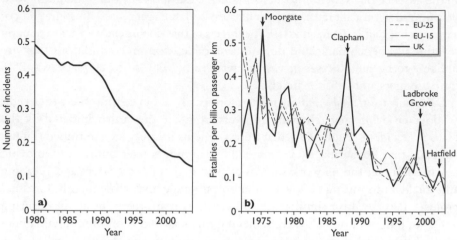

Note: For 2004, data are for the nine-month period from 1 April to 31 December.

Source: Health and Safety Executive (2004)

Financial and economic sustainability

In its executive summary, *Delivering a sustainable railway* states that over £10 billion will be invested in enhancing capacity between 2009 and 2014, with overall government support totalling £15 billion. This constitutes the Statement of Funds Available (SOFA). Yet the 'High Level Output Specification' (HLOS) – a statement of strategic improvements the Transport Secretary wishes the railway industry to secure – indicates a total cash cost of £9 billion, reducing to £6 billion when financing and operating costs are taken into account. The White Paper also states that 'the railway is now in the most stable financial position in 50 years' (DfT, 2007a, p 127), although this claim is somewhat contentious. Data presented in the document (Figure 4.3) show that the majority of funding for the passenger railway currently comes from government support and is at historically high levels. Similarly poor financial performance occurred in 1982 (a year plagued by industrial disputes) and, if sales proceeds are not included, in 1994/95 at the time of privatisation. The best financial performance was in the late 1980s and early 1990s where the commercialisation of British Rail (BR) appeared to be bearing fruit and government support constituted less than 30% of funding. This is confirmed by international comparative studies at the time, which indicated that BR had the highest farebox ratio (proportion of costs covered by commercial revenue) in western Europe (Preston et al, 1994). This performance seemed to be being repeated in the late 1990s as the subsidy reductions from the first round of franchises were becoming apparent. Everything changed, however, with the Hatfield accident, the financial collapse of 13 of the first-round franchises and the need to pay large grants to Railtrack and subsequently Network Rail.

Figure 4.3: Funding of the passenger railway

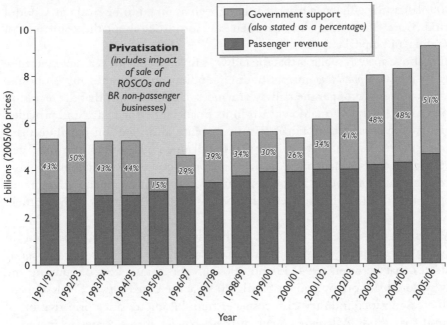

Year

Note: Excludes revenue from property, freight and open access operations, Network Rail's debt and freight grants. Includes all revenue from ticket sales and miscellaneous charges such as parking fees.

Source: ORR (2006)

It is very difficult to put together consistent time-series data on funding because these are affected by alterations in definitions and jurisdictional changes resulting from devolution (Chapter Two). Immediately prior to the sale of BR, government support was around £2.5 billion (in 2002/03 prices) but by the time of the Hatfield accident this had broadly halved. Following the Hatfield accident, however, significant direct subsidy has been given to Railtrack and subsequently Network Rail so that in 2006/07 government support was estimated to be over £5.6 billion. This has, too, involved some increases in revenue support from central government (SRA/DfT) and the Passenger Transport Executives (PTEs), which have also been affected by the pass-through of increased track access charges. With the latest round of franchises, though, revenue support is expected to decrease dramatically so that by 2013/14 it will be around £400 million (in 2002/03 prices). A number of recent winning franchisees are assuming that strong demand and revenue growth and cost control will permit the payment of substantial premia by franchisees to the government towards the end of their franchise terms. But at the same time there is a significant refocusing of subsidy away from train operators and towards the infrastructure authority. Thus, whereas TOCs were in receipt of all substantive government support in 1995/96, by 2013/14 they will only be receiving around 18% of such support. Although this would place Britain on a similar basis to countries such as Sweden, this important change in subsidy policy has generated little public discussion. There is also to be a drastic reduction in direct support to Network Rail at the start of its regulatory 'Control Period 4' (2009/10) as the efficiency gains that have been assumed to be made in 'Control Period 3' are factored in, although there are also issues about the conflation of operating and capital expenses.

The above analysis suggests that the railway's finances are not yet stable, but they may be by 2014 *providing* current trading conditions continue – any economic downturn would scupper the railway's finances in a similar way that the recession of the early 1990s led to a downturn in its financial performance and provided a pretext for privatisation. Financial sustainability also relies on franchise plans coming to fruition, and in particular that the planned increases in non-regulated fares are revenue enhancing. And it relies on Network Rail achieving large efficiency gains of around 5% per annum. Even if all this happens, government support in 2013/14 will in real terms still be almost double that before the Hatfield crash in financial year 2000/01.

Moreover, this increase in public funding is accompanied by an increase in industry costs that has yet to be adequately explained. *Delivering a sustainable railway* indicates that between 1994/95 and 2004/05 the annual cost of running the railway doubled. Work by Andrew Smith (2006) at the University of Leeds suggests an increase in total industry cash costs per train kilometre since privatisation of around two-thirds. A large element of these cost increases relates to increased capital expenditure as a renewals backlog, which emerged following the Hatfield accident, was addressed. This may be a temporary phenomenon that disappears in the fullness of time and helps explain much of the planned reduction in government support. But Nash and Smith (2006) also found a 47.5% increase in TOC costs between 1999/2000 and 2003/04, while passenger train kilometres only increased by 6.2% (indicating a 38.8% increase in unit costs). The causes of these increases are more difficult to explain (and the increases themselves are not uncontentious). Labour costs have increased (in total by 32.7%), split almost equally between increased head count and wage rates (see also MacKinnon et al, 2008a). A number of other explanations are possible, including increased fuel costs, and TOCs taking on greater responsibilities for rolling stock and infrastructure (especially stations), maintenance and renewal. There is some evidence that cost increases were greatest where franchises were renegotiated or transformed into 'cost plus' contracts. To the extent that most of these have been refranchised, these cost increases may also be temporary.

But there is also the strong possibility that some of the cost increases are symptomatic of the privatised structure, with high transaction and regulatory costs. Certainly there is a longstanding concern that the capital costs of railways have increased, exemplified by the West Coast Main Line Passenger Upgrade (PUG). The costs of PUG increased from £2.2 billion in 1997 (for a scheme to be completed in 2005), through £5.8 billion in 1999 (but with an upgraded specification), an estimated £7.5 billion in 2001 (*Rail*, 2001) and up to £13 billion by 2002. The scheme will finally be completed by the end of 2008 at a cost of almost £9 billion. Industry analyst Roger Ford believes that, compared with BR, under Railtrack the costs for upgrades and modernisation projects increased by 150% and costs for maintenance increased by 50% (*Modern Railways*, 2001). Network Rail has dealt with some of these issues by bringing in-house many engineering functions that were previously contracted out (by Railtrack) and by developing its capabilities as a smart procurer.

The true picture with respect to investment is also difficult to determine. Despite an initial investment hiatus, particularly with respect to rolling stock around the time of privatisation, there has subsequently been something of a boom in rail investment, at least in terms of expenditure. It now looks as though this boom is beginning to wane, at least in England (Figure 4.4). Recent investment peaked in 2003/04, which is related to the West Coast Main Line PUG. The break in the data series in Figure 4.4 is followed by proposed HLOS expenditure. These HLOS investments are additional to other investments being made by the TOCs, Rolling Stock Companies (ROSCOs) and Network Rail but it seems clear that the funding of the HLOS requirements on their own does not represent an investment programme on the scale of the 1950s Modernisation Plan. Furthermore, it is not immediately evident that, in real terms, the total investment in rail improvements between 2009 and 2014 will be greater than 2004-09, despite the White Paper's claims.

So if the rail industry is not yet financially sustainable, to what extent is it economically sustainable? While the large increases in usage of passenger and freight services indicate that the industry is doing something right, it can be

Figure 4.4: Investment in national rail (exludes Channel Tunnel rail link)

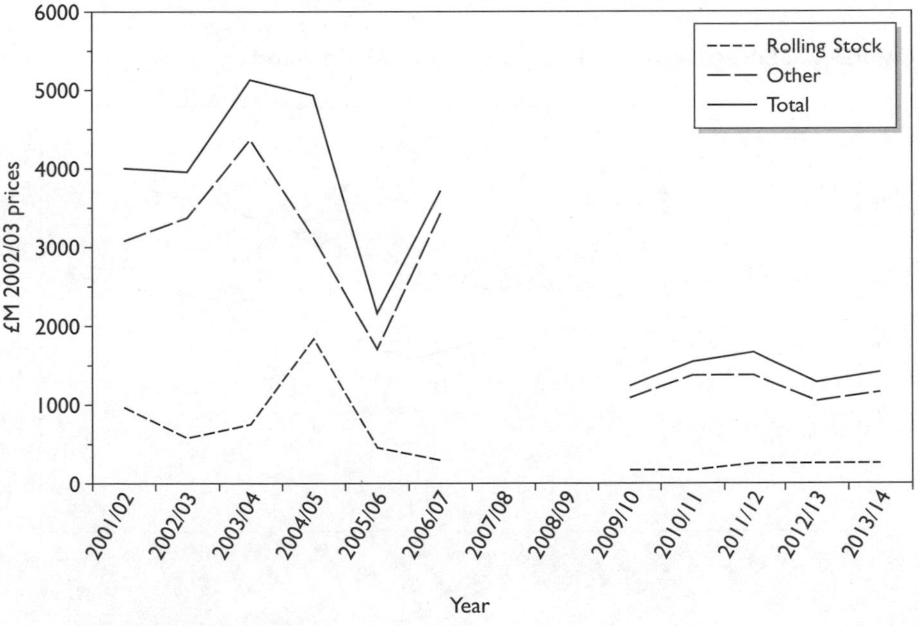

Source: DfT (2007a); ORR (2007)

suggested that around 84% of passenger growth (see also Wardman, 2005) and 46% of freight growth can be attributed to rising national income (Figures 4.5 and 4.6). For freight, much of the rest of the growth may be ascribed to falling tariffs, with Drew (2006) estimating a decrease of around one-third between 1995 and 2004, although these reductions are associated with rail freight deregulation, as well as the earlier deregulation of end markets (for example power generation). The Eddington Report (Eddington, 2006) also raises some questions about the economic sustainability of rail. This report included an evidence base of around 170 transport schemes, although these were dominated by road schemes, with data for only seven rail schemes and 23 local public transport schemes (Table 4.1). What is more, these schemes seem to represent modest value for money with five of the rail schemes and 10 of the public transport schemes having benefit-cost ratios (BCRs) – using the New Approach to Appraisal (NATA; see Chapter One) – of below two. By contrast, only five out of 91 Highways Agency road schemes and four out of 48 local road schemes had such low BCRs. An issue here is the inflated cost of rail schemes. Affuso et al (2000) have suggested that in Britain, the average price for upgrading a line to high speed running might be £3.4 million per kilometre, while the cost of a new high speed line might be £7 million per kilometre.[5] In earlier work, Box (1992) estimated that a kilometre of new double track in 1991 cost £4 million per kilometre under BR at 1999/00 prices, with the corresponding price for track upgrading of around £0.8 million per kilometre.

It is within this context that Eddington (2006) was cautious about investment in new high speed rail lines, a caution that has also been adopted by *Delivering a sustainable railway* (although this has considered the use of the former Great Central

Figure 4.5: Forecast and actual passenger rail demand

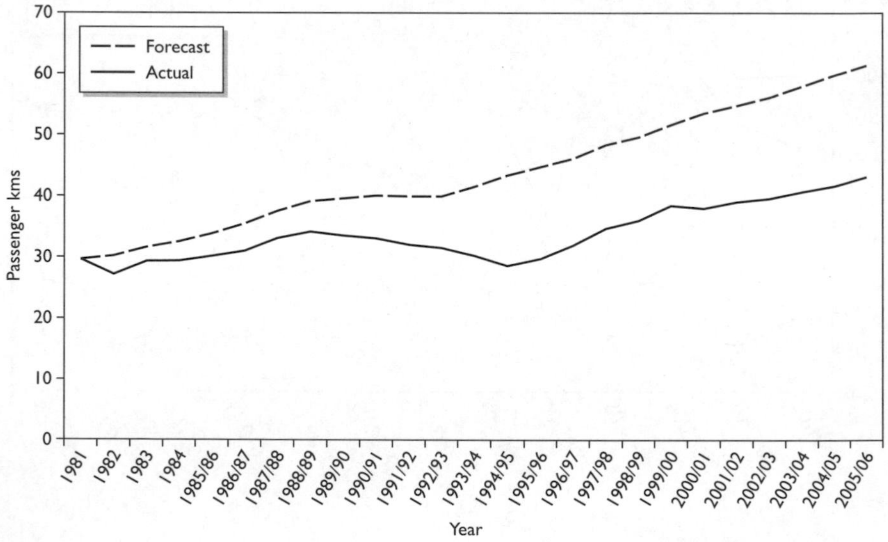

Source: ORR (2007)

Figure 4.6: Forecast and actual freight rail demand

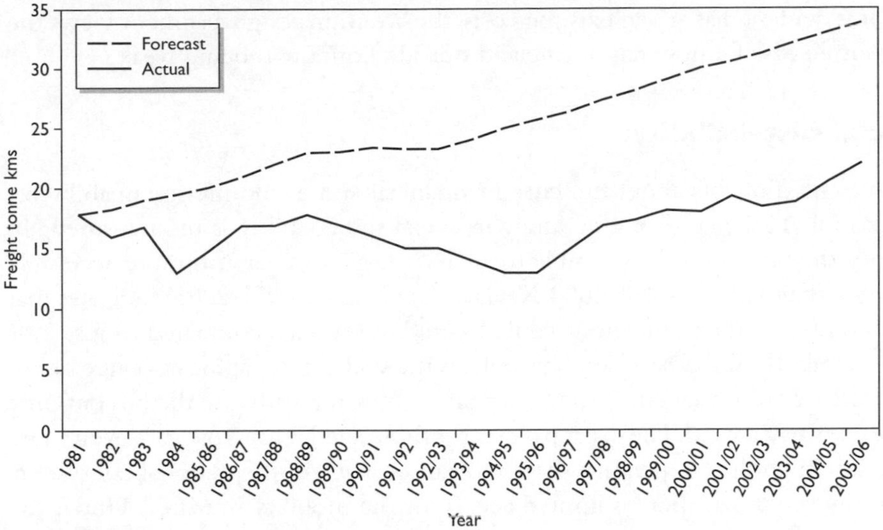

Source: ORR (2007)

alignment for high speed services between London and the West Midlands). The two rail schemes that were considered in detail by Eddington were both cross-London schemes – the north-south Thameslink Upgrade and the east-west Crossrail scheme. Both are being funded despite relatively modest BCRs of 2.1 and 1.6 respectively (see also Chapter One). One of the arguments used is that conventional cost-benefit analysis fails to take into account the claimed wider economic benefits of these schemes that will encourage employment growth in Central London. Work by Dan Graham indicates that workers in Central London are more productive than workers elsewhere, and if these 'agglomeration benefits' are taken into account the BCR for the Thameslink scheme increases to 3.0 and for Crossrail it goes up to 2.6 (Graham, 2006). There is an issue of causation here – whether high wages in London represent higher productivity or higher labour costs – and the extent to which agglomeration diseconomies (high land costs, pollution, congestion, social problems) may offset some of these benefits. There

Table 4.1: Investment returns from transport schemes considered by the Eddington study (number of schemes)

	Highways Agency road schemes	Local road schemes	Local public transport schemes	Rail schemes
Benefit-cost ratio ≥ 2.0	86	44	13	2
Benefit-cost ratio < 2.0	5	4	10	5
Total	91	48	23	7

Source: Based on Eddington (2006)

are also concerns about the appropriateness of the cost-benefit methodology, but it is evident that, given existing costs, the Westminster government views the economic case for new rail in England outside London as being weak.

Social sustainability

I have raised doubts about the current financial and economic sustainability of the national rail network. But surely its social sustainability is more assured? In theory, the rail system is accessible to all; in reality, however, it is more accessible to some than to others. The 2004 *National Travel Survey* (DfT, 2005) indicates that around 60% of the population regularly use bus services, compared to just 20% who regularly use rail services. This reflects the wider geographic coverage of bus networks. For those aged 60 to 69, just under 60% regularly use the bus but only 10% regularly use rail. The discrepancies for those aged 70 and over are even more marked. In part this represents the Victorian heritage of the national rail system, with the result that there is limited access for the mobility impaired. Under the 'Access for All' programme, the government has earmarked £370 million for step-free access at 92 priority stations (DfT, 2006), but it would clearly be prohibitively expensive to ensure that all 2,520 stations (and the trains serving them) meet the standards of the 2005 Disability Discrimination Act. At the European level, the proposed TSI-PRM (Technical Specification for Interoperability – Persons with Restricted Mobility) will also be relevant. A further explanation for the relatively low use of rail by older people may be the increasingly more generous concessionary fare schemes that are offered on rival bus systems (Chapter Five).

Table 4.2 shows that rail users, and particularly commuters and business travellers, tend to be drawn from higher income groups. Whereas around 35% of households have annual incomes of over £35,000, roughly 47% of rail users come from households with incomes above this level. The split by purpose is informative in that 50% of commuters and 56% of business travellers come from households with incomes over £35,000, compared with only 31% of leisure travellers. These results suggest that, overall, in terms of income distribution government support for rail may be viewed as regressive, although support for leisure travel by rail might be viewed as progressive.

Rail is not a public good in the way that roads are because users can be easily excluded through pricing. An inquiry by the House of Commons' Transport Committee highlighted issues concerning the fairness of fares (House of Commons, 2006a); the *National Passenger Survey* indicated that only 45% of rail users were satisfied with the value for money that rail offered, with particularly low ratings for London and the south east of England, compared to an 80% satisfaction rating for rail overall (Passengerfocus, 2007). Certain headline fares attracted particular attention, especially Virgin West Coast's standard open return between Manchester and London, which was priced at around £200 and had increased by 80% between 1995 and 2005. Intermodal comparisons indicated that since 1975 rail fares had increased in real terms by 70%, while car operating

Table 4.2: Rail travel by household income, 2007 (%)

	Commuting	Business	Leisure	Total rail	Total households 2005/06
Below £7000	4	6	14	7	7
£7,000-£12,500	5	6	13	8	8
£12,501-£17,500	8	7	13	9	15
£17,501-£35,000	32	25	29	30	34
£35,001-£50,000	26	22	16	23	20
£50,001-£75,000	16	19	9	15	7
More than £75,000	8	15	6	9	8

Source: DfT (2007b)

costs had decreased by 11% (Figure 1.1, p 15). The RMT Union claimed that comparable fares in continental Europe were half or less of those in Britain and, for example, an annual season ticket from Milton Keynes to London was more expensive than a pass for the entire German network. The Association of Train Operating Companies (ATOC) countered that such comparisons were invalid given the greater range of tickets (including advance purchase) in Britain, (House of Commons, 2006a) but this merely served to highlight the complexity of the fares system. The *National fares manual* had some 70 fare types and some 760 validity conditions. The fact that different TOCs were responsible for the fares for different origin and destination pairs led to some strange anomalies. A through Virgin Trains ticket between Penzance and Birmingham, for instance, was priced at £97.80, but an informed traveller would buy two tickets, one from Penzance to Cheltenham (First Great Western) and a second from Cheltenham to Birmingham (Arriva Trains Wales), at a combined cost of £74.90 and a saving of 23%. Given that all Penzance to Birmingham trains call at Cheltenham, the combined ticket would always be valid. Many other instances of this type were brought to the attention of the Committee.

The government's response in *Delivering a sustainable railway* (DfT, 2007a) was to propose a simplification of the fares system into four broad bands (Anytime, Off-peak, Super Off-peak and Advance) and to hold off from deregulating Saver fares even though the White Paper states that the case for such a reform is strong.[6] Saver fares are aimed at leisure travellers and the analysis above suggests that the regulation of these fares could be equitable. In fact, there may be an argument for more innovative fare products to be introduced, not least network cards, particularly in the off-peak period, but it is clear that the government's intentions are for rail fares overall to rise. Although this will help achieve financial sustainability targets, there will be a conflict with the social role of railways and this issue is currently being brushed aside by ministers.

Environmental sustainability

It has long been argued that rail has an environmental advantage over most other forms of transport (see, for example, TEST, 1991), and this was confirmed by analysis undertaken for *Delivering a sustainable railway*. Figure 4.7 shows that rail does indeed appear to have advantages, particularly in terms of carbon dioxide (CO_2) emissions, but its benefits over the car in terms of nitrogen oxides (NO_x) and particulate matter (PM_{10}) have been eroded and it emits more sulphur dioxide than other modes. These results are sensitive to assumptions concerning vehicles, fuels/power sources used and load factors, but there is an impression that rail has lost some of its benefits over other modes. Writers in the technical press, such as Roger Ford, have noted that new trains in Britain (and the rest of Europe) have tended to get heavier and as a result are less energy efficient than they could be, at the same time as cars have become more efficient (although see Chapter Three).

An upshot of this is illustrated by Table 4.3. At first glance this appears promising for rail. There has been a 22% decrease in CO_2 emissions per passenger kilometre since 1995/96, but at the same time there has been a large increase in passenger kilometres (44%) over this period so that overall carbon emissions from the rail

Figure 4.7: Emissions of CO_2, PM_{10}, NO_x and SO_2 from different modes

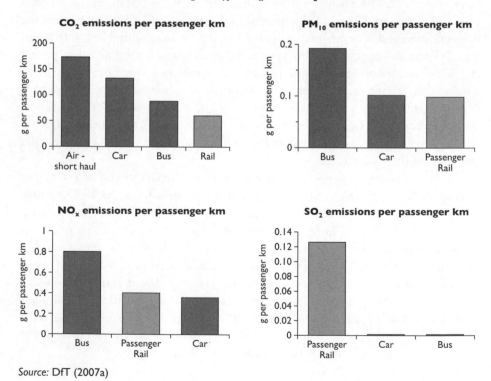

Source: DfT (2007a)

industry are up by 12%; reductions in carbon intensity (of almost 15% per train kilometre) have been offset by increased output. The table also suggests that, in terms of carbon emissions, electric traction currently has a strong advantage over diesel traction, which makes *Delivering a sustainable railway*'s rejection of electrification perplexing, particularly given the economic case established in research for the Rail Safety and Standards Board (Atkins, 2007) and the Scottish Government's decision to sanction significant electrification starting with the Edinburgh and Glasgow main line (for more on longer-term Scottish electrification proposals, see Scottish Executive, 2006). The White Paper argues that rail's main environmental role should be to increase capacity, given its green advantage over other modes, but others caution that if the mode is in danger of losing this advantage efforts should be made to secure 'quick wins' such as the promotion of regenerative braking, in-vehicle energy monitoring and eco-driving (see, for example, Palacin and Kemp, 2005). Given the recommendations of the Stern Review for an 80% reduction in the UK's carbon footprint by the middle of the century (Stern, 2006), it is likely that the environmental performance of rail will come under greater scrutiny in the future.

Environmental issues have framed the debate surrounding the extent to which high speed rail should replace short-haul aviation (Chapter Seven). A number of reports have expounded the environmental advantages of rail in these circumstances (CfIT, 2001; RCEP, 2002), although Eddington (2006) was less supportive on the basis of calculations using load factors and an electricity generation mix that were unfavourable to rail.

Is Labour really delivering a sustainable railway?

New Labour's decision to deal with the railways as they found them initially appeared to be successful. Demand, supply and investment were up and financial support was declining. A cost-benefit analysis of the reforms around this time suggested strongly positive results (Pollitt and Smith, 2002), although this analysis did not attempt to quantify the transitional costs of implementing the privatisation reforms. And then came the Hatfield accident. Reliability collapsed, Railtrack and

Table 4.3: Estimates of CO_2 emissions by mode, and change since 1995/96

Mode	Emissions gCO_2/pkm	% change since 1995/96
Passenger rail – diesel	74	−16
Passenger rail – electric	54	−26
Passenger rail – overall	61	−22
Car and taxi	106	−8
Domestic air	231	+5

Note: g = gram; pkm = passenger kilometre. 2004 figures for car, taxi and air; 2005/06 figures for rail.

Source: ATOC (2007)

over half the franchised train operators failed, capital and operating costs soared and subsidies sky-rocketed. The ensuing crisis resulted in two White Papers (DfT, 2004, 2007a) and the 2005 Railways Act. The policy response has been piecemeal but has essentially involved more governmental control. The franchising process has been taken within the DfT and franchises are more tightly specified than ever before. Network Rail, while notionally a private company, has members rather than shareholders – one of these is the DfT and there are also a number of other governmental bodies represented. The rail industry is also tightly controlled by the ORR. Strategic decisions with respect to infrastructure and technology investment appear to be determined by the DfT. It is tempting to think of this as a form of backdoor nationalisation but that would be something of a misnomer as train operations remain firmly in private hands. What has occurred might be better described as apologetic reregulation.

An important question is whether this latest phase of rail reforms will work. We have seen that there is still a long way to go until a sustainable railway is delivered. Finances may not be as stable as *Delivering a sustainable railway* claims, the social role of the mode still remains loosely defined and its environmental credentials could be improved. Rail's economic performance has been eroded by high costs, its social performance by high fares, and its environmental performance by slow technological change. On top of all this, it has been impacted by institutional fragmentation. The Westminster government's solution to financial problems – raising fares – is likely to lead to further problems, but there may be an argument that the operational context is more amenable to success than previously. The industry has matured and there appear fewer institutional and personality clashes than in the earlier phases of reform. Train operating companies and Network Rail work together in Integrated Control Centres and talk of virtual integration, although some of the old Railtrack tensions still seem to exist. It will of course be important to avoid another set of events such as that after the Hatfield accident, and a point of debate here is the extent to which increasing industry maturity on its own is capable of delivering sustained operational improvements – and, for that matter, greater economic, social and environmental sustainability – without further institutional reform. In other words, is the industry 'sustainable', in terms of its governance and institutional resilience (see Deakin, 2003)? In any response to this question, one problem is determining the counterfactual: what would alternative governance regimes have achieved? Devolution gives some scope for comparative analysis.

The railways in Northern Ireland have remained under public control and are currently operated by an integrated public transport operator, Translink. The railway in Northern Ireland is tiny compared to that in Britain, having some 330 route kilometres and 58 stations compared to 15,795 kilometres and 2,520 stations in Britain. It is, though, interesting to note that rail demand is growing. Between 1999/2000 and 2006/07, passenger journeys increased by 60% and passenger kilometres by 20%. It is also interesting to note that rail costs do not seem to have increased in the same way as on the mainland. Salveson (2001) found that the reinstatement of the Bleach Green–Antrim route was undertaken on time and on budget at a cost of only around £0.7 million per kilometre, although this is a single line with two passing loops and a maximum speed of 90 miles per hour. Despite these successes, Northern Ireland Railways (NIR) has been heavily loss making and there has been recent consideration of a system shut-down, although this was dismissed by members of the Legislative Assembly and indeed there has been significant investment in new trains and line reconstruction (MacKinnon et al, 2008b).

In Scotland and Wales, the 1993 Railways Act applies as it does in England although both devolved administrations have demonstrated much stronger leadership and a more positive vision for the mode. As part of the devolution process, the Scottish Executive (now Scottish Government) has taken over responsibility for letting the ScotRail franchise and the Welsh Assembly Government is a co-signatory to the Wales and Borders franchise (Chapter Two). This contrasts with the six English PTEs that lost their co-signatory status as a result of the 2005 Railways Act. As in Northern Ireland, devolution has given a major impetus to rail investment: in Scotland five new lines have been/are being progressed (Larkhall-Milngavie, Sirling-Alloa-Kincardine, the Glasgow Airport Rail Link (GARL), the Waverley Line to the Borders and Airdrie–Bathgate), although the Edinburgh Airport Link (EARL) fell victim to the change in political control in 2007; and in Wales the Vale of Glamorgan and Ebbw Vale lines have been reopened. Moreover, there are plans to substantially improve services between Glasgow and Edinburgh – in part by electrifying more of the Central Belt rail network and accelerating journey times – and north-south services in Wales. All of this is in direct contrast to England where the emphasis has been on reducing costs, and it is therefore clear that devolution has led to a divergence in rail policy between Westminster and the devolved administrations, a position also illustrated by experience in London (Chapter Nine). There is less certainty over whether these institutional developments have assisted the delivery of a sustainable railway from a UK perspective, since it is arguably in the major English conurbations where rail can do most to achieve broader sustainability objectives.

Perhaps the objectives of sustainability (and its triarchy of economy, society and environment) are better understood than before in the current 'hands-on' regime, but there is a long way to go. Indeed, New Labour's ambivalence to the rail structure it inherited may have rubbed off on the civil servants. Whereas the privatisation of the rail systems was pushed as much by mandarins like Sir Steve Robson as by politicians (Wolmar, 2001; Gourvish, 2002), *A new deal for transport* (DETR, 1998) had no such champions. Mike Mitchell and his colleagues at the DfT now have a much clearer view of their mission (essentially cost control), but there will continue to be concern about civil servants running the railway. Indeed, a reading of *Delivering a sustainable railway* has a rather odd feel about it because it is written by civil servants largely about themselves. It is likely that calls for a more hands-off agency will strengthen particularly when public funding is under better control. Similarly, there will continue to be concerns over Network

Rail's governance structure: while these are likely to be ignored if the company performs reasonably well, the case for change will be irresistible if its performance deteriorates further after its renewed difficulties in early 2008 (or, for that matter, if it performs too well).

The most likely changes may be with franchising, which the Transport Committee of the House of Commons (2006b, p 11) described as a 'muddle', and where the one-size-fits-all policy will appear inappropriate as a chasm emerges between those operators paying premia and those continuing to receive large subsidies. The former, largely based on the intercity and long-distance commuter routes, might be best franchised by longer, more loosely specified contracts, administered on the basis of net cost, as now. By contrast, the social railway – short-distance commuter networks and regional services – might be franchised by shorter, more tightly specified contracts (particularly with respect to fares) and administered on the basis of gross costs. The new London Rail franchise, won by the Hong Kong Mass Transit Railway (MTR) in conjunction with Laing Rail[7] and specified by TfL (Figure 9.2, p 197), is a forerunner of this type of franchise. Distinguishing between social and commercial franchises also has some support from international comparative studies (Thompson, 2007). Such distinctions may also be emphasised by changes in ticketing and retail distribution. For the commercial services, advance purchase is likely to become more prevalent, as is single-leg pricing, with increased delivery over mobile phone technology. For more socially oriented services, smartcards may be expected to become more common, following the success of Oyster in London, which might require further simplification of fares. In the medium term, some technological convergence may be expected with, for example, smartcards being mounted on mobile phones.

Open access appears to have worked well for the rail freight industry – even if there has not been a radical change in industry structure, with only two significant new entrants (GB Railfreight and Direct Rail Services) – suggesting that the market is at least partially contestable. This arrangement has been less widespread in the passenger sector but Hull Trains has been successful and this has encouraged a number of imitators including Grand Central, the introduction of whose Sunderland service was so hotly contested by GNER. Ultimately, though, while entry into niche passenger markets may be beneficial, the promotion of more direct competition is probably neither desirable (because it results in too much service at too high fares) or feasible (because of scarce capacity) (Preston et al, 1999). Nevertheless, the perceived success of open access may provide a barrier to calls for vertical reintegration, and certainly the rail freight industry has vigorously opposed such calls. The Conservative Party appears to favour some integration at the route level, however, and the Scottish Labour Party considered proposing vertical reintegration before the 2007 Holyrood election. There have also been calls for experimentation with such reintegration in other relatively self-contained parts of the network such as Merseyrail, not least because this would provide some yardstick competition for Network Rail.

To answer this chapter's rhetorical question, rail can have a sustainable future, but, as for many other transport modes, it is not yet fully articulated and the latest rail White Paper should be seen as the starting point rather than the finishing line. This is particularly the case with regard to the mode's role within a broader sustainable transport strategy. In part this is due to the current industrial structure, which despite government protestations to the contrary, is not yet sustainable. It is also related to the difficulties in achieving joined-up government, with a particular disconnect between rail policy and planning policy, with, for example, little consideration of the opportunities for rail of the designated Growth Areas in the south east of England. Fares policy provides another manifestation of this disconnect, with there having been little consideration as to whether redirecting subsidy towards lower fares might assist in achieving wider sustainability goals. A public-sector oriented solution to these problems might see the DfT's rail division and Network Rail merge to form a Railways Agency akin to the Highways Agency, with local services devolved to relevant local authorities, a solution that would also allow further devolution of rail powers, especially in Scotland. A private-sector oriented solution might see Network Rail's functions taken over by TOCs, for which some of the larger operators have actively canvassed (Stagecoach Group, 2001; *The Independent*, 2004), possibly accompanied by a widening of open access provisions for passenger services (on the latter, see Glaister, 2004). A regulatory solution might see the franchising role of DfT taken over by the ORR (see also Helm, 2000). The underlying goal should be to reduce the industry's transaction and regulatory costs and promote productive efficiency – hence reducing unit operating and capital costs. If rail's underlying finances can be improved in this way, economic, social and environmental sustainability will more easily follow.

Notes

[1] The Office of the Rail Regulator became the Office of Rail Regulation in 2004, as a result of the 2003 Railways and Transport Safety Act. In the first phase of the moderation of competition regulations, flows that constituted more than 0.2% of a franchisee's revenue were protected from competition. In the second phase, which commenced in September 1999, entry was possible on up to 20% of a franchisee's revenue on registered flows. This second phase officially ended in 2002 and was eventually replaced by a regime in which there is no official contractual moderation of competition. The current procedures and criteria for granting track access rights do, however, preclude services that are 'primarily abstractive', and this acts as an informal moderation of competition.

[2] And, actually, the Labour Party, as opposed to the government – see *The Guardian* (2004).

[3] This typically means that after the first four years of the franchise contract have passed (or earlier where negotiations have taken place): 50% of any fares revenues in excess of 102% of the TOC's original forecasts are shared with the DfT; the DfT makes a contribution equivalent to 50% of any revenue shortfall below 98% of the TOC's original forecast; and for any shortfall below 96%, the DfT's contribution increases to 80%.

[4] Now trading as First Capital Connect.

[5] This figure is incidentally very close to the cost of TGV Est, the most recent high speed line to be opened in France.

[6] Editors' note: in April 2008 ATOC announced with great fanfare that the simplification of fares along the lines suggested in the White Paper would take place in two stages – in May and September of that year (see www.nationalrail.co.uk/simplefares). ATOC's claim is rather spurious, however. Athough four bands of fares have indeed been adopted, there is still, as far as we can see from the National Rail Enquiries website (www.nationalrail.co.uk), a range of ticket types available within the 'Advance' band (the first to be introduced) and this varies between TOCs.

[7] Laing Rail was acquired by Deutsche Bahn AG, the German state railway, in January 2008.

References

Affuso, L., Masson, J. and Newbery, D. (2000) *Comparing investments on new transport infrastructure: Road vs railways?*, Cambridge: Department of Applied Economics, University of Cambridge.

Atkins (2007) *Study on further electrification of Britain's railway network*, Report T633, London: RSSB.

ATOC (Association of Train Operating Companies) (2007) *Baseline energy statement*, London: ATOC.

Box, D. (1992) 'Costing passenger railways', in N. Harris and E. Godward (eds) *Planning passenger railways*, Glossop: Transport Publishing Co.

CfIT (Commission for Integrated Transport) (2001) *A comparative study of the environmental effects of rail and short-haul air travel*, London: CfIT.

Deakin, M. (2003) 'The New Deal for Transport: the BEQUEST protocol for assessing the sustainability of urban development', in J. Hine and J. Preston (eds) *Integrated futures and transport choices*, Aldershot: Ashgate.

DETR (Department of the Environment, Transport and the Regions) (1998) *A new deal for transport: Better for everyone*, Cm 3950, London: The Stationery Office.

DETR (2000) *Transport 2010: The 10-year plan for transport*, London: DETR.

DfT (Department for Transport) (2004) *The future of rail*, Cm 6233, London: The Stationery Office.

DfT (2005) *National travel survey: 2004*, London DfT, www.dft.gov.uk/pgr/statistics/datatablespublications/personal/mainresults/nts2004/nationaltravelsurvey2004a (accessed 8 January 2008).

DfT (2006) *Access for all: The accessibility strategy for Great Britain's railway*, London: DfT.

DfT (2007a) *Delivering a sustainable railway*, Cm 7176, London: The Stationery Office.

DfT (in association with Transport Scotland) (2007b) *National rail travel survey*, Provisional 2007 report, London: DfT.

Drew, J. (2006) 'The benefits and costs of vertical separation and open access', Paper presented at the European Transport Conference, the Netherlands, 20 September, Strasbourg.

Eddington, R. (2006) *The Eddington transport study: The case for action: Sir Rod Eddington's advice to the government*, London: The Stationery Office, www.dft.gov. uk/162259/187604/206711/executivesummary (accessed 8 January 2008).

Glaister, S. (2004) *British rail privatisation: Competition destroyed by politics*, Occasional Paper 23, Bath: Centre for Regulated Industries.

Gourvish, T. (2002) *British rail 1974-97: From integration to privatisation*, Oxford: Oxford University Press.

Graham, D. (2006) *Investigating the link between productivity and agglomeration for UK industries*, Report for the DfT, London: Imperial College.

Health and Safety Executive (2004) *Annual report on railway safety*, London: HSE.

Helm, D. (2000) *A critique of rail regulation: The Beesley lectures in regulation*, London: Institute of Economic Affairs and the London Business School.

House of Commons (20056a) *How fair are the fares? Train fares and ticketing*, Sixth report of the House of Commons Transport Committee, Session 2005-06, HC 700-I, www. publications.parliament.uk/pa/cm200506/cmselect/cmtran/700/70002.htm (accessed 8 January 2008).

House of Commons (2006b) *Passenger rail franchising*, Fourteenth report of the House of Commons Transport Committee, Session 2005-06, HC 1354, www.publications. parliament.uk/pa/cm200506/cmselect/cmtran/1354/1354.pdf (accessed 8 January 2008).

Labour Party (1997) *New Labour: Because Britain deserves better*, www.psr.keele.ac.uk/area/ uk/man/lab97.htm (accessed 10 January 2008).

MacKinnon, D., Cumbers, A. and Shaw, J. (2008a) 'Rescaling employment relations: key outcomes of change in the privatised rail industry', *Environment and Planning A*, 40, pp 1347-69.

MacKinnon, D., Shaw, J. and Docherty, I. (2008b) *Diverging mobilities? Devolution, transport and policy innovation*, Oxford: Elsevier.

Modern Railways (2001) 638, November, p 18.

Nash, C. and Smith, A. (2006) 'Passenger rail franchising – British experience', ECMT Workshop on Competitive Tendering for Passenger Rail Services, 12 January.

National Audit Office (2004) *Network rail: Making a fresh start*, HC532, London: The Stationery Office.

ORR (Office of Rail Regulation) (2006) *National rail trends 2005-2006*, London: ORR.

ORR (2007) *National rail trends 2006-2007*, London: ORR.

Palacin, R. and Kemp, R. (2005) 'Living up to the myth by enhancing the sustainability of rail', Presented to Excellence in Railway Systems Engineering and Integration conference, 25 November, Derby.

Passengerfocus (2007) National Passenger Survey, spring 2007, London: Passenger Focus, www.passengerfocus.org.uk/news-and-publications/document-search/document. asp?dsid=1043 (accessed 10 January 2008).

Pollitt, M. and Smith, A. (2002) 'The restructuring and privatisation of British Rail: was it really that bad?', *Fiscal Studies*, 23, pp 463-502.

Preston, J. (2002) 'Railtrack: problems, solutions and an absolution', Paper presented to the UTSG Annual Conference, Napier University, Edinburgh, 4 January.

Preston, J., Whelan, G. and Wardman, M. (1999) 'An analysis of the potential for on-track competition in the British passenger rail industry', *Journal of Transport Economics and Policy*, 33, pp 77-94.

Preston, J., Garlick, M., Hodgson, F., Nash, C. and Shires, J. (1994) *European railway comparisons: Final report*, Working Paper 418, Leeds: Institute for Transport Studies, University of Leeds.

Rail (2001) 422, November, pp 4–5.

RCEP (Royal Commission on Environmental Pollution) (2002) *The environmental effects of civil aircraft in flight*, London: RCEP.

Salveson, P. (2001) *Beeching in reverse: The case for a programme of line and station re-openings*, Huddersfield: Transport Research and Information Network.

Scottish Executive (2006) *Scotland's railways*, Edinburgh: Scottish Executive, www.scotland. gov.uk/Resource/Doc/157764/0042650.pdf (accessed 10 January 2008).

Shaw, J. (2000) *Competition, regulation and the privatisation of British Rail*, Aldershot: Ashgate.

Shaw, J. and Farrington, J. (2003) 'A railway renaissance?', in I. Docherty and J. Shaw (eds) *A new deal for transport? The UK's struggle with the sustainable transport agenda*, Oxford: Blackwell.

Smith, A. (2006) 'Are Britain's railways costing too much? Perspectives based on TFP comparisons with British Rail 1963-2002', *Journal of Transport Economics and Policy*, 40, pp 1–44.

Stagecoach Group (2001) 'Press release: Stagecoach study into vertical integration for rail', 7 November, www.stagecoachplc.com/scg/media/press/pr2001/2001-11-07/ (accessed 10 January 2008).

Stern, N. (2006) *Stern review on the economics of climate change*, London: HM Treasury, www. hm-treasury.gov.uk/independent_reviews/stern_review_economics_climate_change/ sternreview_index.cfm (accessed 8 January 2008).

TEST (1991) *Wrong side of the tracks? Impacts of road and rail transport on the environment: A basis for discussion*, London: TEST.

The Guardian (2004) 'Rail vote embarrassment for Blair', 28 September 28, http://politics. guardian.co.uk/labour2004/story/0,,1314600,00.html (accessed 10 January 2008).

The Independent (1995) 'Blair on defensive over rail', 16 January, http://findarticles.com/ p/articles/mi_qn4158/is_19950116/ai_n14871782 (accessed 10 January 2008).

The Independent (2004) 'FirstGroup to press for control over track', 4 November, http:// news.independent.co.uk/business/news/article18624.ece (accessed 10 January 2008).

The Times (2008) 'Network failed', 4 January, www.timesonline.co.uk/tol/comment/ leading_article/article3129295.ece (accessed 10 January 2008).

Thompson, L. (2007) 'Competitive tendering in railways: What can we learn from experience?', in *Competitive tendering of rail services*, Paris: OECD Publishing.

TSSA (Transport Salaried Staffs' Association) (2007) *Public ownership: The right track for our railway*, London: TSSA, www.epolitix.com/NR/rdonlyres/C1D40BD8-E125-43D1- 92F5-C4983495E60B/0/Alternativepositionbriefing.pdf (accessed 10 January 2008).

Wardman, M. (2005) *Demand for rail travel and the effects of external factors*, Leeds: Institute for Transport Studies, University of Leeds.

Wolmar, C. (2001) *Broken rails: How privatisation wrecked Britain's railways*, London: Aurum Press.

Wolmar, C. (2007) *Fire and steam: A new history of the railways in Britain*, London: Atlantic Books.

FIVE

Buses and light rail: stalled en route?

Richard D. Knowles and Pedro Abrantes

Better-quality public transport was heralded by incoming Labour ministers as the key to persuading some car users to switch modes for some journeys, thereby reducing car use and urban traffic congestion (DETR, 1997, 1998). As large-scale improvement was needed quickly, the main focus was on buses, which are the main mode of local public transport everywhere except in Central and Inner London. The image change sought was encapsulated in the title of the buses policy document *From workhorse to thoroughbred* (DETR, 1999), and Quality Partnerships (QPs) were seen as the way to produce better local bus services and reverse the 50-year decline in bus use. Voluntary cooperation between local authorities could give buses priority on the roads and in return private bus companies would invest in higher-quality buses. Light rail was considered to be expensive and unable to deliver improvements quickly but still viable where it was part of a coherent urban public transport strategy. Improved public transport was also a prerequisite for making restraint of car traffic acceptable. The 2000 Transport Act introduced the idea of Statutory Quality Partnerships (SQPs) to cover facilities and vehicle standards in a legally binding agreement, and also offered councils an option of partial reregulation in the form of Quality Contracts (QCs) if partnerships were not delivering patronage growth targets (Davison and Knowles, 2006). Quality Contracts would give exclusive access to designated routes but would not be approved by the government unless they were the only practicable way to meet local authority targets. Also in 2000, *Transport 2010: The 10-year plan* (DETR, 2000) introduced national targets for Britain of a 10% growth in local bus usage and a 100% growth in light rail usage by 2010/11; 25 new light rail schemes were also to be built. Whereas the concept of an integrated transport policy had been promulgated UK-wide in 1998, the governance landscape in relation to the formulation and delivery of transport policy objectives and targets was fundamentally changed by devolution in 1999/2000 (Chapter Two). This chapter demonstrates that these new governance arrangements have promoted differences in both bus and light rail policies and their outcomes in the constituent parts of the UK over the last few years.

The UK bus industry

As a result of deregulation, privatisation and governance reform, bus market structure varies markedly across the UK. In London, Transport for London (TfL), sets fares and plans packages of routes, which are then franchised to private sector bus operators by tender (Chapter Nine). In Northern Ireland public transport is planned and operated mainly by public sector companies (operating under the 'Translink' banner) responding directly to the Northern Ireland Minister for Regional Development. In the rest of the country private operators are expected to plan and operate profitable networks with public financial support only via fuel duty exemption and payments for concessionary fares. Local authorities can then choose to put to tender, at their own expense, the operation of specific services or routes deemed non-commercial by operators. In the English conurbations an additional layer of (statutory) Passenger Transport Authorities and Executives (PTAs/PTEs) oversees public transport across all the local authority areas but has no highway powers.

A new deal for transport (DETR, 1998) recognised the failure of deregulation and privatisation to reverse the severe decline in bus patronage and advocated greater public sector intervention. Great emphasis was placed on better public transport integration, for example by making multi-operator area-wide ticketing schemes possible and promoting the central provision of information, but these would rely on local authority delivery through cooperation with private operators. In England, *From workhorse to thoroughbred* recognised that it was essential to remove the stigma attached to bus use in order to attract passengers back from the car.[1] The QPs and QCs, promoted partly as a way to address this issue, also reflected the government's expectations that local authorities and PTA/Es should be better able to influence network planning and service quality. The introduction of five-year Local Transport Plans (LTPs) (Chapters Two and Ten) gave local authorities and PTA/Es the opportunity and means to influence bus transport by tapping into additional government funding proposed in *Transport 2010* (DETR, 2000). As we have noted, ministers expected in return a 10% growth in national bus patronage between 2000 and 2010.

In 2002, however, this bus target was amended to a combined 12% national growth target for bus and light rail usage, as bus patronage continued to decline outside London. This became a series of regional targets in 2004, but all were quietly dropped in 2007 (DETR, 1998; DfT, 2004). Despite declining bus usage, the 2004 Transport White Paper – *The future of transport* (DfT, 2004) – continued to advocate partnership working as the key to promoting bus travel. The 2007 Local Transport Bill for England proposed enhancements to QPs, easier ways of introducing QCs, reliability agreements between local authorities/PTEs and operators and the combination of highway and public transport powers within renamed Integrated Transport Authorities in PTE areas. Fuel duty exemption was to be withdrawn and the money reallocated to local authorities/PTEs so that better targeting of subsidy could take place. Meanwhile, free off-peak local bus travel for the over sixties and disabled people had been provided with government funding since April 2006 within each English local authority or PTE area and was widened to any trip within England from April 2008. Free concessionary bus travel in Wales, Northern Ireland and Scotland introduced at different times since 2002, and earlier in London, had increased bus patronage. An unintended consequence of devolution is the creation of a border barrier on these concessions between England and both Wales and Scotland.

Bus industry performance

After five years of fairly stable demand prior to 1985, deregulation and privatisation brought about a severe decline in bus patronage coupled with a steep increase in real bus fares due to subsidy reduction (Table 5.1). Between 1985/86 and 1996/97, bus passenger numbers dropped by a striking 40% in PTE areas and over 20% elsewhere, while real bus fares rose by 50% in PTE areas and by 10% in other places. A 25% increase in bus vehicle kilometres in PTE areas and around 15% elsewhere – partly due to greater use of single-decker buses and midi buses – was attributed to initial on-road competition, although this often resulted in a worsening safety record, rising bus congestion and a weakening user perception of bus services (Mackie and Preston, 1996). Operating costs fell mainly due to more efficient working practices, but also to reductions in both wage rates and the workforce. In London, where the bus network remained integrated and largely unchanged, patronage remained stable in spite of an increase in fares of over 30%.

By 1996/97, significant market concentration had taken place in the bus industry leading to reduced on-street competition, greater network stability and more passenger confidence (Mackie and Preston, 1996). Although the decline in bus patronage slowed down, usage in PTE areas kept falling at an annual average of 1.5%. After a period of stability until 2000/01, bus patronage in the English shires followed a similar downward trend; indeed, in England's regions between 2000/01 and 2005/06, only Greater Manchester achieved patronage growth. Demand fell most dramatically in the West Midlands' non-PTE areas (–19%), the north east (–16%) and in South Yorkshire (–14%). London's franchised bus system in contrast carried 10% more passengers in the four-year period to 2000/01, and witnessed a further 48% increase up to 2006/07 coinciding with the extensive priority and frequency improvements put in place prior to the introduction of congestion charging in Central London in 2003 (Chapter Nine). London's

Table 5.1: Bus passenger journeys by area (millions)

Area	a	b	c	d	a–d	b–c	c–d	b–d
	1996/97	2000/01	2005/06	2006/07	%	%	%	%
London	1,230	1,347	1,881	1,993	62	40	6	48
PTE areas	1,310	1,203	1,117	1,109	–15	–7	–1	–8
English shires	1,304	1,292	1,198	1,269	–3	–7	6	–2
Scotland	478	458	477	482	1	4	1	5
Wales	133	119	118	119	–11	–1	1	0

Source of raw data: DfT (2007a)

increase alone was enough to deliver the original *Transport 2010* 10% national growth target by 2006/07, by offsetting declines elsewhere (Figure 5.1). Bus usage outside of London has increased since 2005/06 after the introduction of free off-peak concessionary travel for the over sixties (patronage among this group grew by an average 25% in four of the PTE areas; MVA, 2007). In Scotland, bus subsidies were doubled to stabilise fares and allow the introduction of free off-peak concessionary travel in 2002, enabling the long decline in bus patronage to be reversed sooner than in any other part of Britain outside London. Similarly, bus patronage in Wales stabilised from 2000/01 onwards.

With the exception of London and Scotland, fares had been growing at a rate of around 2% per year above inflation, due to rising fuel prices, wages and traffic congestion, with the greatest increases taking place in the PTE areas (Table 5.2). The fall in average fares in 2006/07 in England outside London merely reflected the effects of introducing free off-peak concessionary fares. Although London's operating costs rose by nearly 25% above inflation, its real fares rose much less than elsewhere as TfL increased bus subsidies dramatically from 2000. London now receives over four times the total amount of subsidy in PTE areas and almost twice the amount for the whole of the rest of England (Table 5.3). In Scotland fares actually fell in real terms from 2000/01 until 2005/06 following devolution.

Table 5.2: Fare index at current prices (1996/97 = 100)

Area	a	b	c	d
	1996/97	2000/01	2005/06	2006/07
London	100	100	105	110
PTE areas	100	108	124	121
English shires	100	109	125	115
Scotland	100	107	106	107
Wales	100	111	123	126

Source: DfT (2007a)

Table 5.3: Bus support by area at current prices (£ million)

Area	a	b	c	d	a–d	b–c	c–d	b–d
	1996/97	2000/01	2005/06	2006/07	%	%	%	%
London	12	84	596	625	5108	610	5	644
PTE areas	106	104	116	128	21	12	10	23
English shires	83	133	240	253	205	80	5	90
Scotland	26	28	45	N/A	N/A	61	N/A	N/A
Wales	8	16	28	30	275	75	7	88

Source of raw data: DfT (2007a)

Figure 5.1: Bus patronage change by region, 2000/01-2006/07

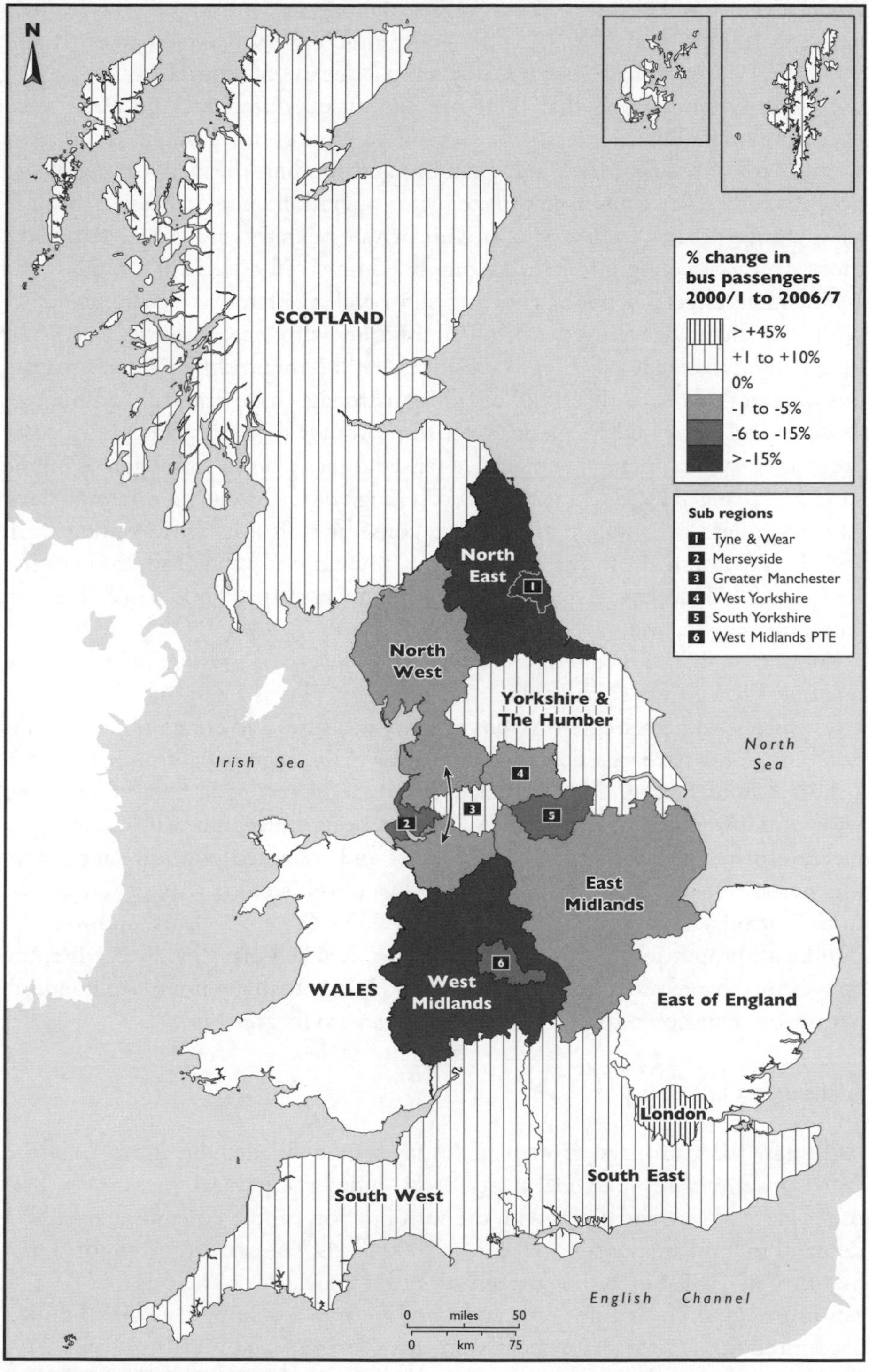

N

SCOTLAND

**% change in
bus passengers
2000/1 to 2006/7**

> +45%
+1 to +10%
0%
-1 to -5%
-6 to -15%
> -15%

Sub regions
1 Tyne & Wear
2 Merseyside
3 Greater Manchester
4 West Yorkshire
5 South Yorkshire
6 West Midlands PTE

North
East

North
West

Yorkshire &
The Humber

Irish Sea

*North
Sea*

East
Midlands

WALES

West
Midlands

East of England

London

South West

South East

English Channel

0 miles 50
0 km 75

Source of raw data: DFT (2007b)

Bus vehicle kilometres have been growing in London but declining elsewhere especially in the PTE areas. While vehicle kilometres in London rose by 10% between 1996/97 and 2000/01 and then by another 25% between 2000/01 and 2006/07, PTE areas have seen a steady annual decline of around 1.5%.

This discussion shows that there are significant differences between areas operating under different regulatory regimes. In London, the public sector plays a major role in setting fares and planning and funding the network, with the potential efficiency gains from private sector operation being harnessed through a franchising process. In the rest of Britain, private operators are expected to make those decisions taking into account purely commercial criteria. If a route is not achieving its target revenue a private operator will raise fares, reduce frequency or withdraw the service altogether. Only in this case will a local authority or PTA/E be called on to decide whether to subsidise a replacement.[2] In PTE areas, private bus operators, faced with a trend of falling patronage, have gradually withdrawn services and decreased frequencies on some routes to reduce operating costs. Steep increases in operating costs were passed directly on to passengers as public subsidies changed little. As a result of worsening service levels and increased fares, patronage kept declining, with negative consequences for highway congestion and the environment. In the shire areas, a doubling of public subsidy between 1997 and 2004 meant that total vehicle kilometres remained fairly stable, although patronage kept falling.

London, with its franchised bus market, offers a very contrasting picture where bus travel has grown remarkably in recent years. This is a response to a rise in bus vehicle kilometres, extensive bus priority measures and congestion charging, which together have significantly reduced travel times on radial routes, provided a more comprehensive 24/7 coverage of services, a complete fleet of low floor buses and lower fares in real terms. All this has been underpinned by a substantial increase in public subsidy for bus transport and sustained political support for this mode (Hendy, 2007). The growth in bus travel is often wrongly attributed to the introduction of congestion charging alone; Table 5.2 clearly shows that a significant proportion of this growth had already taken place by 2003 when the congestion charge was introduced and White (2007) attributes just 6% of London's patronage increase up to 2005/06 to the Charge (Chapter Nine).

A changing bus policy?

Although the patronage growth in London quickly met the initial *Transport 2010* target of a 10% national increase, this hides a very bleak picture for most other parts of England. Even with the introduction of free concessionary travel, demand in most areas is still well below 2000 levels. The situation was not always like this: in 1985, before bus deregulation, PTE areas accounted for 43% of all bus journeys, shire areas for 33% and London only a quarter. By 2005, London accounted for 43% of all journeys, shire areas for 30% and PTE areas only 27%. London also consumes 63% of all public subsidies for bus services. While the bus has been recognised as a vital part of London's transport system, in other large urban areas deregulation has undermined attempts to stem its continuing decline. It is clear, however, that the government is not prepared to finance London-style fare subsidies and frequency increases elsewhere; deregulation has been retained because of proven cost savings to the Exchequer, even though in the long run it could generate higher costs due to increased congestion and carbon emissions, and more demand for road-building and maintenance. Experience in London and other European cities (CfIT, 2001) shows that successful public transport systems require substantial subsidy, and this is likely to be the case even more in English towns and cities where shrinking demand is unlikely to prompt private operators to invest.

In spite of the national decline in bus usage there have been a few cases, such as Cambridge, Oxford and York, of impressive network-wide growth within a deregulated environment (DETR, 1998; DfT, 2004, 2006). They are all freestanding historic small cities with a fairly dense and compact centre containing substantial employment and major tourist attractions. Due to space and conservation restrictions, highway capacity and car parking are considerably less than in other towns of similar size. These constraints have contributed to political support for significant bus improvements, including extensive priority along radial routes, real-time information systems, free park and ride sites with heavily subsidised bus fares, investment in information and marketing campaigns. The success of the park and ride systems (Parkhurst, 2000) is as much due to high city centre parking charges as the bus priority and quality measures. Quality Partnerships with bus operators have contributed increased service frequencies and new high-quality bus fleets.

These case studies show the importance of partnership working and a package of integrated measures, but they also highlight the key role of local politicians and highway authorities in delivering bus priority measures and setting parking charges. This has proven difficult in conurbation areas where public transport and highway powers are held by PTEs and local authorities respectively (NERA, 2006), and reallocation of road space from cars to buses is a sensitive political issue. While higher-quality vehicles, strong marketing campaigns and the 'partnership' brand attract passengers, it is unlikely that they will be retained unless the key service variables (travel time, reliability, fares) become and remain competitive in relation to the car (TAS, 2001). Reliability agreements between operators and local authorities/PTEs are therefore a welcome feature of the 2007 Transport Bill. It will allow operators to appeal to the Traffic Commissioner if local road conditions are significantly affecting the reliability of its services, therefore putting pressure on local authorities to introduce priority measures.

The hostility among drivers to reallocating road space remains a significant political conundrum and the government demonstrates a lack of political leadership in passing the buck for introducing pro bus measures and road pricing to local politicians (Chapter Three). It is important to note also that the improvements to bus services mentioned above have been financed from successful LTP bids awarded competitively among local authorities: so even if political consensus is obtained, LTP funding will need to be significantly increased by government.

Despite the sustained decline in bus travel outside London, the government remains committed to bus deregulation and advocates more effective partnerships between local authorities and operators (DfT, 2004, 2006, 2007b). In the 2000 Transport Act, QCs would have given exclusive franchises to designated routes, like in the London system, but none have been applied for as the government would not approve them unless they were the 'only practicable way' to meet local authority bus patronage targets (Mackie, 1999). Bus operators continue to oppose QCs as franchised operations, awarded by competitive tender, are less profitable than deregulated monopolies. The 2007 Local Transport Bill proposes that SQPs can be extended to cover minimum frequencies, service timing and maximum fares but changes since the draft Bill give operators an 'admissible objections' veto, and although the criteria for QCs have been simplified, new proposals must be vetted by a non-elected Approvals Board (DfT, 2007c). Both of these caveats can be interpreted as victories for the bus operators in the face of government failure to stand up to vested interests (Chapters One and Ten).

The North Sheffield SQP signed in autumn 2007 is the only SQP in the seven years since they became permissible under the 2000 Transport Act because of the difficulty in persuading private bus operators to sign statutory agreements (Bristow et al, 2001). One barrier to SQPs is the threat that the Office of Fair Trading could deem them anti-competitive and block progress towards partnership working altogether. While formal agreements would protect bus company investment, the lack of competition on most bus corridors and the near monopoly or market dominance in most districts makes SQPs unnecessary from an operator's perspective (Table 5.4; Figure 5.2) (Mackie and Preston, 1996; Mackie, 1999; NERA, 2006; Knowles and Ametepe, 2007). For these reasons successful partnerships continue to develop as informal agreements based on the good faith and willingness of both parties: where local authorities and PTEs can muster political support for significant enhancements to public transport infrastructure, operators should be happy to contribute quality enhancements, but they are unlikely to give local authorities and PTEs control over such a vital commercial tool as fare levels.

Quality Contracts were unworkable under the 2000 Transport Act's provisions, although they were an acknowledgement that London's franchise system had been able to achieve similar cost reductions to full deregulation without the latter's negative impact on patronage. It remains doubtful that the 2007 Local Transport Bill's slightly simpler QC application process will result in any being implemented as the operators have threatened legal action to oppose the introduction of any of the proposed new-style SQPs as they want to protect their profitable deregulated monopolies (CILT, 2007). Without consensus between local authorities/PTEs and operators, as well as the expectation of significant patronage growth as in Greater Manchester's July 2007 Transport Innovation Fund (TIF) Bid, SQPs and QCs are unlikely to be approved (Sørenssen et al, 2007).

Table 5.4: Bus market dominance along selected corridors in Greater Manchester and Merseyside districts in 2006 (bus kilometres)

Corridor	District	Company	End-to-end services market share (%)	Single fare
A662/A635 Ashton New Road	Manchester & Tameside	Stagecoach/ Magic Bus	100	£1.70/£1.30
A56 Chester Road	Manchester & Trafford	Arriva	100	£2.40
A62 Oldham Road	Manchester & Oldham	First	100	£2.60
A561/A565 Southport	Liverpool & Sefton	Arriva	100	£1.50
A561 Speke corridor	Liverpool (to Speke)	Arriva	100	£2.00
A59/A506 Kirby	Liverpool & Knowsley	Stagecoach	81[1]	£1.50
A6 Stockport Road	Manchester & Stockport	Stagecoach/ Magic Bus	66.7[2]	£2.30/£1.90
A34 Wilmslow Road	Manchester	Stagecoach/ Magic Bus	41.9[3]	£1.90/£0.90

Notes: [1] Arriva 19% deregistered route from 3 September 2006: Stagecoach = 100%.

[2] UK North 33.3% (single fare £1.75) until Traffic Commissioner suspended Operator Licence in December 2006: Stagecoach = 100%.

[3] Bullocks 19.4%; Finglands 19.4%; and UK North 19.4% until Traffic Commissioner suspended UK North's Operator Licence in December 2006. Single fares to East Didsbury of £1.35, £1.00 and £1.40 respectively. Stagecoach = 61.3%.

Source: Knowles and Ametepe (2007)

Figure 5.2: Bus market dominance in PTE areas, 2004

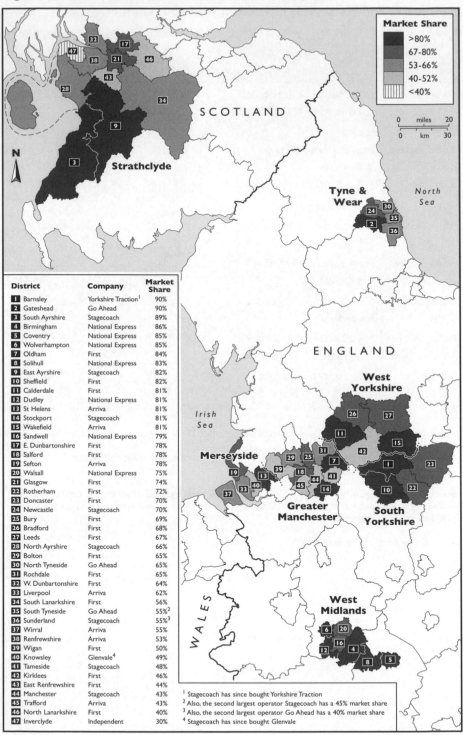

District	Company	Market Share
1 Barnsley	Yorkshire Traction[1]	90%
2 Gateshead	Go Ahead	90%
3 South Ayrshire	Stagecoach	89%
4 Birmingham	National Express	86%
5 Coventry	National Express	85%
6 Wolverhampton	National Express	85%
7 Oldham	First	84%
8 Solihull	National Express	83%
9 East Ayrshire	Stagecoach	82%
10 Sheffield	First	82%
11 Calderdale	First	81%
12 Dudley	National Express	81%
13 St Helens	Arriva	81%
14 Stockport	Stagecoach	81%
15 Wakefield	Arriva	81%
16 Sandwell	National Express	79%
17 E. Dunbartonshire	First	78%
18 Salford	First	78%
19 Sefton	Arriva	78%
20 Walsall	National Express	75%
21 Glasgow	First	74%
22 Rotherham	First	72%
23 Doncaster	First	70%
24 Newcastle	Stagecoach	70%
25 Bury	First	69%
26 Bradford	First	68%
27 Leeds	First	67%
28 North Ayrshire	Stagecoach	66%
29 Bolton	First	65%
30 North Tyneside	Go Ahead	65%
31 Rochdale	First	65%
32 W. Dunbartonshire	First	64%
33 Liverpool	Arriva	62%
34 South Lanarkshire	First	56%
35 South Tyneside	Go Ahead	55%[2]
36 Sunderland	Stagecoach	55%[3]
37 Wirral	Arriva	55%
38 Renfrewshire	Arriva	53%
39 Wigan	First	50%
40 Knowsley	Glenvale[4]	49%
41 Tameside	Stagecoach	48%
42 Kirklees	First	46%
43 East Renfrewshire	First	44%
44 Manchester	Stagecoach	43%
45 Trafford	Arriva	43%
46 North Lanarkshire	First	40%
47 Inverclyde	Independent	30%

[1] Stagecoach has since bought Yorkshire Traction
[2] Also, the second largest operator Stagecoach has a 45% market share
[3] Also, the second largest operator Go Ahead has a 40% market share
[4] Stagecoach has since bought Glenvale

Source of data: pteg

Light rail

Since the 1970s, most of Britain's conurbations and big cities have considered investment in light rail systems on congested radial corridors. Light rail's advantages include much lower costs than for either new underground metros or suburban railways and the ability to carry many more passengers at higher speeds than quality bus corridors, which are less likely to attract motorists to switch modes and thus tackle urban congestion (Knowles 1992; Knowles and White, 2003; Davison and Knowles, 2006). Light rail systems are costly – from £5 million to £25 million per two-way route kilometre – but their frequent, fast and reliable services to the heart of a city centre and a bright, modern image offer an attractive journey proposition. Although light rail vehicles cost up to £2.15 million each compared with between £120,000 and £200,000 for buses, they can carry up to three times more passengers and have a much longer operating life (CfIT, 2005). Light rail's average speeds of 15 to 35 kilometres per hour are also much higher than for buses in mixed traffic (6 to 25 kilometres per hour) and even better with segregated right of way (light rail 25–50+ kilometres per hour) (Hass-Klau and Crampton, 2001; pteg, 2005; Vuchic, 2007).

Conservative and Labour governments alike have rarely decided to give grants for part-funding of light rail schemes because of their high cost and very long lead-in times. It usually takes at least 10 years in Britain to open new light rail routes because of legal, planning and financing delays, compared with just three years and six months from preliminary study to opening for Lyon's first two tram routes in France (pteg, 2004; Knowles, 2007). Indeed, Grant Thornton (2008) notes that Britain's conurbations have been talking about light rail systems longer than it has taken many continental cities to actually build them. This reluctance by successive British governments to support light rail is despite its operational advantages and its effective role as a catalyst for urban regeneration. Up to the year 2000, many light rail schemes had been rejected and only six systems were in operation after more than 20 years of proposals. Government policies that had hindered light rail schemes included local bus deregulation outside London (which undermined bus/light rail integration), the 1989 requirement for non-user benefits to exceed the amount of government light rail grant, the preference for investment in cheaper bus QPs from 1997, and the *New deal for transport*'s (DETR, 1998) requirement that road-user tolls or workplace parking charges had to be introduced as part of the funding for light rail projects (Knowles, 2007). This was in spite of Manchester Metrolink Phase 1 quickly exceeding its patronage targets and achieving an unexpected and substantial modal shift from former car users of 21% of total light rail passengers, and Transport and Works Act Orders offering quicker and cheaper legal powers to allow construction (Knowles, 1996; Knowles and White, 2003).

Against this background, the targets in *Transport 2010* – advanced in the light of Parliamentary Select Committee support for light rail in appropriate circumstances – to double light rail use and invest in 25 schemes were unsurprisingly seen as important elements of plans to improve accessibility and personal mobility in larger urban areas (House of Commons, 2000). Indeed, this apparent shift in policy briefly heralded a new dawn for light rail in Britain (or, at least, in England) and was based on an assumption that £2.6 billion of public and private sector investment would become available (DETR, 2000; Docherty, 2001). From a baseline figure of 124 million light rail passengers in 2000/01, *Transport 2010* assumed at least 248 million passengers per year by 2010/11, but this target failed to distinguish between new traffic from opening new light rail systems or extensions and traffic growth on existing routes. Worse still, this target was abandoned after just two years in 2002 and, as we have seen, subsumed within a combined 12% growth target for bus and light rail, which in turn was abandoned in 2007.

By 2004 just two new light rail schemes had opened, in Sunderland and Nottingham, and only the Docklands Light Railway's (DLR's) London City Airport extension was under construction. The target of 25 new light rail lines in 10 years, already in jeopardy, became completely untenable in July 2004 when the government rejected bids to part-fund new light rail schemes in Leeds, Liverpool and Portsmouth and three extensions to Greater Manchester's Metrolink (Clark, 2004; Wainwright, 2004; House of Commons, 2005a; Fowler, 2006). Ministers were quick to endorse a National Audit Office (2004) report, which criticised light rail's value for money on the basis of costs and performance, and expressed concerns about substantial increases in projected capital costs. The report's main conclusions were advanced in the context of a loss of private sector confidence in railway investment and operation after the collapse of Railtrack, losses in constructing Nottingham Express Transit, financial problems at Croydon Tramlink and the early termination of several rail passenger franchises (Knowles, 2004, 2007). The government was less keen, however, to acknowledge that the report was not entirely critical. Recommendations to improve the prospects of light rail transport – better integration with bus services, improvements in park and ride, priority in traffic and procurement procedures, less utility diversion, track sharing with heavy rail and conversion from heavy rail – were all largely ignored. Instead, ministers reiterated the hollow commitment that congestion charges, something they were unwilling to support at the national level, were an option that would allow local authorities to raise extra funds if they still wished to take forward light rail schemes.

The government's attitude to light rail is particularly unfortunate given that, despite its barely disguised hostility towards the mode, in overall terms it has performed rather well. Modal shift from car to light rail has been around 20% at peak periods and 12.5 to 20% off-peak, much higher than the average for guided bus (3%) and for quality bus schemes (4 to 6.5%) (CfIT, 2005; pteg, 2005). In the 10 years after 1997, light rail passengers increased by 128%, while distance travelled rose by 130% (Table 5.5). This growth was greater than in any other rail sector, and light rail now provides a small but growing share of public transport in London and five of England's provincial conurbations and larger cities. From the publication of *Transport 2010* to 2006/07, light rail's proportion of all rail and local bus passengers in Britain increased from 1.9 to 2.4% and of just rail passengers from 6.0 to 7.5% (DfT, 2005a, 2007b). Some of this growth was due to the opening of new supertram systems in Croydon in May 2000 and Nottingham in March 2004, and to short extensions of the segregated and more heavily engineered DLR and the Tyne and Wear Metro. By 2006/07 the DLR alone had over a third of all light rail passengers in Britain and was the fastest-growing light rail system – this reflects its key role in facilitating extensive office development and employment in Canary Wharf and in regenerating the Royal Docks area – and both the DLR and Croydon Tramlink benefit from being part of London's integrated, intermodal transport system. Elsewhere, light rail competes with deregulated bus services.

Almost at the same time as the government cancelled the proposed light rail schemes in Leeds, Liverpool, Manchester and Portsmouth, several schemes in London, including extensions to the DLR, the integration of the East London Line into the London Overground rail network and Crossrail – the last of these alone being allocated £5 billion of government grant towards its £16 billion total cost – were confirmed. This prompted accusations of bias in favour of London (Kelso, 2004; Wainwright, 2004), although the successful 2012 Olympic Bid undoubtedly helped the city obtain higher priority for transport funding from the Department for Transport (DfT); the then Mayor of London, Ken Livingstone, pointed out that '[w]ithout the bid we would have never got the East London line improvements through. It was bottom of the Strategic Rail Authority's list of priorities but the bid got it up the list and the improvements are happening' (quoted in Kelso, 2004). Since 2004, TfL's Five-Year Investment Programme funded the opening of another DLR extension to London City Airport and North Woolwich in December 2005, and its further extension under the River Thames to Woolwich Arsenal, opening in 2009 (TfL, 2006a, 2006b).

What future for light rail in the UK?

In 2005 the Westminster government reiterated its view that light rail was too expensive when it largely rejected the House of Commons Transport Committee's critical report on government light rail policy (House of Commons, 2005a, 2005b). The DfT's year-long delay in publishing its largely unchanged light rail guidance (in December 2006) on the circumstances under which it will consider light rail schemes, signified its continuing indifference to light rail solutions. At the end of 2007, the only other planned light rail schemes with full or part-funding in place in England were:

Table 5.5: English light rail patronage changes

System	Passengers (millions)			Change		Passenger kilometers (millions)			Change	
	a	b	c	a–c	b–c	a	b	c	a–c	b–c
	1996/97	2000/01	2006/07	%	%	1996/97	2000/01	2006/07	%	%
Docklands Light Railway[1]	16.7	38.4	63.9	283	66	86.0	200.1	300.6	250	50
Tyne & Wear[2]	35.4	32.5	37.9	7	17	245.3	229.2	294.8	16	29
Manchester	13.4	17.2	19.8	48	15	85.6	152.3	207.6	143	36
Sheffield	7.8	11.1	14.0	80	26	28.9	38.0	42.0	45	11
Croydon[3]	N/A	15.0	24.6	N/A	64	N/A	96.0	127.9	N/A	33
West Midlands	N/A	5.4	4.9	N/A	–9	N/A	56.8	51.4	N/A	–9
Nottingham[4]	N/A	N/A	10.1	N/A	N/A	N/A	N/A	43.3	N/A	N/A
Blackpool[5]	4.9	4.1	3.4	–31	–17	14.9	12.6	10.4	–30	–17
TOTAL	78.2	123.7	178.6	128	44	469.7	784.0	1,078.0	130	38

Notes:

[1] Docklands Light Railway opened in 1987, extended to Bank in 1991, Beckton in March 1994, Lewisham in November 1999 and London City Airport and North Woolwich in December 2005.

[2] Tyne & Wear Metro opened in stages between 1980 and 1984, extended to Newcastle Airport in 1991 and Sunderland in March 2002.

[3] Croydon Tramlink opened in May 2000.

[4] Nottingham Express Transit opened in March 2004.

[5] Blackpool Corporation Tramway opened in 1885; 1996/97 passenger kilometres are estimated.

Sources of raw data: DfT (2005a, 2005b, 2007b); Knowles and White (2003)

- the conversion to DLR, funded by TfL from its Five-Year Investment Programme, of the Canning Town to Stratford section of the heavy rail North London Line, with an extension to Stratford International, opening in 2010 to serve the 2012 London Olympic Games site and the Channel Tunnel High Speed Rail Link (TfL, 2006c);
- Manchester Metrolink Phase 3a to Chorlton, Droylsden, Oldham and Rochdale, after £520 million of government funding was reinstated in December 2004 following a successful local private and public sector campaign, although the need to retender and the absence of inflation proofing left a £200 million shortfall (Knowles, 2007). Funding for the remainder of Metrolink Phase 3 to Manchester Airport and Ashton under Lyne and through Oldham and Rochdale town centres formed part of Greater Manchester's TIF bid to the government in July 2007;
- a Metrolink spur to Media City/BBC at Salford Quays costing about £20 million, funded by Salford City Council with £8 million contributed by the North West Regional Development Agency.

In Scotland, meanwhile, the minority SNP government acquiesced to providing £375 million part-funding of Edinburgh's £498 million tram scheme (£45 million is being provided by Edinburgh Council) after losing a parliamentary vote in June 2007. The scheme was supported by the previous Labour/Liberal Democrat coalition, and final business case approval was given by a combination of Labour, Liberal Democrats and Conservatives on Edinburgh Council in autumn 2007 with construction commencing in early 2008 (City of Edinburgh Council, 2006; *Transport Times*, 2007a, 2007b). How ironic that Labour pushed through Edinburgh's trams after light rail schemes in four English cities had been vetoed by an Edinburgh Labour MP, Alistair Darling, in his capacity as Secretary of State for Transport.

Thus, after 25 years of dashed hopes for light rail in Britain, it is now clear that its future expansion, at least in England, will be limited unless a range of alternative capital funding sources is identified to lessen dependence on central government funding. Although the government's 2005 announcement of the TIF could help to fund some light rail schemes, it is open to bids from all transport modes; in any case, most cities still regard the introduction of congestion charging or a workplace parking levy – a requirement of the TIF process (Chapter Three) – as politically dangerous and Edinburgh lost a referendum by a 3:1 ratio on the issue in February 2005 (Gaunt et al, 2007). In contrast to the situation in England, France has opened many new light rail systems based on funding from local and regional government and the local business community (Knowles, 2007). In the US, cuts in federal funding resulted in local referendums to seek voter approval for hypothecated fuel or sales tax increases, and total spending on transit has continued to grow due to increased state and local funding. The UK's compact geography makes locally differentiated sales tax and road fuel duty unrealistic, and while the business community criticises the poor quality of the country's urban transport systems, it has resisted supplementary national business rates to help invest in the better-quality public transport with lower fares experienced in most of Europe. Alternatively, a set proportion of business rates could be hypothecated for planned transport investment over a sustained period, although a French-style *Versement Transport* – a dedicated payroll tax – is unlikely as again it would be perceived by the business community as an additional burden on their competitiveness (see Grant Thornton, 2008, for more analysis on these potential revenue generation options).

In summary, then, *Transport 2010* targets to double light rail use by 2010/11 and build 25 new light rail systems were scrapped after just two years when the government decided it would only part-fund a handful of new light rail schemes. The National Audit Office's (2004) report appears to have been used selectively to justify the rejection of light rail schemes, while other countries have managed to substantially reduce light rail's capital costs as well as devising alternative funding sources to lessen or abandon dependence on central government funding. Despite the government's partial reinstatement of Manchester Metrolink's Phase 3, it is still unlikely that further light rail schemes will be built elsewhere in England outside London unless new funding sources are secured to wholly or partly replace government capital grants.

In light of all this, some local authorities have adopted Bus Rapid Transit (BRT) measures in an attempt to keep some form of high-quality public transport investment programme alive. BRT is a cheaper alternative to light rail with renowned flagship systems in Curitiba, Brazil and Bogotá, Colombia (TRB, 2003; BRT-UK, 2007). The idea is that if buses are freed from general road traffic congestion by running on dedicated roadways (usually with better buses, waiting facilities and information, and pre-payment of fares) they can perform nearly as well as light rail at lower cost and with more operational flexibility as the non-dedicated elements of their routes can be changed. They can also be implemented much more quickly. Bus Rapid Transit is by no means an optimal solution, however, because buses cannot carry the same volume of passengers, are slower than light rail with poorer acceleration and ride comfort and nor are buses able to produce as much modal shift from cars due to their poorer image. Existing BRT systems in the UK include those in Bradford, Crawley, Dartford, Edinburgh, Leeds, Runcorn New Town and York. Leeds City Council and Metro have now proposed a BRT alternative to their Supertram scheme, and South Yorkshire has recently followed suit, endorsing BRT in favour of earlier light rail plans between Sheffield and Rotherham. The shift in government mood away from light rail schemes and towards bus-based alternatives suggests that high-priority bus systems are likely to play an increasing role in the major English conurbations, even though they have not been given any concrete backing in the 2007 Transport Bill (Atkins, 2005; CfIT, 2005). It remains to be seen whether funding for BRT schemes will be assembled and how they will be implemented given their significant highway capacity requirements.

Conclusion

A decade after the publication of *A new deal for transport* (DETR, 1998), the government's policies for England have failed, except in London, to achieve its own targets for local buses and light rail, which it set out in *Transport 2010* (DETR, 2000). In short, this is due to a lack of political leadership and a failure to take on the powerful vested interests of the large private bus companies. Local bus transport in London, Scotland and Wales has benefited from different governance environments that have enabled additional transport spending and earlier introduction of generous national concessionary fares schemes (Chapter One). London has also retained the advantage of a locally managed, franchised bus network and a multimodal transport system with integrated fares and services. Outside of London the UK continues to invest much less in local public transport than most of its European neighbours (Chapter Ten), and the continuation of bus deregulation in the rest of Britain remains a major obstacle to the integration of services and fares both between and within transport modes. While very recent growth in bus use in the English provincial conurbations and shires – resulting from free off-peak bus fares for the over sixties from April 2006 – and continuing growth in light rail use marks a limited revival in public transport, aspirations for widespread modal switch from car to bus and reductions in traffic congestion have not been achieved.

The current debate on bus policy seems to have moved on significantly from the clear-cut arguments in 1985 for and against deregulation and privatisation (Beesley and Glaister, 1985; Gwilliam et al, 1985). It is clear from experience in London, and to some extent in Scotland, that a significant degree of regulatory intervention and increased public subsidy are needed to reverse the decline in bus patronage. A franchising system like the one in London puts sustainability and integration at the heart of network planning and pricing, while successfully managing to introduce competition in tendering for contracts and therefore efficiency in network operations. Elsewhere deregulated monopolies are more profitable to bus companies than competitively tendered franchises so it is no surprise that QCs are fiercely opposed by private sector operators. The government thinks that such monopolies are less costly to the Exchequer, although this may only be a short-term advantage as the number of subsidised services increases with decreasing patronage and increasing highway congestion. For some local authorities the deregulated system is a convenient scapegoat to hide their reluctance to provide greater bus priority, and the success of a few voluntary QPs continues to be used by the bus operators, some local authorities and the DfT as justification of the status quo.

Notes

[1] Conservative Prime Minister Margaret Thatcher is often credited with the statement that 'anyone seen in a bus over the age of 26 is a failure in life' although there is still disagreement as to its author.

[2] In PTE areas, subsidised services represent around 20% of total vehicle kilometres.

References

Atkins (2005) *Study of high quality buses in Leeds*, Report to the Department for Transport, London: DfT, www.dft.gov.uk/pgr/regional/buses/study/ (accessed 23 September 2007).

Beesley, M. and Glaister, S. (1985) 'Deregulating the bus industry: a response', *Transport Reviews*, 5, pp 133–42.

Bristow, A., Shires, J. and Mackie, P. (2001) 'Quality Bus Partnerships: new evidence on performance', Paper presented at the World Conference on Transport Research, South Korea.

BRT-UK (2007) *Buses as rapid transit: A transport revolution in waiting*, Edinburgh: BRT-UK.

CILT (Chartered Institute of Logistics and Transport) (2007) *CILT response to draft Local Transport Bill (via John Carr)*, Corby: CILT.

City of Edinburgh Council (2006) 'Edinburgh's world-class tram network one step closer', Press Release, 26 January.

Clark, A. (2004) 'How Prescott's masterplan was dumped', *The Guardian*, 21 July.

CfIT (Commission for Integrated Transport) (2001) *Study of European best practice in the delivery of integrated transport*, London: CfIT.

CfIT (2005) *Affordable mass transit guidance: Helping you choose the best system for your area*, London: CfIT.

Davison, L. and Knowles, R. (2006) 'Bus Quality Partnerships, modal shift and traffic decongestion', *Journal of Transport Geography*, 14, pp 177–94.

DETR (Department of the Environment, Transport and the Regions) (1997) *Developing an integrated transport policy*, London: DETR.

DETR (1998) *A new deal for transport: Better for everyone*, Cm 3950, London: The Stationery Office.

DETR (1999) *From workhorse to thoroughbred: A better role for bus travel*, London: DETR.

DETR (2000) *Transport 2010: The ten-year plan*, London: The Stationery Office.

DfT (Department for Transport) (2004) *The future of transport: A network for 2030*, Cm 6234, London: The Stationery Office.

DfT (2005a) *Transport statistics Great Britain 2005*, London: DfT.

DfT (2005b) *Light rail statistics – England: Key facts*, London: The Stationery Office.

DfT (2006) *Putting passengers first*, London: DfT.

DfT (2007a) *Transport statistics Great Britain 2007*, London: DfT.

DfT (2007b) *Public transport statistics bulletin GB: 2007 edition*, London: DfT.

DfT (2007c) *Local Transport Bill*, London: The Stationery Office.

Docherty, I. (2001) 'Interrogating the ten-year transport plan', *Area*, 33, pp 321–8.

Fowler, D. (2006) 'Merseytram case against Darling hits court buffers', *Transport Times*, 14, 10 February.

Gaunt, M., Rye, T. and Allen, S. (2007) 'Public acceptability of road user charging: the case of Edinburgh and the 2005 referendum', *Transport Reviews*, 27, pp 85-102.

Grant Thornton (2008) *Connecting for competitiveness: The future of transport in the UK city regions*, London: Grant Thornton LLP.

Gwilliam, K., Nash, C. and Mackie, P. (1985) 'Deregulating the bus industry in Britain: the case against, *Transport Reviews*, 5, pp 105-32.

Hass-Klau, C. and Crampton, G. (2001) 'Bus or light rail – which is best?', in T. Grayling (ed) *Any more fares? Delivering better bus services*, London: IPPR.

Hendy, P. (2007) Keynote address given to the 1st Public Transport Conference, University of Leeds, 18 October.

House of Commons (2000) *Light rapid transport systems*, Eighth report of the Environment, Transport and Regional Affairs Select Committee, HC 153, London: The Stationery Office.

House of Commons (2005a) *Integrated transport: The future of light rail and modern trams in the United Kingdom*, Tenth report of the Transport Committee, Session 2004-05, HC 378-1, London: The Stationery Office.

House of Commons (2005b) *Government response to the Committee's 10th report of session 2004-05*, HC 526, London: The Stationery Office.

Kelso, P. (2004) 'New London stadium not for football', *The Guardian*, 6 October.

Knowles, R. (1992) 'Light rail transport', in J. Whitelegg (ed) *Traffic congestion: Is there a way out?*, Hawes: Leading Edge Press, pp 107-33.

Knowles, R. (1996) 'Transport impacts of Greater Manchester's Metrolink light rail system', *Journal of Transport Geography*, 4, pp 1-14.

Knowles, R. (2004) 'Impacts of privatising Britain's rail passenger services – franchising, re-franchising and Ten Year Transport Plan targets', *Environment & Planning A*, 36, pp 2065-87.

Knowles, R. (2007) 'What future for light rail in the UK after Ten Year Transport Plan targets are scrapped?', *Transport Policy*, 14, pp 81-93.

Knowles, R. and Ametepe, A. (2007) 'Bus patronage, bus deregulation and Ten Year Transport Plan targets in gateway cities: the case of Greater Manchester and Merseyside', *North West Geography*, 7(2), pp 1-11.

Knowles, R. and White, P. (2003) 'Light rail and London Underground', in I. Docherty and J. Shaw (eds) *A new deal for transport?*, Oxford: Blackwell Publishing, pp 135-57.

Mackie, P. (1999) 'Quality Bus Partnerships: implications for market performance', Paper presented at the Sixth International Conference on Competition and Ownership in Land Passenger Transport, Cape Town, South Africa.

Mackie, P. and Preston, J. (1996) *The local bus market: A case study of regulatory change*, Aldershot: Avebury.

MVA (2007) *Recent evidence on bus fare elasticities for older and disabled concessionary passengers*, Report for the Passenger Transport Executive Group, London: MVA Consultancy.

National Audit Office (2004) *Improving public transport in England through light rail*, Report by the Comptroller and Auditor General, HC 518, Session 2003-2004, London: The Stationery Office.

NERA (2006) *The decline in bus services in English PTE areas: The quest for a solution*, London: NERA Economic Consulting.

Parkhurst, G. (2000) 'Influence of bus-based park and ride facilities on users' car traffic', *Transport Policy*, 7, pp 159-72.

pteg (Passenger Transport Executive Group) (2004) *We must learn from the French on tram schemes*, Leeds: pteg.

pteg (2005) *What light rail can do for cities: A review of the evidence: Final Report*, Leeds: pteg.

Sørenssen, C., Gudmundsson, H. and Bergström, T. (2007) 'Bus transport in Manchester: between new public management regimes and sustainable transport aspirations – an "outside" view from Scandinavia', Paper presented at a workshop on Governance Structures, Public Bus Transport and Sustainable Mobility, Greater Manchester Passenger Transport Executive, Manchester, 28 November.

TAS (2001) *Quality Bus Partnerships good practice guide*, Preston: TAS Partnership.

TfL (Transport for London) (2006a) *Docklands Light Railway: London City Airport extension*, London: TfL.

TfL (2006b) *Docklands Light Railway: Woolwich Arsenal extension*, London: TfL.

TfL (2006c) *Docklands Light Railway: Stratford International extension*, London: TfL.

Transport Times (2007a) 'State of the art trams on the way for Edinburgh', October, p 11.

Transport Times (2007b) 'Vote paves the way for 2008 start on Edinburgh Tram', November, p 11.

TRB (Transportation Research Board) (2003) *TCRP report 90 – bus rapid transit (volume 1)*, Washington, DC: TRB, http://onlinepubs.trb.org/onlinepubs/tcrp/tcrp_rpt_90v1.pdf (accessed 27 September 2007).

Vuchic, V. (2007) *Urban transit: Systems and technology*, Hoboken, NJ: Wiley.

Wainwright, M. (2004) 'Rejection of northern tram plans prompts suspicions of London bias', *The Guardian*, 21 July.

White, P. (2007) 'Factors behind recent patronage trends in Britain and their implications for future policy', Paper presented at the Threadbo 10 Conference, Hamilton Island, Australia, 12-17 August.

SIX

Walking and cycling: easy wins for a sustainable transport policy?

Rodney Tolley

Given that walking and cycling require little collective intervention to make possible, beyond the manufacture of shoes, clothing and bicycles and the construction and maintenance of basic infrastructure, it is not surprising that they are often regarded as the most obvious candidates for modes satisfying Bill Black's definition of sustainable transport as 'transport that meets the needs of the present without compromising the ability of future generations to meet their own needs' (Black, 1996, after the World Commission on Environment and Development, 1987). Yet it could easily be argued that this substantially underplays the worth of these simple yet highly effective forms of transport. Adopting the three-way economic/environmental/social conception of sustainability outlined in Chapter One, walking and cycling move from being 'benign' modes exerting very little environmental damage, to positive 'active' or 'personal' modes, which encourage myriad economic and social connections for very modest environmental costs. This should not come as a surprise, but is often overlooked given the generally negative language that characterises the sustainable transport narrative. In the midst of the transport 'crisis', generated in large part by a car-dominated transport system that does not meet our current needs nearly as well as it might – with worsening congestion, and with safety, environmental quality, social inclusion, community cohesion and personal and public health all compromised by the growth in car use – it is probably inevitable that the debate over what to do should be framed in terms of trying not to make things even worse.

Escaping, however, from this somewhat depressing analytical paradigm to a more positive, normative approach to promoting active travel alters the picture completely. As H. G. Wells is reputed to have said, 'when I see an adult on a bicycle, I have hope for the human race'. The same is true for walking, since it is the fundamental, ubiquitous means for us as human individuals to meet one another and engage in conversation, learning and other social processes. Walking is one of the first things a child wants to do, and one of the last things an adult wants to give up (London Walking Forum, 2000), yet as a society we have been taking walking for granted. It also has the very useful side-effect of making us fitter and less likely to be overweight, even if undertaken to modest extent (Sloman, 2006). Jacobs (1961) famously pointed to the ultimate importance of walking as the mechanism that turns roads into streets where social interaction and economic exchange flourish, long before the Pedestrians' Association renamed itself as 'Living Streets' (Pedestrians' Association, 2001).

But our society has become so genuinely car dependent that many of the most basic activities – food shopping and travelling to school – now require vehicular travel for many people, not only because our land-use patterns have evolved to privilege the car, but also because we have lost our appreciation of the utility of walking and cycling as modes of transport in their own right (Docherty and Hall, 1998). For example, in Germany, in one generation, the increase in car use has not led to more trips, more activities or time saved for the average person. Instead, the extra speed conferred by the car is consumed in longer trips, so that people now have to travel further to access the same things that were accessed locally a generation ago (Brög, 1995). Activities are not more accessible (indeed for many people, they are markedly less so given the deepening social inequality that car-based planning often brings; see Schaeffer and Sclar, 1975), but people on the whole are more mobile, and this increase in the consumption of motorised transport has significant impacts on sustainability. The premise of this chapter is therefore that there is an undeniable imperative not only for us to switch to more sustainable forms of transport (which includes public transport), but also for large proportions of our travel to be moved to the *most* sustainable forms – walking and cycling – not just for environmental reasons, but also to promote better economic and social outcomes as well.

As is documented throughout the book, transport policy in the UK has generally been about accommodating increasing flows of motorised traffic, and then about trying to avoid doing very much at all once the true nature of transport's impact on the global environment became apparent (Chapter One). Walking and cycling have not been seen as viable alternatives to the car in the same way as motorised public transport modes have, and, indeed, such planning as there has been for them has usually been focused on trying to protect the two activities from the worst impacts of cars and lorry traffic. This is not unimportant given that British cyclists have traditionally been expected to share the road with motor vehicles, rather than the pavement with pedestrians, which is the case in much of continental Europe, but obscures the fact that many of the everyday trips we make by motorised modes are in fact extremely amenable to walking or cycling (Banister and Gallent, 1998). But the lowly overall importance of the two modes is not surprising, given that walking and cycling policy has long been regarded as among the least glamorous aspects of transport planning, but also because the car-dependent psyche of many people today is reflected in their everyday habits towards pedestrians, cyclists and the spaces they use.

The importance of walking and cycling

The policy amnesia over the role of walking in everyday life is reflected in the fact that until very recently it was difficult to appreciate fully how important the activity was in Britain; the first reasonably comprehensive statistical picture of walking only became available in 1998, with the publication of *Transport statistics report: Walking in Great Britain* (DETR, 1998a). Data are now more readily available from the National Travel Surveys. Although there is some likelihood of undercounting of short trips, walking accounts for 2.8% of the total distance travelled and is still the dominant mode of transport for short journeys (DfT, 2007a). Of all trips made in Britain, 22% are still under one mile in length and almost 80% of these are made on foot. Around 40% of all education journeys, one quarter of all shopping journeys and a quarter of social/entertainment journeys are walked. Despite its importance, however, the amount of walking has declined. The average British resident made 249 trips on foot in 2006 compared with 292 in 1995/97, a decrease of 15%. By 2003, the proportion of all journeys made on foot in the UK since the mid-1990s had fallen from 33% to 27%, although it has remained at roughly this level since.

At the outset, it should be stressed that much of this walking is not transport as such, in that people need not be attempting to reach a particular destination to be pedestrians (that is, walking as an 'access mode' (LPAC, 1997). Walking is also an 'access sub-mode', as it is the main way of getting to public transport services. In fact, as walking is an integral element of all trips for non-disabled people, it may be thought of as the 'oil' that helps the transport system to run more smoothly. Walking (like cycling) can also be a 'recreation/leisure mode' – including walking for the sake of it, playing and walking the dog. And finally, it can be a 'circulation/exchange mode', where people carry out a range of non-transport activities on foot in public spaces, such as window shopping, chatting to neighbours and friends and having a drink at a pavement café, which Jane Jacobs (1961) famously explored. In other words, walking is not just transport, but a vital part of our use of public spaces.

Cycling on public highways has been in general decline in Britain since the 1970s, both in the number of journeys made and the total distance travelled, so that only about 2% of all journeys are now made by bicycle. There are marked variations from city to city, however, with usage as high as 18% of all trips in York (DETR, 1999). As if to demonstrate the different purposes of active travel, there have been steady increases in the number of people cycling for recreation since the mid-1980s: it appears that many Britons now see cycling as a healthy recreation activity rather than as a useful everyday mode of transport. For example, research undertaken in Scotland in 2005 found that 54% of adults and fully 86% of children regarded leisure as the main reason for owning a bicycle (Scottish Executive, 2005).[1] This growth is drawing attention to differing interpretations of the walking and cycling statistics. Sustrans argues that usage of the National Cycle Network by both pedestrians and cyclists has grown over and above increased usage associated with new routes every year since monitoring began in 2000 (Sustrans, 2007a). By contrast, as we have noted, the National Travel Survey for Great Britain has, in recent years, shown no growth in cycling and a decline and then flattening off in walking trips. One of the reasons for this discrepancy is perhaps the high number of both walking and cycling trips being made on traffic-free routes across the Network in circumstances where, in Sustrans' view, the National Travel Survey does not adequately record trips being made on these routes.

As with walking, it is clear that there is great potential for increasing the levels of cycling in Britain. Most trips in urban areas are very short. For example, nearly 70% of all journeys are under five miles in length; 41% are under two miles, and, as we have seen, 22% are under one mile (DfT, 2007a). Even in the case of journeys undertaken by car, around 60% are below five miles in length. Average trip lengths to education and shopping in 2006 are 3.3 miles and 4.2 miles respectively. Commuting distances, although rising on average, are frequently walkable or cyclable by the majority of the population. Fifteen million people in the UK own a bicycle, yet only 3.6 million use one regularly.

The sustainability benefits of walking and cycling

The principal sustainability benefits of cycling are listed in Box 6.1, many of which also apply to walking. Although this framework is more than 25 years old, it remains relevant and, indeed, some of its contents have become more pressing issues in recent times, given the increasing attention paid to the obesity 'epidemic' (see Prentice and Jebb, 1995; Sloman, 2006). In particular, it is the significance of the health benefits of walking and cycling that has been increasingly appreciated over the past two decades, whether conceived of narrowly in terms of personal benefits or more broadly in terms of public health, and which has led to the wider appreciation of 'active travel' as a positive public policy tool in the UK and elsewhere (Lopez-Zetina et al, 2006; Lindstrom, 2007; Sustrans, 2007b). To take walking first, it is the most natural form of physical activity and has been described as 'the nearest activity to perfect exercise' (Morris and Hardman, 1997, p 306). It can be enjoyed by people of most physical conditions and ages, and requires little in the way of skill or specialist equipment. Evidence indicates that regular walking contributes to reductions in heart disease, diabetes, osteoporosis, colon cancer, obesity and depression. It is now central to health promotion activity in the UK, not least because, being easy to incorporate into daily lives and split into 'bite-sized chunks', it is actually more likely to be taken up by people and maintained, especially since this means it 'doesn't feel like exercise'.

Box 6.1: Why plan for cyclists?

It is a cheap way of providing mobility
Cost effectiveness is an important criterion for determining the priorities for investment. Money spent on removing the constraints on cycling can significantly increase the availability of transport for a large section of the community. The provision of routes for bicycles gives people 'freeways' for the price of footpaths.

It makes efficient use of space

In congested urban areas, space is a valuable resource. Bicycles take up little space when moving; the capacity of a road is increased approximately 10 times if bicycles are used instead of cars. Furthermore, bicycle parking does not rank in the same class as car parking; between 10 and 15 bicycles can be parked in one car-parking space.

It contributes to energy conservation

Energy conservation is now a priority in most countries. A cyclist can travel about 2,500 kilometres on the energy equivalent of five litres of petrol.

It keeps people fit and healthy

Regular cycling reduces body weight, reduces heart disease, lessens tension, improves sleep and therefore reduces the cost of health services. It has also been shown to increase people's efficiency at work.

It is an equitable means of transport

More people can afford the running costs of a bicycle than any other means of transport and the capital cost is less than a week's wages in most developed countries. The bicycle is a simple piece of machinery to understand and maintain, and thus gives people greater control over their lives.

It can cut death and injury on the roads

The annual toll of deaths and injuries to cyclists is appalling. Many are killed and injured through no fault of their own. Cheap and well-tried measures can be used to save lives and injuries.

It is a quick means of transport

Door-to-door travel times for urban journeys between four and six kilometres (the vast majority of urban journeys) can be quicker by bicycle than any other means of transport.

It is a reliable means of transport

Bicycles are less likely to break down than other means of transport and are unhindered by traffic jams.

It provides mobility to practically everyone

Many of the old, the young and people from the other minority groups who will never be able to use cars, can ride bicycles.

It is a benign means of transport

The bicycle is noiseless, pollution-free and does not significantly encroach on other people's lives.

Source: Adapted from Hudson (1982)

The personal health benefits of cycling are, arguably, even greater than walking because it is also an aerobic activity, which uses major muscle groups, has the potential to raise the heart rate to an extent that benefits cardiovascular health and expends significant amounts of energy. The results have been well documented: regular cyclists are fitter and live longer than non-cyclists (Cavill, 2003). To take just one example, the Copenhagen Heart Study found that those who did not cycle to work experienced a 39% higher mortality rate than those who did (Andersen, 2000).

Despite the obvious focus on individual health, the major benefits of more people walking and cycling are experienced by the population in general. First, more cycling and walking (at the expense of car use) would significantly improve local air quality and reduce greenhouse gas emissions. Up to 24,000 vulnerable people die prematurely each year and similar numbers are admitted to hospital, because of exposure to air pollution from particulates, ozone and sulphur dioxide, most of which is related to road traffic (DH, 1998). A second public benefit advantage is reduced risk of road traffic injury. A disproportionate number of victims of crashes are pedestrians and cyclists, accounting for about 20% of those involved in serious accidents in the World Health Organization's (WHO's) European Region (WHO, 2002). This is frequently interpreted as meaning that these are inherently dangerous modes, which need therefore to be reduced if we are to have greater safety overall. Yet even in what could currently be regarded as a hostile environment for cycling in Britain, the benefits from regular cycling in terms of life years gained through improved fitness of regular cyclists outweigh the life years lost in cycling crashes – and the ratio may be as high as 20:1 (Hillman, 1993). Moreover, if the cycling environment were to be made less intimidating (for example, by reducing traffic speeds and constructing more cycle paths and lanes) the benefits would be greater still. Partly this is because existing cyclists would be less likely to come into fatal conflict with cars, but it is also because such improvements would help to release the known latent demand for cycling, and thus save even more lives as more people cycle and fewer people drive.

Thus, in contrast to received wisdom, the riskiness of cycling is inversely related to the level of cycle use. For example, the three European countries with the most cycling (Denmark, the Netherlands and Sweden) have fatality rates for cyclists per 100 million kilometres (62.5 million miles) ranging from 1.6 to 2.3. In the countries with the least cycling (Austria, Britain and Italy) they range from 6.0 to 11.0 (WALCYING, 1997). Clearly, as the amount of cycling increases to a critical mass, traffic arrangements have to be made to accommodate it and car drivers have to adapt their behaviour to share the space with cyclists, producing not only more cycling safety, but more safety for motorised modes too. As one analyst puts it, 'proper planning for cycling and walking is a catalyst for road safety' (Wittink, 2003, p 172).

A final public health benefit is that more cycling and walking would lead to greater social interaction and improve 'social capital', a concept being linked increasingly to health, and also to economic development (Percy-Smith, 2000).

Busy streets sever communities and discourage children from playing, and from walking and cycling to school. By contrast, 'liveable streets' filled with people on foot or two wheels encourage social interaction, build social capital and diminish the fear of crime. They can even help stimulate the economy, especially when effectively integrated with major new public transport investment (Hall and Hass-Klau, 1985; Marshall and Harrison, 2007), as a senior transport planner in Nantes explained to Iain Docherty during his research on the impact of the tramway in that city. Pressed on his assertion that the installation of the tram network had generated one new pedestrian trip for every one new tram ride, the planner explained that:

> 'Before the tram, people would drive to work, eat their lunch at their desk and drive home. Now, because the city centre environment is so much better because of the tram and less traffic, people come to work on the tram, and go out to eat more often at lunchtime. And they also go to the shops, do other things during the day. That's where the extra trip on foot comes from.'

These broader benefits of walking and cycling should therefore not be underestimated, since 'bowling alone' (Puttnam, 2000) isn't as much fun as doing so with friends, and eating a sandwich lunch at your desk doesn't encourage work–life balance, or stimulate the creative café society on which innovation and economic development is increasingly claimed to depend (Florida, 2005).

Obstacles to walking and cycling

Understanding why people walk less than they once did and (much) less than they could requires an appreciation of the many real or perceived deterrents to going out on foot. Among the most important physical deterrents are personal safety and fear of crime, speeding traffic, lack of seating and inadequate pavements (made worse by posts, guard rails, traffic signs, grit bins, sandwich boards, commercial waste, wheelie bins and insensitively parked cars, such as that seen in Figure 6.1; see also Goodman and Tolley, 2003). The difficulty experienced in crossing roads is a worsening problem:

> We are corralled behind long lengths of guard railing, forced into dark and dangerous subways and made to endure long waits at pedestrian crossings.... For once all that has to be done to see the difficulties is to step outside the Palace of Westminster.... Here in the heart of our largest and richest city [London], by the nation's best known buildings, it is impossible to cross some of the roads. (House of Commons, 2001, p ix)

Figure 6.1: A motorist in Gateshead, England, responds to the reallocation of road space from the car to buses and cyclists

© Iain Docherty

Beyond these physical issues – which have been highlighted by the success of the Royal Borough of Kensington and Chelsea's (RBKC's) pilot project to *remove* guard rails and other street furniture from Kensington High Street (RBKC, 2008; Figure 6.2) – three other obstacles to walking need to be stressed. One is the problem of land-use planning and the location of facilities. Distances between homes, shops and schools are increasing, not only because of planning decisions, but also because of the unintended consequences of other public policies, such as increased choice in school education and the rebuilding of major hospitals in less-congested, cheaper edge-of-town sites.[2] For example, the percentage of homes within a six-minute walk of shops selling food fell from 68% to 57% between 1989/91 and 1998/2000. Connected to this is a second issue, that of time, with people feeling that their busy, multitasking lifestyles simply do not allow enough time for them to walk (Goodman, 2001). A third problem is the 'invisibility' of walking identified earlier in the chapter. Even though walking accounts for such a large proportion of modal share, particularly for short journeys, it is still often overlooked in policy and in planning. 'Walking is 'hidden', as it is 'so basic to all planning and transport activities, and so undemanding in terms of government finance, that it somehow slips through the net in strategy formulation' (MTRU, 1996). Walking does not attract big budgets and championing pedestrian issues does not normally further planners' careers.

This lack of professional focus is compounded by the failure of the public to bring the problems walking faces to the attention of planners and politicians. This is because few people see themselves as pedestrians (compared to those

Figure 6.2: New streetscape in Kensington High Street, London

Source: RBKC (2008)

who identify with being drivers or cyclists) and so campaigners are scattered and lack influence. Transport officers in local authorities cannot justify to their committees the expense of providing for walking, as 'they do not have the active and well informed allies on the outside to help demonstrate that "the public" actually wants money spent on facilities for pedestrians' (Gaffron, 2000, p 11). This lack of really powerful lobby or advocacy groups thereby compounds the problem of the invisibility of walking, although it should be recognised that things have begun to improve somewhat with the development of personal travel planning initiatives made possible by advances in information and communications technology (Chapter Eleven).

The obstacles to everyday cycling are primarily related to the environment in which it takes place. It is an open-air mode relying on human power and is vulnerable to threat by vehicles, especially when cyclists are asked to share road space with general traffic, or with buses in bus lanes, the latter an especial peculiarity of the UK. Potential cyclists are deterred by physical barriers such as gradients, heavy traffic and excessive speeds, by the lack of cycle storage and facilities such as showers at workplaces, and also to some extent by the macho image portrayed by some cyclists.[3] Moreover, the quality of schemes attempting to overcome these problems has been widely criticised: at a series of seminars on promoting cycling in 2001, practitioners repeatedly noted that the levels of cycling were being depressed by the poor quality of UK cycling schemes, including conflict with pedestrians on shared-use paths, lack of continuity of routes, dangerous road junction design and poor cycle facilities at destinations (Jones, 2001). Four of the five standard cycle route design criteria – coherence, directness, attractiveness, safety and comfort – are frequently ignored, with safety often pursued at the expense of the others by, for example, installing barriers, staggered crossings and routes through subways, all of which make routes less coherent and direct, and more uncomfortable and unattractive (and which also risk destroying the quality of the urban realm, especially for pedestrians; see Badland and Schofield, 2005). These problems have been ascribed to inadequate guidance from central government, to lack of support from senior management and councillors and to inadequate training of staff (Gaffron, 2000).

It is critical to understand, however, that even top-quality infrastructure – the 'hardware' – will not increase levels of cycling without the 'software' of attitude shifting and behaviour change. For example, the low social status accorded to cyclists has been identified as a major dissuasive factor to cycling (Finch and Morgan, 1985). Much research since has re-emphasised this crucial point. While cycle facilities can make cycling safer and are popular, they do not in themselves lead to more cycling. The genuine culture change in getting people to consider cycling as a feasible alternative to the car is much more important (Davies et al, 1997). A key part of this is likely to be some sort of fiscal recognition of cycling to work, which is not only a direct incentive, but also signals that cycling is a serious activity, with valued public benefits. Whereas company cars have long enjoyed tax breaks (although these are now diminishing), as have public transport season tickets in many parts of Europe, (modestly) paying people to cycle to work rather than use a motorised alternative is a new and radical initiative, but one with the potential to bring about meaningful modal shift if combined with improved cycle infrastructure (Wardman et al, 2007).

The changing UK policy context for non-motorised transport

Under the Thatcher administrations from 1979 to 1990, support for walking and cycling was almost non-existent. Writing in 1993, John Adams argued that government transport policy was 'clear, coherent and powerful'. It consisted of promoting an explosive growth in the modern means of travel (cars and planes) and phasing out the 'old-fashioned' means of movement, bicycle, bus and train. The bicycle was, he said, 'clearly heading the way of the horse and cart'. What he called the Department of Transport's (DoT's) 'most impressive achievement – the reduction of walking' – was largely undocumented because 'the Department's statisticians did not consider walking to be a form of transport and did not collect information about it' (Adams, 1993, pp 73-7).

By 1996, definite policy support for cycling was becoming clearer as the DoT launched *The national cycling strategy* (NCS) (DoT, 1996a) in the light of important research especially on cycle safety (BMA, 1992). It had targets – for doubling the number of trips by bicycle on 1996 figures by the end of 2002, and doubling them again by 2012 – and included a model local cycling strategy for local authorities.

The NCS was also supported, from the mid-1990s, by a range of policies that have had the effect of raising the profile of cycling, such as school and company travel plans, safe routes to school, new casualty reduction targets, home zones, quiet lanes, traffic calming, government reviews of speed and changes in planning guidance. Within this overall policy framework, air quality and health issues continued to push cycling up the agenda, and the mode received a further boost when the National Cycle Network reached 5,000 miles in June 2000 (Lumsdon and Mitchell, 1999).

These gains for sustainable transport were not limited to cycling. In 1996 a discussion document from the Walking Steering Group recognised that to be successful, walking must be considered as part of an overall strategy and not just in isolation (DoT, 1996b). The opportunity to do this came in July 1998, with the publication of the New Labour government's White Paper *A new deal for transport: Better for everyone* (DETR, 1998b). For walking and cycling, the New Deal was to make these modes more attractive, safer and therefore more viable alternative modes of transport, contributing to the idea that their improved integration with motorised modes would represent a significant carrot to behaviour change.

Thus, the mid-1990s saw a considerable shift in favour of green modes – at least rhetorically – as, for a short time, motoring groups, environmentalists and politicians seemed to agree that things could not continue the way they were. But, as Lynn Sloman (2003, p 474) put it, 'almost as soon as the consensus formed, it fell apart'. As other chapters discuss, the final White Paper was itself a rather compromised version of the transport ideas that had prevailed in Labour's policy statements in 1996 and 1997, and which signposted the government's subsequent retreat from the sustainable transport agenda more generally (Docherty, 2003). Then, ministers began to argue that government policy should tackle the adverse *impacts* of traffic, rather than traffic *volumes* themselves (DETR, 2000a). Of course, for walking and cycling this was a crucial shift in direction, because it opened the door to new road-building and meant that the 'non-congestion' consequences of traffic – danger, severance, social exclusion, noise and so on – would get worse, not better. And so, therefore, would conditions for walking and cycling.

The reversal in Labour government policy after 1998 particularly impacted on walking. Following consultation in 1997 the intention had been to publish a National Walking Strategy (NWS) in April 1998. But by then the government was retreating from its White Paper vision and was becoming increasingly nervous about promoting walking, lest it be seen as 'anti-car'. This was made much worse by John Prescott's decision (when Secretary of State for Transport) to travel the 250 or so yards from his hotel to the Labour Party conference venue in 1998 by car. By referring to him habitually as 'Two Jags' Prescott, the tabloids fuelled government concern that the publication of a walking strategy would precipitate general derision and Pythonesque 'Ministry of Silly Walks' headlines. The promised strategy was repeatedly delayed and then eventually replaced by an advice document *Encouraging walking: Advice to local authorities*, which was published without a launch or other publicity in 2000 (DETR, 2000b).

If the intention was to remove the 'embarrassing' issue of walking from the transport debate, it was conspicuously unsuccessful. The failure to produce a strategy contributed to the House of Commons' Environment, Transport and Regional Affairs Committee deciding late in 2000 to examine the government's record on walking. The Committee identified the need to adopt, first, planning policies to promote high-density, mixed-use, compact cities, which keep distances short and, second, recommendations for transport strategies that give priority to and promote walking, produce better conditions for pedestrians, restrain traffic and more effectively manage public space (House of Commons, 2001). The government's Social Exclusion Unit was also criticised for realising only belatedly that members of poorer households walk more than others, are more likely to be killed by motorists and lack access to many facilities including shops and medical services, despite this having been apparent to accessibility planners and social inclusion researchers for many years following work such as that of Schaeffer and Sclar in the 1970s (Schaeffer and Sclar, 1975). It was felt that tackling these problems in deprived areas could divert urban regeneration funds from other, higher-profile investments in housing, schools and other public services, a timely reminder of the cross-cutting nature of walking in terms of both its general importance but also its vulnerability to shifts in political fashion.

The Committee was, however, clear that the primary difficulty with walking was the attitude to it held by politicians with responsibility for transport. Defending the fact that of the thousands employed by the huge Department for the Environment, Transport and the Regions, only *two* staff were in post to deal with walking – despite walking accounting for nearly one-third of trips – the Minister of State for Transport said in evidence, 'I suspect it is about right ... because most of us know how to do it.... I just think that you can therefore take a lot for granted when it comes to walking'. The Committee tartly observed that 'on this basis a large part of the Government machine could be wound up tomorrow' (House of Commons, 2001, p xxxiii). Moreover, the Committee noted the widespread criticism of the government for producing an advice note rather than a strategy, which had diminished the importance of walking in the eyes of local authorities, other organisations and professionals. In particular, it had been argued that a NWS would have acted as a trigger to the production of local walking strategies in the same way that the NCS had spurred publication of local versions (Gaffron, 2000).

The Committee recommended the establishment of a NWS that would indicate (a) the criteria against which local strategies would be examined for the purpose of funding, (b) a shift of priorities in respect of policies and spending in its overall transport strategy and (c) how different government departments will coordinate policies to facilitate and promote walking. The Committee was of the view that guidance should be issued under the headings of 'changing priorities', 'funding', 'planning', 'conditions for walking', 'quality of design', 'campaigns to promote walking' and 'research'. The establishment of a National Walking Forum was also recommended, which would exchange best practice, advise on government policy, examine Local Transport Plans (LTPs – Chapter Two), monitor progress and publish a training strategy. Clearly irritated by the relentless criticism contained within the report, the government first reacted by trying unsuccessfully to block the re-appointment of the Committee's chair, the late Gwyneth Dunwoody, but its formal response, published in November 2001, was more measured (HM Government, 2001). Indeed, the document's upbeat tone on walking took many by surprise. Although it rejected targets and the mooted National Walking Forum, it recommended that local authorities should be encouraged to develop pedestrian-friendly environments, remove guard rails and staggered crossings, observe new policy guidance from government and communicate good practice through a new interactive walking website. Above all, though, was a significant reversal of policy, which would henceforth be one of promoting the mode, driven by a newly written action plan. Could walking, always the Cinderella of transport modes, go to the ball after all?

Walking, cycling and the sustainable transport agenda

When *Walking and cycling: An action plan* finally appeared in 2004 (DfT, 2004), it was a much more honest document than might have been expected given the government's earlier tendencies towards bluster and then denial with regards to the efficacy of its sustainable transport policies. Reviewing current progress and formally abandoning the NCS targets, the document was at least candid in its admission that – despite the successes of some proactive local authorities – the overall level of walking and cycling in England had not risen above the baseline level of 1996. The plan did, however, note that the government remained committed to working towards these targets in an aspirational sense, setting out a list of (familiar) policies designed to achieve this, including improving walking and cycling infrastructure, associated 'hard' interventions such as better land-use planning and investment in the public realm, and also 'soft' measures such as designating home zones and mainstreaming consideration of the needs of cyclists and pedestrians into other areas of policy, especially tackling crime, the fear of crime and antisocial behaviour. In other parts of the UK, walking and cycling strategies developed by the devolved administrations identified similar aspirations and interventions (DRDNI, 2003; Welsh Assembly Government, 2003).

Evidence in the aftermath of the action plan supports both pessimistic and optimistic views of non-motorised transport futures in the UK. On a pessimistic note, there is the failure so far to make any real progress towards meeting the targets set in the NCS. More optimistic – and realistic – is the assertion in 2007 by Cycling England, the body set up to deliver the government's planned cycling investment in England, that there could still be 'a net increase in cycling levels in England of at least 20% by 2012' given current investment levels (Cycling England, 2007, unpaginated). Cycling England's report, *Bike for the future II*, goes on to say that the original NCS target of quadrupling cycling remains possible, but does not place a timeframe on its eventual achievement. It does, however, note the case of London, which is on course to meet this target by 2025. More optimistic still is that public attitudes to cycling might be changing – in December 2007, the National Lottery's public vote on which third sector project should win £50 million of good causes funding was won by Sustrans and its proposals to enhance and extent the National Cycle Network that it has worked hard to develop and promote (BLF, 2007; Sustrans, 2007c). Moreover, the Sustainable Travel Towns project, which was trialled in Darlington, Peterborough and Worcester, was reporting by November 2007 substantial increases in walking (especially) but also cycling, from the application of 'soft' behaviour change interventions, particularly personalised travel planning (*Local Transport Today*, 2007; see also the discussion of 'smart' measures in Chapter Eleven).

Optimism about the future of cycling must be tempered with the cold realities of the limited financial resources available for investment in new infrastructure and education campaigns. The funding issue is key because it is a litmus test of government's real priorities in its spending plans. It is, of course, very difficult to identify exactly how much is being spent on non-motorised modes, because road maintenance, lighting installation or speed reduction measures, for example, may benefit walkers and cyclists as well as motorists. Early in New Labour's first term of office, when it was suggested to the then minister Lord Macdonald that the government puts emphasis on large-scale schemes, he simply agreed. He explained that this is not because they were more cost effective, but instead because their 'impact' and 'value for money' are more easily measured through the methodology 'that is available to the Treasury' (House of Commons, 2001, p xliii). This was an extraordinary statement. It implied that building large schemes with measured positive value is more worthwhile than building small-scale schemes because their value cannot be measured. Of course, this is nonsense. It is simply untrue that small-scale schemes cannot be measured: indeed, there are plentiful examples of such schemes producing very high rates of return in their first year, such as the 526% first-year rate of return for the pedestrian priority signals installed in Hull in 1997 (IHIE, 2001). More accurately, it seems that Treasury methodologies were being used to conceal the fact that, as the Committee Report commented, 'the government is simply not interested in appraising small schemes', an issue that it said 'must be addressed' (House of Commons, 2001, p xliii). More recently, Cycling England (2007) has estimated that its programme of interventions should achieve a benefit-cost ratio of between 3 and 4.5:1, levels that many larger transport schemes – especially major rail projects – would be more than proud of (Chapters One and Four).

Also important is Labour's attempt to pursue sustainability while retaining the political support of motorists, so that one of its key messages has become that car *ownership* should increase but car *use* should decrease. Continental countries with higher car ownership levels but lower levels of use are frequently cited, conveniently forgetting that these countries have much better public transport and superior conditions for walking and cycling. Without great expenditure on better facilities for pedestrians and cyclists, one can anticipate continuation of existing trends in Britain where the purchase of a car is a precursor to increased travel distances and sharply reduced levels of walking, in particular.

Looking to the future, despite the pro-motoring backlash against sustainable transport policies described in this chapter and throughout the book, reasons for optimism for the future of cycling and walking can be found. Perhaps most important is the fact that the Department for Transport's (DfT's) (2004) walking and cycling action plan was published at all. Its candour, and its restatement of established policy objectives and tools, is important in setting out a renewed commitment to (the pursuit of) better performance, in spite of the dropping of explicit targets. In England, the plan should, with the help of a focused delivery body, help inform policies in many other relevant government departments and agencies apart from transport, so that consideration of walking and cycling breaks out from its traditional narrow policy base. These include those on crime and disorder, health and social inclusion, progress in none of which, arguably, can be delivered without walkable public space. Another hopeful signal has emerged from Scotland, where the Scottish Government's budget allocated a significant increase in support for active travel (which includes walking, cycling and travel planning) for 2008-09 compared to the previous year, which will be sustained for three years and fully ringfenced.

It is unlikely that future events would bear out a wholly optimistic or pessimistic scenario; some combination is more probable, with the balance of wins and losses determining how the progress of the modes is judged. It is, however, possible that the experience of the two modes might actually be different from one another. Indeed, in a way, and despite the recent positive statements outlined above, the prospects for cycling seem if anything less positive than those for walking, as a consequence of the government's redefinition of the fundamental transport problem as one of the need to reduce traffic to that of reducing congestion. This means that the future is likely to be one of more cars, travelling further if not faster, and given that an enduring obstacle to encouraging bicycle use has been the speed and volume of traffic, it follows that getting people to take up cycling in the future is likely to be harder, not easier. It is difficult to see levels of cycling being increased in the face of continuing increases in motorised traffic – the lesson of London, where cycling has increased at the same time as traffic has decreased thanks to the congestion charge, should be explored.

The principal way of reconciling more traffic and more cycling would be to construct a complete network of (primarily) off-road cycle facilities in British towns and cities. Technically this is feasible, although it would pose major problems in dense centres. In resource terms too it is possible, as such measures designed to encourage modal switching from the car should logically be funded from what is currently spent on providing for cars. But the real barrier is the lack of political will. Although some cities are exceptions – York, Cambridge and to a lesser extent Edinburgh are notable examples – the great majority of authorities see cycling as a bolt-on extra to existing transport policies and are in no way ready to countenance the notion of restraining car traffic in order to make more space for cyclists.

In contrast to the situation for cycling, there have been some policy shifts that make the promotion of walking easier and less contentious. A combination of the 'liveability' agenda, a real and undeniable urban renaissance driven by strong employment growth and investment in new city-centre consumption opportunities (Begg, 2001; Harrison, 2007), and strategic economic development policies focused on developing competitive *places* (Marshall and Harrison, 2007; Grant Thornton, 2008), makes this possible. In 2001, Tony Blair gave a speech about local quality of life, or 'liveability', in which for the first time government acknowledged the importance to people of high-quality public spaces, reduced danger from traffic, and a clean, well-managed, safe and secure street environment: 'Towns, cities, regions and countries that provide safe and attractive places for people to live and work will be the winners. For Britain to prosper, we need to make such places the rule, not the exception' (Blair, 2001). The primary aim of such urban renaissance is to create people-friendly urban areas by enhancing their quality and environment and, in turn, to improve their amenity, viability and vitality. The creation of safe and attractive pedestrian environments in towns and cities is a necessary condition for success and is central to improving them for shoppers, visitors, workers and residents alike. In other words, quite apart from pro-walking arguments based on sustainability, the environment or social inclusion, there is a strong business case for improving walking conditions, as Blair was implying. There is indeed emerging evidence that more walking and cycling produce strong economic benefits for towns and cities. The economic regeneration of Birmingham city centre following its spectacular transformation from a 'motor city' into an attractive place to stroll, linger and shop is probably the best of many examples in Britain.

This changed perspective may allow walking to escape from its traditional home in Britain – the local authority 'safety ghetto' – and become much better connected to issues of town and city-centre management, or urban regeneration, while at national level creating powerful synergies with, for example, strategies on social inclusion and crime reduction. Indeed, in the future, it may be that the way to promote walking will be to stop talking about walking; that is, rather than promote walking as transport to get somewhere, it may be more effective to promote the things you can do when out walking – window shopping, strolling, people watching, playing and so on. The focus effectively would shift from the activity of walking to the creation of high-quality environments in which walking becomes a natural and pleasurable activity, an approach endorsed by the DfT's (2007b) *Manual for streets* (which is regarded by the Cycle Campaign Network (2006, p 1) as perhaps being 'the most influential document on urban design in 50 years').

Conclusions

As for many other aspects of *A new deal for transport* (DETR, 1998b), policy for cycling and walking got off to an inconspicuous start, before getting even worse in many respects. Wracked by nervousness over being perceived as anti-car, central government lost focus on the potential of the active modes, and adopted the ostrich mentality all too often favoured by ministers and civil servants faced with difficult policy problems to address. Unlike some other aspects of transport policy, there are at least some 'green shoots', not least the (perhaps unintended) spur to walking generated by the recovery of many of Britain's larger cities, the slowly improving attitudes to cycling resulting from recognition of the success of organisations such as Sustrans and the National Cycle Network as a facilitator of the leisure cycling that people genuinely seem to enjoy, and the quiet hard work of some local authorities and major employers in promoting personal travel planning as part of their wider travel strategies (Dickinson et al, 2003; DfT, 2007c).

In spite of these causes for optimism, the promotion of walking and cycling still all too often takes place in a policy vacuum, without any serious consideration given to the necessary trade-off between trips by different modes: a classic example of the silo mentality in action. Given that the overall number of trips per person is relatively stable at about three per day, it follows that an increase in the number of trips by one mode must be at the expense of another. Therefore the sustainability goal should not be, for example, to increase walking as this might be at the expense of cycling, yielding no sustainability gain. Similarly, increasing walking *and* cycling may be achieved by reducing bus trips, again being effectively 'sustainability-neutral', as car traffic would be untouched. In other words, it is of limited benefit in sustainability terms to increase walking and cycling unless, at the same time, car traffic is reduced by a concomitant amount. The goal is less car traffic, not *just* more walking and cycling, and here the key is to reduce trip lengths in order to lessen environmental damage and increase the chance of the trip being made on foot or by bicycle. While longer journeys need to be switched from car to public transport, it is the 70% of all journeys that are under eight miles that need to be the focus, as these are either cyclable or walkable – yet are increasingly being driven.

In her classic text, *Life and death of American cities*, Jane Jacobs (1961) suggested that the key factor in creating 'liveable cities' is to establish a mixed land-use pattern that decreases distances between facilities. This results in an environment with heavy pedestrian activity, a reduced level of interference from motorised traffic, informal supervision by everyone and a sense of ownership of public space. After all, 'if a city is to be "liveable", it has to be "walkable"' (Pharoah, 1992, p 10). Thus, in the architect Jan Gehl's cryptic phrase, 'there is much more to walking than walking' (Gehl, 2000, unpaginated). Although the wider planning and economic development policy direction in the UK has gone some way to rediscovering the Roman maxim, *via vita est* (streets are life), there is still a long way to go before this becomes embedded in policy development and implementation to the extent that active planning for walking and cycling is regarded as an essential, valuable and worthwhile endeavour.

So while there have been green gains for walking and cycling under Labour, they are set in a sea of red losses. Although the DfT has been the source of much best practice guidance, the same DfT is, simultaneously, accepting and anticipating rising volumes of motorised traffic, and this failure to grasp the nettle of traffic reduction sits extremely uneasily with goals of increasing trips by bicycle and, to a lesser degree, on foot. Indeed, only if government shows much greater leadership in directing efforts to reduce traffic are we likely to see a significant shift from the car towards non-motorised modes. There is currently no sign that it is prepared to do so, and yet again it might be left to local authorities, and perhaps the devolved administrations, to show the way forward. And so we come back to the introductory comments in this chapter, and to one of the key themes of the book as a whole. Better transport policy, in this case for walking and cycling, *is* possible, but is more likely if the narrative of sustainable transport considers more carefully and proactively the potential to improve all three aspects of sustainability – the economic and the social as well as the environmental.

Notes

[1] It would no doubt also be interesting to calculate how much car traffic is generated by people going to the gym to exercise on machines that are designed to enable static walking and cycling.

[2] An excellent example of the latter is the relocation of the (admittedly first-rate) new Edinburgh Royal Infirmary from a highly accessible location in the very centre of the city to the kind of site on the urban fringe more commonly associated with out-of-town shopping centres.

[3] Hence Lynn Sloman's (2006) memorable call for 'cycling without spandex' in her book *Car sick*.

References

Adams, J. (1993) 'No need for discussion – the policy is now in place!', in P. Stonham (ed) *Local transport today and tomorrow*, London: Local Transport Today Ltd, pp 73-7.

Andersen, L. (2000) 'All-cause mortality associated with physical activity during leisure time, work, sports, and cycling to work', *Archives of Internal Medicine*, 160, pp 1621-8.

Badland, H. and Schofield, G. (2005) 'Transport, urban design and physical activity: and evidence-based update', *Transportation Research Part D*, 10, pp 177-96.

Banister, C. and Gallent, N. (1998) 'Trends in commuting in England and Wales – becoming less sustainable?', *Area*, 30, pp 331-41.

Begg, I. (2001) *Urban competitiveness: Policies for dynamic cities*, Bristol: The Policy Press.

Black, W. (1996) 'Sustainable transportation: a US perspective', *Journal of Transport Geography*, 4, pp 151-9.

Blair, T. (2001) Address to Groundwork seminar, Croydon, 24 April.

BLF (Big Lottery Fund) (2007) *Sustrans' Connect2 wins £50million prize*, www.biglotteryfund.org.uk/prog_the_peoples_50_million.htm (accessed 8 January 2008).

BMA (British Medical Association) (1992) *Cycling: Towards health and safety*, Oxford: Oxford University Press.

Brög, W. (1995) *Strategy for the systematic promotion of the use of bicycles*, Munich: Socialdata.

Cavill, N. (2003) 'The potential for non–motorised transport for promoting health', in R. Tolley (ed) *Sustainable transport: Planning for walking and cycling in urban environments*, Cambridge: Woodhead Publishing.

Cycle Campaign Network (2006) *CCN news*, 83, July, p 1.

Cycling England (2007) *Bike for the future II: A funding strategy for national investment in cycling to 2012*, www.cyclingengland.co.uk/library.php?c=17&n=Home (accessed 8 January 2008).

Davies, D., Halliday, M., Mayes, M. and Pocock, R. (1997) *Attitudes to cycling: A qualitative study and conceptual framework, Report 266*, Crowthorne: Transport Research Laboratory.

DETR (Department for the Environment, Transport and the Regions) (1998a) *Transport statistics report: Walking in Great Britain*, London: The Stationery Office.

DETR (1998b) *A new deal for transport: Better for everyone*, Cm 3950, London: The Stationery Office.

DETR (1999) *Cycling in Great Britain, personal travel factsheet*, London: DETR.

DETR (2000a) *Transport 2010: The 10-year plan*, London: The Stationery Office.

DETR (2000b) *Encouraging walking: Advice to local authorities*, London: DETR.

DfT (Department for Transport) (2004) *Walking and cycling: An action plan*, www.dft.gov.uk/pgr/sustainable/walking/actionplan/walkingandcyclinganactionplan (accessed 25 April 2008).

DfT (2007a) *Transport statistics bulletin, National Travel Survey: 2006*, London: DfT.

DfT (2007b) *Manual for streets*, www.dft.gov.uk/pgr/sustainable/manforstreets/ (accessed 25 April 2008).

DfT (2007c) *Making personal travel planning work: Research report*, London: DfT, www.dft.gov.uk/pgr/sustainable/travelplans/ptp/makingptpworkresearch (accessed 8 January 2008).

DH (Department of Health) (1998) *Quantification of the effects of air pollution on health in the UK*, London: DH.

Dickinson, J., Kingham, S., Copsey, S. and Pearlman Hougie, D. (2003) 'Employer travel plans, cycling and gender: will travel plan measures improve the outlook for cycling to work in the UK?', *Transportation Research Part D*, 8, 53–67.

Docherty, I. (2003) 'Policy, politics and sustainable transport: the nature of Labour's dilemma', in I. Docherty and J. Shaw (eds) (2003) *A new deal for transport? The UK's struggle with the sustainable transport agenda*, Oxford: Blackwell.

Docherty, I. and Hall, D. (1998) 'Which travel choices for Scotland?', *Scottish Geographical Journal*, 115, pp 193–209.

DoT (Department of Transport) (1996a) *The national cycling strategy*, London: HMSO.

DoT (1996b) *Developing a strategy for walking*, London: London.

DRDNI (Department for Regional Development Northern Ireland) (2003) *Walking Northern Ireland: An action plan*, Belfast: DRDNI.

Finch, H. and Morgan, J. (1985) *Attitudes to cycling*, Report RR14, Crowthorne: Transport Research Laboratory.

Florida, R. (2005) *Cities and the creative class*, New York: Routledge.

Gaffron, P. (2000) 'Walking and cycling: does common neglect equal common interests?', *World Transport Policy and Practice*, 6, pp 8-13.

Gehl, J. (2000) 'There is much more to walking than walking', Keynote address to the first Walk21 International Walking Conference, London.

Goodman, R. (2001) 'A traveller in time: understanding deterrents to walking to work', *World Transport Policy and Practice*, 7, pp 50-4.

Goodman, R. and Tolley, R. (2003) 'The decline of everyday walking in the UK: explanations and policy implications', in R. Tolley (ed) *The greening of urban transport: Planning for walking and cycling in western cities* (2nd edition), Chichester: John Wiley.

Grant Thornton (2008) *Connecting for competitiveness: The future of transport in the UK city regions*, London: Grant Thornton LLP.

Hall, P. and Hass-Klau, C. (1985) *Can rail save the city?*, Aldershot: Gower.

Harrison, J. (2007) 'From competitive regions to competitive city-regions: a new orthodoxy, but some old mistakes', *Journal of Economic Geography*, 7, pp 311-32.

Hillman, M. (1993) 'Cycling and the promotion of health', *Policy Studies*, 14, pp 49-58.

HM Government (2001) *The government's response to the Environment, Transport and Regional Affairs Committee's report on walking in towns and cities*, London: DfT.

House of Commons (2001) *Walking in towns and cities*, Eleventh report of the Environment, Transport and Regional Affairs Committee, Session 2000-2001, HC 167-I, London: The Stationery Office.

Hudson, M. (1982) *Bicycle planning, policy and practice*, London: Architectural Press.

IHIE (Institute of Highway Incorporated Engineers) (2001) *Safe roads for all: A guide to road danger reduction*, York: Road Danger Reduction Forum.

Jacobs, J. (1961) *Death and life of great American cities*, New York: Random House.

Jones, M. (2001) 'Promoting cycling in the UK – problems experienced by the practitioners', *World Transport Policy and Practice*, 7, 7-12.

Lindstrom, M. (2007) 'Means of transportation to work and overweight and obesity: a population-based study in southern Sweden', *Preventive Medicine*, doi:10.1016/j.ypmed.2007.07.012

Local Transport Today (2007) 481, 8 November, pp 12-15.

London Walking Forum (2000) *Walking: Making it happen*, London: London Walking Forum.

Lopez-Zetina, J., Lee, H. and Friis, R. (2006) 'The link between obesity and the built environment: evidence from an ecological analysis of obesity and vehicle miles of travel in California', *Health and Place*, 12, pp 656-64.

LPAC (London Planning Advisory Committee) (1997) *Putting London back on its feet: A strategy for walking in Central London*, London: LPAC.

Lumsdon, L. and Mitchell, J. (1999) 'Walking, transport and health: do we have the right prescription?', *Journal of Health Promotion International*, 14, pp 271-9.

Marshall, A. and Harrison, B. (2007) *Connecting cities: Local transport, economic connectivity, and economic growth*, London: IPPR.

Morris, J. and Hardman, A. (1997) 'Walking to health', *Sports Medicine*, 23, pp 306-32.

MTRU (Metropolitan Transport Research Unit) (1996) *Putting London back on its feet, the why, how and who of developing a strategy for walking in London*, London: LPAC and MTRU.

Pedestrians' Association (2001) *A manifesto for living streets*, London: Pedestrians' Association.

Percy-Smith, J. (2000) *Policy responses to social exclusion: Towards inclusion?*, Milton Keynes: Open University Press.

Pharoah, T. (1992) *Less traffic, better towns*, London: Friends of the Earth.

Prentice, A. and Jebb, S. (1995) 'Obesity in Britain: gluttony or sloth?', *British Medical Journal*, 311, pp 437-9.

Puttnam, D. (2000) *Bowling alone: The collapse and revival of American community*, New York: Simon Schuster.

RBKC (Royal Borough of Kensington and Chelsea) (2008) *Kensington High Street improvements*, www.rbkc.gov.uk/EnvironmentalServices/general/hsk_intro.asp (accessed 8 January 2008).

Schaeffer, K. and Sclar, E. (1975) *Access for all: Transportation and urban growth*, London: Penguin.

Scottish Executive (2005) *Transport research series: Cycling in Scotland*, Edinburgh: Scottish Executive.

Sloman, L. (2003) 'The politics of changing to green modes', in R. Tolley (ed) *Sustainable transport: Planning for walking and cycling in urban environments*, Cambridge: Woodhead Publishing.

Sloman, L. (2006) *Car sick: Solutions for our car-addicted culture*, Totnes: Green Books.

Sustrans (2007a) *The National Cycle Network route user monitoring report*, Newcastle: Sustrans.

Sustrans (2007b) *The value of investment in active travel*, www.sustrans.org.uk/default. asp?sID=1146564740234 (accessed 8 January 2008).

Sustrans (2007c) *£50 million won and we couldn't have done it without you!*, www. sustransconnect2.org.uk/ (accessed 8 January 2008).

WALCYING (1997) *How to enhance walking and cycling instead of shorter car trips and to make these modes safer*, Reports 1 and 4, Lund and Vienna: Lund University and Factum.

Wardman, M., Tight, M. and Page, M. (2007) 'Factors influencing the propensity to cycle to work', *Transportation Research Part A*, 41, pp 339-50.

Welsh Assembly Government (2003) *Walking and cycling strategy for Wales*, Cardiff: WAG.

WHO (World Health Organization) (2002) *Physical activity through transport as part of daily activities*, Copenhagen: WHO, Regional Office for Europe.

Wittink, R. (2003) 'Road safety has much to gain by the integration of cycle planning', in R. Tolley (ed) *Sustainable transport: Planning for walking and cycling in urban areas*, Cambridge: Woodhead Publishing.

World Commission on Environment and Development (1987) *Our common inheritance*, Oxford: Oxford University Press.

SEVEN

UK air travel: taking off for growth?

Brian Graham

The publication of the White Paper *A new deal for transport* (DETR, 1998) presaged a period of intensive study into the UK air transport industry that, by way of the interim consultation paper on air transport policy, *The future of aviation* (DETR, 2000), culminated in the 2003 White Paper, *The future of air transport* (DfT, 2003). The last of these itself generated a further raft of studies in advance of the *Air transport White Paper progress report* (DfT, 2006). These key documents and their supporting papers are characterised by several recurring themes. First, the issue of airport capacity, and particularly its shortage in south east England, has dominated government thinking. Second, there remains an uneasy and unresolved conflict between controlling the environmental costs of civil aviation, the fastest growing source of carbon emissions, and fostering its contribution to the UK national and regional economies. Meanwhile, the entire supply side of the air transport industry has been revolutionised by: the growth of low-cost carriers (LCCs); their impact on the business structures of 'legacy' carriers; the privatisation and commercialisation of the bigger airports into 'cathedrals' of consumerism; and, not least, the security controls that have also transformed them into a traveller's dystopia.

This chapter addresses this policy debate and at least some of its myriad contradictions. (The focus is entirely on passenger air transport, space precluding an adequate consideration of air freight.) Following a brief introductory contextual discussion that summarises the strategies advanced in the milestone policy documents, the content is divided into three principal sections. First, I examine trends in UK air travel since 1998, focusing on the issues of airport capacity and the step-changes brought about by the LCCs. Second, the chapter turns to the more recent and current policy context introduced by the 2003 White Paper. This is concerned essentially with a tripartite interweaving of national and regional responses, mediated through the wider context of European Union (EU) policy. While UK air transport policy remains a matter reserved for central government, devolved regional administrations can influence airport policy and air transport provision through the planning process and strategies for regional economic development. Both national and regional policies have to be compliant, however, with the legislation that created and maintains the EU Single Aviation Market fully implemented in 1997. Finally, the chapter addresses the contested interconnections between air transport's role in sustaining economic development and the costs of its rapidly growing environmental externalities.

The future of air transport in the UK

The discussion of air transport in *A new deal for transport* (DETR, 1998) was dominated by the issue of scarce airport capacity in south east England. The region's five principal airports – Heathrow, Gatwick, Stansted, Luton and London City – handled over 100 million passengers in 1998, accounting for no less than 64% of total UK terminal passengers (CAA, 1999). By 2006, this had fallen to 58.2%, reflecting, primarily, dramatic growth in passenger traffic at some regional airports precipitated by LCC market entry. The issue of scarce airport capacity in south east England was regarded as being so crucial that the entire analysis of air transport in *A new deal for transport* was couched within the overriding constraint that it must not prejudice the then ongoing public inquiry into the construction of Heathrow's Terminal 5, which finally opened in March 2008.[1] Moreover, the government was also committed to preparing a UK airports policy looking some 30 years ahead, a pledge that materialised in the 2003 aviation White Paper (DfT, 2003).

More generally, *A new deal for transport* did reflect – albeit in rather vague terms – the then rapidly growing importance of environmental issues concerned with air transport, advancing three specific and not easily reconciled dimensions in its analysis of air transport: the relationship of the mode to environmental sustainability; the integration of air and ground transport modes; and the contribution of air transport to regional development and regeneration. Specifically, the question of surface access to airports was seen as being crucial to the environmental impact of air transport and the White Paper advocated the integration of airports into local transport plans and wider national rail and coach networks. In line with the 'polluter pays' principle, the aviation industry was expected to help fund new rail infrastructure. *A new deal for transport* also proposed that each airport should organise an Air Transport Forum, which would include all the various stakeholders involved in the relationship between the airport and its local area, recognising that planning permission for any form of airport capacity enhancement is dependent on satisfying the demands of local communities and planning authorities.

It was further assumed that airports could not be viewed in isolation but should 'both compete with ... and complement each other' (DETR, 1998, p 77). Thus, regional airports potentially offered one means of relieving congestion in south east England, prompting the release of 'soundly-financed local authority airports [such as Manchester] from public sector borrowing controls' (DETR, 1998, p 78) and allowing non-EU foreign carriers open access to all UK airports, excepting Heathrow and Gatwick, provided that UK airlines could operate on the same routes. Partly through lack of evidence, little was said about the role of air transport in regional economic development but *A new deal for transport* precipitated an intensive period of research at both national and regional scales into this and other areas, which culminated in the 2003 White Paper *The future of air transport* (Graham, B. 2003).

The future of air transport sets out a 'sustainable' strategic framework for the development of airport capacity in the UK over the 30-year period out to around 2030. Although environmental concerns are foregrounded in what is claimed to be a balanced approach, the only policy advocated is emissions trading despite aviation being excluded from the Kyoto Protocol, while international aviation is left out of the UK government's 60% carbon reduction target. The focus of the White Paper is directed far more firmly at airport capacity both in terms of making better use of existing facilities but also in adding to them. It is not, of course, the role of government to build airports or add runways and the White Paper does not formally authorise or preclude any development and normal planning processes. But it does endorse capacity expansion based on various growth scenarios, leading to well-versed accusations that it is no more than an exercise in 'predict and provide' (Chapters One and Three). In one strong critique, Riddington (2006, p 311) sees the projections in *The future of air transport* as diagnostic of a top-down approach in which forecasts are 'largely based on the UK growth rate multiplied by some unchanging income elasticity'. 'For London', he argues, 'the problem is capacity and [thus] "forecast and allocate" makes a great deal of sense', whereas in Scotland and elsewhere outside the south east, the problem is 'the best way to develop international services [while] capacity is not a major problem' (Riddington, 2006, p 309). Albeit a pertinent conclusion, this does underplay the importance of capacity constraints for the regions in that they require services to the south east hub airports, especially Heathrow, which is the most constrained, for access to intercontinental networks. As the Civil Aviation Authority (CAA) (CAA, 2007a, p 6) observes, 'the scarcity (and consequent value) of slots at Heathrow continues to be perceived as a threat to more marginal domestic services'. Regions have been gradually losing such services (although three links – Belfast International, Inverness and Jersey – were actually reinstated between 2004 and 2008) and the White Paper proposed, if necessary, the imposition of EU 'public service obligations' (PSOs) to protect slots but also encouraged regional Route Development Funds (RDFs) to promote new services at airports outside the south east.

The White Paper's 'central' scenario forecasts that UK air travel demand will grow to 465 million passengers per annum by 2030 (compared to 228 million in 2005). To accommodate this growth, it supported a new third runway at Heathrow by around 2015, providing it could be demonstrated that there was strict adherence to environmental limits including noise and nitrogen oxide (NO_x) emissions. It was proposed that this would be shorter than the existing two runways and likely to be dedicated to shorter-haul services. Second runways were recommended at Stansted (after 2015), Birmingham (around 2016) and Edinburgh (around 2020 at the earliest). In addition, the White Paper also supported a swathe of capacity increases – terminals, aprons, runway extensions – at almost all the more important regional airports. This reflected the methodology used in the White Paper, which effectively allocated capacity growth around the UK. Despite this general support for expansion, proposals for new runways at Nottingham East Midlands and Luton and a proposed new airport north of Bristol were not supported in the interests of making better use of existing capacity.

Trends in UK air travel since 1998

While the policy direction since 1998 has been driven by concerns over airport and airspace capacity, it has also been shaped by, and forced to respond to, radical changes in the UK air transport industry. Although this is a complex and ever-shifting field (Graham and Shaw, 2008), four trends are particularly relevant here: the growth of LCCs and their impact on the 'legacy' airlines; traffic growth at regional airports; the intercontinental market; and airport management strategies.

LCCs

It is now accepted that the growth of the low-cost sector has been the most dramatic repercussion of the liberalisation of the EU aviation market, which was finally completed in 1997. Not only is this the fastest growth market sector in UK air transport but the rise of the LCCs has also forced the legacy carriers into quite dramatic changes in their business strategies. Thus, there has been a step-change in the nature of the liberalised airline industry since the 1990s: 'Cost reduction is no longer a short-term response to declining yields or falling load factors. It is a continued and permanent requirement if airlines are to be profitable' (Doganis, 2001, p 222). The network carriers have been forced to reduce labour costs (through layoffs, wage and benefit cutbacks, and shedding pension benefit plans), lower their own fares for point-to-point services, reduce the standard of cabin service, and promote electronic booking on the Internet. In the UK, British Airways (BA) has been compelled to focus on its core business, the hubs at Heathrow and, to a lesser extent, Gatwick, while offloading peripheral routes and dropping its regional subsidiary, BA Connect, which was merged with the LCC Flybe in 2007 (Dennis, 2007). It has also wound down the idea of franchises with other UK carriers, terminating an agreement with the Scottish carrier Loganair from 2008 and acquiescing to bmi and easyJet taking over, respectively, British Mediterranean and GB Airways.

In round terms, LCCs accounted for about 20% of all European air traffic in 2005, although this rises to about 50% in the British Isles–continental Europe market, while the sector's growth rate is much greater than that of the legacy carriers (AEA, 2006). Capitalising on their 'first-mover' advantage (Francis et al, 2006), the two largest European LCCs – Ryanair and easyJet – carried 42.5 million and 28 million passengers respectively in 2006, placing both in the world top 20 by this measure. By comparison, BA carried 33.1 million passengers (*Airline Business*, 2007).

When *A new deal for transport* was published in 1998, total LCC traffic in the UK was around 7 million passengers (Graham and Dennis, 2007). Despite this rapid development, however, a major study by the CAA found little evidence that, in aggregate terms, LCCs have 'significantly affected overall rates of traffic growth', which have remained fairly constant at 5-6% per annum since the mid-1990s (CAA, 2006, p 3). Individual airports may show very high percentage increases in traffic but, overall, LCC growth has been at the expense of the full service/legacy carriers and, even more so, of the charter airlines, which have been forced to focus on more 'exotic' long-haul destinations. Market entry by a powerful LCC such as Ryanair on a city-pair has a real competitive impact on incumbents, which lose market share or are even forced to abandon services (Pitfield, 2007).

Thus, the key step-change is not growth per se but the availability of low and unrestricted fares and a very considerable increase in choice of destinations and airports. Network expansion and passenger growth is driven by the additional capacity being added by the airlines. Quite how long this process can continue is open to question but route selection often appears to be little more than casual, driven by the availability of subsidies of one form or another:

> It was all about the deals on offer from the airports.... [Michael] O'Leary (Chief Executive Office [CEO], Ryanair) had no time for demographics or detailed market research. He needed routes for his planes, and he needed money from the airports to keep his costs down. So the airports prepared to offer the best deals got the routes. (Ryanair executive, cited in Ruddock, 2007, p 325)

The balance between leisure and business traffic varies depending on the nature of services at a particular airport but the former predominates. At Stansted, 82% of passengers are travelling for this reason, compared to 65% at Heathrow. Although it is claimed that LCCs are promoting social inclusion in allowing more people to fly, there is little evidence that the 'LCCs are appealing to the less wealthy ... [but] seem to be encouraging more frequent flying ... in some cases influenced by the existence of a second home' (Graham, B., 2006, pp 19-20). The CAA (2006) found no real 'democratisation' effect, there being little evidence of any major change, especially in the leisure market, in the type of people flying compared to the mid-1990s. While this finding challenges popular perceptions (and even 'empirical experience') of low-cost air travel and despite the significant increase in the total number of people flying, it is the middle- and higher-income socioeconomic groups who are 'flying more often than in the past, and often on shorter trips' (CAA, 2006, p 5). Indeed, there is also evidence that people suspend their 'normal' judgement when it comes to travelling by air for leisure reasons. One recent Scandinavian study (Holden, 2007, p 189) demonstrates that a green attitude is 'a better predictor of sustainable everyday mobility than of ... leisure-time mobility', even to the extent that membership of an environmental organisation correlated positively (and significantly) with energy consumption for long-distance leisure travel by plane. Holden attributes this surprising result to a sense of powerlessness but also to a desire for personal indulgence.

In catering for latent demand at regional airports and in stimulating new markets largely based on leisure travel, UK-based LCCs have salient market advantages. Although their operations and bases now extend across the entire EU, the domestic and Britain–island of Ireland (effectively a domestic market) services form the backbone of both Ryanair's and easyJet's networks, demand being fostered by the UK's fractured geography and road congestion, combined with infrastructural deficiencies and the high 'walk-up' fares of conventional rail. In Britain and Ireland, LCCs already have more than 30% of the market (EC, 2005).

Geography confers further benefits to UK-based LCCs in that they are heavily dependent on cross-water routes between the UK/Ireland and continental Europe. While these serve a wide variety of destinations, the key markets are the principal Mediterranean cities and 'sunspots' and winter ski resorts. Ryanair, in particular, is aggressively entering the Iberian market. The second-home market is especially strong in France, Spain and Portugal and helps support, for example, a number of routes between the UK and small French regional airports. west–east routes have grown significantly with the 2004 and 2007 expansions of the EU, which, in addition to opening up new tourist markets, have also encouraged substantial immigration into the UK, especially from Poland but also from Latvia and Lithuania. Low-cost carriers are clearly facilitating the movement of migrant labour and the CAA (2006) found significant evidence that inbound traffic to the UK has increased. Moreover, its study shows that migration is followed by 'visiting friends and relations' traffic, which is the fastest-growing segment of inbound traffic at both Luton and Stansted in recent years, accounting for almost 50% of inbound trips.

Traffic growth at regional airports

As the CAA (2005, p ix) clearly demonstrates, there has been a 'period of substantial and sustained growth' in services from UK regional airports since around 1990. While often derived from very low base figures, the percentage increases are frequently dramatic (Table 7.1). In part, this trend can be explained by EU liberalisation and the concomitant growth of LCCs, which has realised the potential for direct services from regional airports to continental (and Irish) destinations. Again, the provision of new services has unlocked the latent demand for passengers wanting to travel from local airports, where passenger numbers have increased at 7% per annum since 2000 (CAA, 2007a). The growth of traffic has been most marked in international scheduled flights, which increased from 6.2 million in 1990 to 29.8 million in 2004 and in services to the London area (excluding Heathrow). Both Ryanair and easyJet have based aircraft at a number of airports while the smaller LCCs such as bmibaby, Flybe and Jet2 have also established themselves at particular regional airports (Figure 7.1). Not all inter-regional air travel is provided by low-cost operators and there remains some limited scope for niche business operators such as bmi Regional and Eastern Airways, both of which use small aircraft on predominantly low-volume but high-yield business routes, especially along the east coast.

Table 7.1: Terminal passengers at selected UK airports, 2001 and 2006

Airport	2006		2001		% change 2001-06
	Number of terminal passengers	% of passengers at all UK airports	Number of terminal passengers	% of passengers at all UK airports	
Heathrow	67,339	28.6	60,453	33.4	11.4
Gatwick	34,080	14.5	31,097	17.2	9.6
Stansted	23,680	10.1	13,654	7.5	73.4
Manchester	22,124	9.4	19,082	10.5	15.9
Luton	9,415	4.0	6,540	3.6	44.0
Birmingham	9,056	3.9	7,712	4.3	17.4
Glasgow	8,802	3.8	7,243	4.0	21.8
Edinburgh	8,607	3.7	6,038	3.3	42.5
Bristol	5,710	2.4	2,673	1.5	113.6
Newcastle	5,407	2.3	3,376	1.9	60.2
Belfast International	5,015	2.1	3,603	2.0	39.2
Liverpool	4,962	2.1	2,251	1.2	120.4
Nottingham East Midlands	4,721	2.0	2,380	1.3	98.4
Aberdeen	3,163	1.3	2,525	1.4	25.3
Leeds Bradford	2,787	1.2	1,524	0.8	82.9
Prestwick	2,395	1.0	1,232	0.7	94.4
London City	2,358	1.0	1,619	0.9	45.7
Belfast City	2,106	0.9	1,192	0.7	76.6
Cardiff Wales	1,993	0.8	1,524	0.8	30.8
Southampton	1,913	0.8	857	0.5	123.3
Exeter	971	0.4	333	0.2	191.7
Bournemouth	961	0.4	265	0.1	263.0
Norwich	745	0.3	390	0.2	91.1
Inverness	671	0.3	343	0.2	95.7
City of Derry	342	0.1	188	0.1	82.2
All UK airports	235,139	100.0	181,195	100.0	29.8

Source: CAA (2007c)

Figure 7.1: Low-cost carrier bases at UK airports, 2007

BE	Flybe
EI	Aer Lingus
FR	Ryanair
LS	Jet2
TOM	Thomsonfly
U2	easyJet
WW	bmibaby
Y2	Flyglobespan

Source: Airline websites

While very high percentage increases in traffic have been characteristic of many regional airports, the two dominant hub airports in the south east of England – Heathrow and Gatwick – have shown much more modest growth (around 3% per year), reflecting their capacity constraints (Figure 7.2). Heathrow's share of terminal passengers at all UK airports fell from 33.4% in 2001 to 28.6% in 2006 while the equivalent figures for Gatwick were 17.2% and 14.5%. Total terminal passengers at the two airports increased by only 11.4% and 9.6% respectively over the same period compared to a UK average of 29.8% (CAA, 2007b). Between 1990 and 2004, the number of domestic destinations served from Heathrow more than halved and while it still has 49% of total terminal passengers (2006) at the five London area airports (Heathrow, Gatwick, Stansted, Luton and London City), this compares to around 80% in 1990 (CAA, 2005, 2007a). The strong traffic growth in the London area is underlined, however, by 73.4% and 44% increases in terminal passengers at Stansted and Luton respectively between 2001 and 2006, these two airports being the principal LCC bases in the south east. Indeed, Ryanair and easyJet account for no less than 85% of Stansted's customer base. Thus, the key statistic is that the five London area airports still accounted for 58.2% of all UK terminal passengers in 2006, compared to 62.55% in 2001, the difference being almost entirely attributable to the growth of LCC services at regional airports.

The intercontinental market

Given the public focus on LCCs, it is easy to underestimate the traditional importance of the UK in the global air transport market. British Airways remains the seventh ranked carrier in the world by revenue passenger kilometre, while the country's second long-haul carrier – Virgin Atlantic – is 29th in the same ranking (*Airline Business*, 2007). At one level, BA is competing with Lufthansa and Air France/KLM for dominance in the European intercontinental market, at another it is fending off the LCCs and trying to defend its core short-haul network. Long-haul liberalisation has been slower than that within the EU but the 2007 EU–US open skies agreement (which came into effect in March 2008) will open up the already relatively liberal transatlantic market and increase the pressure for, and value of, scarce slots at Heathrow and Gatwick. Given that no additional runway capacity is imminent at either, the likelihood is that slots used for short-haul flights with smaller aircraft will be sold off or switched to more profitable long-haul services.

Because London is such an important global air transport hub, about 25% of all international passengers to or from the UK (11 million in 2005) 'are simply making connections between international services' (CAA, 2007c, p 1). More than 30% and 20% of long-haul passengers at Heathrow and Gatwick respectively did not start their journeys in the UK. Although there are concerns that the additional security restrictions imposed at UK airports are compromising the competitive position of Heathrow vis-à-vis its continental competitors, the CAA observes

Figure 7.2: UK airports and terminal passengers, 2006

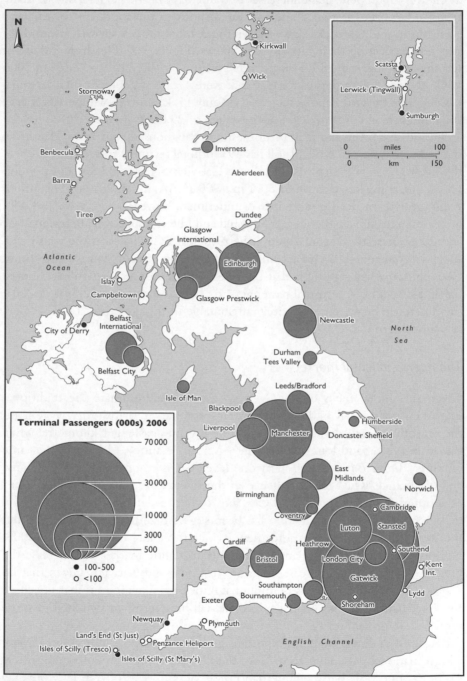

Source: CAA (2007c)

that more liberalised agreements on long-haul services seem to correlate with greater traffic growth. Thus, the inception of the transatlantic open skies agreement may well increase Heathrow's connecting traffic. In 1998, *A new deal for transport* (DETR, 1998) pointed to the potential of diverting or growing traffic at regional airports as one means of using capacity more effectively. While Heathrow and Gatwick still had 89% of UK long-haul traffic in 2005, this compared to 96% in 1996. Long-haul passengers at regional airports increased from 2.7 million in 1996 to 7.2 million in 2006, largely comprising increased leisure traffic and that created by the opening up of spoke routes from their hubs by airlines such as Continental at Newark, NJ and Emirates at Dubai.

Airports

In addition to the roles of European liberalisation and LCCs releasing latent demand at regional airports (that is, more people flying more often), the CAA (2005) argues that the adoption of more commercial strategies by airports is also a prime factor in the growth of regional air services. The airports themselves are now generally privatised although one of the largest – Manchester – remains in local authority hands, albeit operating as a commercial company. The dominant south east airports – Heathrow, Gatwick and Stansted – are all owned by BAA, now a subsidiary of the Spanish company, Ferrovial. In 2007, BAA was referred to the Competition Commission to investigate if this constituted a monopoly and some airlines are calling for the company to be broken up (and the Competition Commission's (2008) 'emerging thinking' report suggests that it is minded to agree with these airlines). Ryanair and easyJet are also objecting vociferously at having to fund the expansion of Stansted (the cost of a new runway is estimated at £2.7 billion) through increased landing charges. Certainly, following the opening of Terminal 5 (which is dedicated to BA) in March 2008, the other terminals at Heathrow will be rebuilt or refurbished and that also must be funded through aeronautical charges.

The profit margins ensuing from the commercialisation of airports, which has led to the largest being indistinguishable from shopping malls, is one reason why airlines are loathe to pay increased charges (Graham, A., 2003). This trend, however, resonates with what the CAA (2005) has termed the 'virtuous circle' airport model (Figure 7.3). In a competitive world, airports compete with each other to attract airlines and services through various incentives including discounted aeronautical charges. The increased passenger throughputs provide, however, a source of ancillary income from retailing, food outlets, car parking and so on. In turn, this income can be invested into improving the airport infrastructure and attracting more services through marketing support and discounts. It has been estimated that higher levels of discounting are occurring where aeronautical revenues are a smaller share of overall revenues than other charges – as at Nottingham East Midlands and Belfast International, both of which have a high proportion of low-cost traffic. Moreover, there is limited evidence that non-aeronautical revenues at certain

Figure 7.3: The 'virtuous cycle' airport model

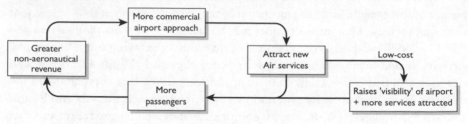

Source: After CAA (2005)

airports have not 'increased to the extent to which they may fully compensate for... reduced aeronautical revenue' (Graham and Dennis, 2007, p 169).

The virtuous circle is also, of course, being undermined by security concerns and the 'knee-jerk' response by government to terrorism or alleged terrorist plots. Airports now generally resemble a totalitarian, securitised, commercialised parallel reality to everyday life: 'All these retail parks, the airport and motorway culture. It's a new kind of hell....' (Ballard, 2006, p 85). (One has only to read Ballard's 2006 novel, *Kingdom come*, to realise that it has, that UK airports are virtually beyond parody.) Docile queues of passengers are herded at length through increasingly ludicrous security controls, threatened by robotic voices endlessly issuing warnings of the dire consequences of non-compliance, while denied the right to reply, anaesthetised only by the retailing delights that await when they finally emerge from this subterranean world populated by privatised, unaccountable, presumably somehow vetted and generally sullen (presumably minimum wage) security staff, meanwhile 'protected' by police armed with weaponry that might be more appropriate to Falluja or Helmand Province. This inefficient, inconsistent, institutionalised harassment of air passengers has become as much about justifying the securocrats and generating profits for private sector 'security' companies as about protecting the public. But airports are also, of course, economic entities, often run by heavily leveraged and indebted companies like BAA whose primary focus is not the UK economy, or dealing with capacity growth, but short-term profit. Given the twin tracks of homeland security and Mammon, it is not surprising that the 'virtuous' airport can be read instead as one of the least redeeming symbols of dystopian postmodernity.

At a more prosaic level, in 1998, *A new deal for transport* (DETR, 1998) flagged up the importance of surface access to airports. Progress on integrating rail and air services has, however, been disappointing. Givoni and Banister (2006) argue for airline and railway integration in which high speed rail (HSR) services are used as spokes to complement or substitute for air services (as has happened, for example, along the Paris–Brussels corridor). They argue that the case has been overlooked at Heathrow and that new runways are not the only means of increasing capacity. Modal substitution by high-speed trains (HSTs) is markedly more effective under airline and railway integration although, even then, it is not a panacea in terms of meeting the forecast growth for UK air services. In Europe,

HSTs can compete effectively with air on intercity pairs of up to three hours and are far more energy efficient than aircraft. The reality is, however, that High Speed 1 (HS1) between St Pancras and the Channel Tunnel, which opened in November 2007, looks like being a unique development rather than initiating a UK HST network (at least in the medium term). Certainly, the Eddington Transport Study (Eddington, 2006) did little for further developments. Thus, while Eurostar can dominate the London–Paris/Brussels markets, and Virgin has taken traffic from the airlines on the conventional, if improved, so-called West Coast mainline, there appears little likelihood that rail will contribute significantly to resolving the projected UK airport capacity crisis. The mode's role is thus largely restricted to the provision of airport–city linkages through conventional rail as at Heathrow and Gatwick, or light rail as at Newcastle. Birmingham, Manchester and Stansted, apart, no other UK airport is integrated directly into national intercity services. Work for the new rail link to Glasgow has started but ambitious plans for an Edinburgh counterpart were radically downscaled in 2007 by the Scottish Government. Thus, UK airports remain predominantly dependent on road surface access; indeed, the high cost of existing airport–city rail fares actively encourages cheaper coach competition.

The policy context since 2003

If the studies preceding the 2003 White Paper were more concerned with the economic contributions of aviation to national and regional economies, the environmental agenda has been increasingly to the fore since then. National initiatives have also been mediated through regional strategies by the devolved administrations while, at a different scale, UK policies are subject to the scrutiny of the European Commission (EC) and its monitoring and administration of the liberalised EU Single Aviation Market.

The national scale

In December 2006, the Department for Transport (DfT) published its Progress Report into the future of air transport. Rejecting the commonly voiced criticism of predict and provide levelled at the 2003 White Paper, it begins with the environmental challenge. The UK aims to reduce carbon emissions, including domestic but not international aviation, by 60% by 2050. In overall terms, the Stern Report (Stern, 2006) calculates that aviation accounts for 1.5% of global greenhouse gas emissions, a figure that comes closer to 3% in Europe; projecting current growth trends, the global statistic would rise to 2.5% by 2050. Stern recommended that aviation should pay its full carbon price, either by higher taxes or emissions trading, noting that the choice of instrument would be driven as much by political viability as by economics.

Nevertheless, the Progress Report also concludes that, irrespective of the cost of oil or slower economic growth, 'the trajectory for air travel is still strongly positive' (DfT, 2006, p 23). As Eddington (2006) shows, despite the problems of slot shortages, congested terminals and security, Heathrow remains the best-connected international airport in the EU while nearly two-thirds of the UK's large towns and cities are within one hour's travel time from a major international airport. The DfT 2006 Progress Report does point, however, to some pulling back from the 2003 capacity enhancement proposals. While a new runway at Edinburgh around 2020 still stands, that proposed for Birmingham will not be operational before 2020 at the earliest. Planning processes for a second runway at Stansted will not be completed before 2010 and no new runway is likely before 2015. The Progress Report estimates that the proposed third runway at Heathrow would be worth £5 billion in net present value terms. Meanwhile, it gives considered support to 'mixed-mode' operations at the airport (operational runways used for both landings and take-offs) to make better use of the existing capacity. These conclusions presaged the publication of the government's consultation paper on adding capacity at Heathrow (DfT, 2007). Of the latter, an editorial in *The Guardian* (2007a, p 38) argued:

> This is not a consultation, nor even an attempt at conversion; it is a lecture.... The document's figures on noise and pollution were provided by Heathrow's owner, BAA – and some of the report's arguments were so lopsided that they too might as well have been. Gordon Brown may have come to power promising greater openness, but this report shows more of the old thinking that always puts growth and business interests first.

While the then Secretary of State for Transport, Ruth Kelly, expressed her disappointment at this 'cynical assessment' (*The Guardian*, 2007b, p 31), she also summed up – perfectly if inadvertently – the argument that air travel is yet another 'tragedy of the commons', the situation in which people believe that any individual sacrifice for the greater good (in this case, the environment) would have no value unless followed by all others (Shaw and Thomas, 2006). According to Kelly, 'If Heathrow is allowed to become uncompetitive, the flights and routes it operates will simply move elsewhere. All it will do is shift capacity over the Channel. It will make us feel pure, but with no benefit to the rest of the planet' (*The Guardian*, 2007c, p 9). The consultation recommends a third runway (2,200 metres in length), a new terminal and mixed-mode operations, which, combined, would potentially enable Heathrow to handle 700,000 air transport movements a year by 2020, 'nearly 50% more than today' (DfT, 2007, p 3), while 'fully meet[ing] the air quality limits', in particular for nitrogen dioxide (NO_2) (DfT, 2007, p 9). That, however, would require the phasing out of older aircraft and substantial improvements in road traffic emissions. Despite the increased traffic, it is claimed that a 57-decibel noise footprint around Heathrow can be sustained (although, again, this is predicated on the phasing-out of older, noisier aircraft). Arguably, the DfT is seeking to 'steamroller' its opponents with an avalanche of statistics and consultation reports, which they cannot hope to challenge effectively but, crucially, the consultation report has nothing to say about climate change and the government's financial estimates as to the value of Heathrow to the national economy have always been contestable because they do not adequately take into account outward flows of discretionary income by UK residents.

Devolved and regional policies

Given that air transport remains a reserved matter for the DfT, the devolved administrations can exert influence only through the planning process for airports and ground linkages, and on realising air transport's potential in helping stimulate regional economic development through enhanced connectivity. There does not appear to be any real disagreement with DfT policy at this level of governance or attempts to undermine it through planning. On the first score, the Scottish Government, for example, is investing in improved ground access to both Glasgow and Edinburgh airports. Second, the devolved administrations have been concerned to exert pressure on the DfT to protect linkages to Heathrow but there has been no policy implementation on this front, not least because of the complications of compliance with EU rules. Thus, until 2007, the principal mechanism of market intervention for devolved UK governments and other English regional administrations was through start-up aid for new air services. There is a very limited use of EU PSO legislation to support routes serving the Scottish Highlands and Islands and one between Cardiff and Anglesey while the Irish government supports a Dublin–City of Derry service. Otherwise, the devolved administrations in Scotland, Northern Ireland and Wales all established air RDFs, principally to stimulate better international connections (Graham and Shaw, 2008; MacKinnon et al, 2008).

The key criteria underpinning RDFs were: that such aid did not discriminate against any user; that it was granted for a limited period; and that all proposed routes were subjected to economic appraisals, which had to demonstrate a net economic benefit to the region (derived from inbound business travel, tourism and direct/indirect/induced employment as well as outbound business travel). It can be argued that the predominance of LCC routes among those funded by RDFs means that the schemes are destined to cater for local outbound leisure traffic rather than attracting inbound tourist and business traffic (Graham and Dennis, 2007), but RDFs do raise the profile of the airports and regions concerned (CAA, 2005) and thus may well have a 'kick-start' or catalytic effect. The Scottish scheme, set up in 2002, has funded over 50 new routes and the modest intervention of the RDF in Northern Ireland, which had only one international service (Belfast International–Amsterdam) in 1999, seems to have been a factor promoting the development of an easyJet base at Belfast International and stimulating subsequent market entry by Aer Lingus, Ryanair, Wizz Air and Jet2. By spring 2008, Northern Ireland was served by more than 20 international city-pairs (albeit most at less than daily frequency).

European Union

Policy making for air transport at both national and regional scales has also to be compliant with European legislation and planning. The EC is the level of governance that deals, for example, with international agreements on intercontinental routes and is responsible for the negotiation of the first and subsequent stages of the open skies agreement with the US. It is overseeing a number of other initiatives on air transport and airspace, two of which have a particular and immediate importance for current UK air transport. These are the guidelines on start-up aid for air routes and the negotiation of an EU Emissions Trading Scheme (ETS).

In the past, various forms of aid were compatible with EU transport policy if such subsidies fostered the development and improved use of the secondary airport structure, which may be underused and representing a cost to the Community as a whole (EC, 2001). Subsidies, however, can also distort competition and this was the basis of the Charleroi ruling of 3 February 2004 in which the EC found that under the 'prudent private investor criterion', Ryanair had been receiving subsidies tantamount to state aid from the airport's owner, the Walloon regional government (EC, 2004; see, also, Barbot, 2006). Subsequent Commission rulings now restrict start-up aid to a maximum of 30% of eligible costs over the period of support and is prohibited at 'large Community airports' (over 10 million passengers per year), while specific EC clearance is required in respect of routes from 'national airports' (5-10 million passengers per year) (EC, 2006). One effective result in the UK has been the closure of the devolved RDFs as present commitments expire.

Although aviation falls outside the Kyoto Protocol adopted in December 1997, the EC wants to include the industry in an EU ETS from 2011 for intra-European travel and 2012 for all EU air travel. The 2006 DfT Progress Report endorses the idea of carbon pricing and gives its support to an EU ETS. The airlines are unhappy about the staggered dates of the implementation of the scheme while its full realisation would require international agreement with, for example, the US, which, currently, does not look as if it might be forthcoming. As the Chief Executive of the International Air Transport Association (IATA), Giovanni Bisignani, has stated: 'This is a global industry and we need a global tool. Regional [carbon] trading schemes will not work. That is why 170 countries will challenge Europe' (*The Guardian*, 2007d, 26). Nevertheless, although UK and European airlines, including most LCCs, would prefer a global solution under the auspices of the International Civil Aviation Organization (ICAO), they are reluctantly supporting the ETS (European Aviation Industry Joint Statement, 2006). The impact of such a scheme would probably be greater on LCCs that are more sensitive to price than on full-service carriers (Frontier Economics, 2006) but it is seen as the least worst option and preferable to taxes designed to push up operating costs. Nevertheless, there is current uncertainty as to how such a scheme would work and also its effects on the price of carbon permits (Bows and Anderson, 2007).

Air transport, economic development and the UK environment

The period since 1998 has seen a considered attempt to weigh up the balance between the environmental costs of aviation and its economic benefits (Graham and Shaw, 2008). These have been both specific to the sector but have also considered its wider implications as in the Stern (2006) and Eddington (2006) Reports. As UK support for an EU ETS indicates, policy seems set to follow the recommendations of the Stern Report that aviation should pay its full economic costs although the scale of the problem is daunting and the policy means for attaining it unclear. The LCCs do try to claim the environmental moral high ground because they are using resources more effectively. Nevertheless, they are promoting growth in air travel, predominantly over shorter distances (Whitelegg and Cambridge, 2004) in narrow-body aircraft with fewer than 200 seats on city-pairs, which could often be served by more sustainable forms of transport such as HSTs or even conventional rail. High-speed trains use electricity that can be generated by different fuels and are arguably cheaper in terms of relative external costs; CO_2 emissions per passenger on a typical 500 kilometre intra-European city-pair range from 1.17kg per kilometre for air travel to only 0.052kg per kilometre for rail (Wit et al, 2002). Eurostar's advertising for HS1 emphasises the term 'carbon neutral'. Conversely, despite their huge environmental cost, the proposals for airport capacity expansion detailed in the 2003 White Paper are mainly to cater for what are essentially subsidised (and from regional airports, predominantly outbound) leisure passengers.

Given the projected growth trends, it is unsurprising, therefore, that there is mounting public opposition in the UK to aviation. This focuses primarily on noise, emissions and capacity issues and is directly related to the increasing volume of traffic and aircraft movements. Public opposition to aviation in general tends to focus primarily on noise rather than emissions although it is now widely recognised that the most serious sustainability impacts of air transport stem from atmospheric pollution (Environmental Change Institute, 2006). Again, although technology has been successful in reducing atmospheric emissions per individual aircraft and passenger, the technological returns are diminishing and being offset by aviation's growth. As one report observes: 'Aviation emissions are a high-stakes issue for UK climate policy. More than any other sector the aviation industry, with its continued reliance on kerosene and its high growth rate, threatens the integrity of the UK long-term climate change target' (Tyndall Centre, 2005, p 49).

The same report observes that both the EC and the UK's national and devolved governments are 'encouraging continued high levels of growth in aviation, whilst simultaneously asserting that they are committed to a policy of substantially reducing carbon emissions' (Tyndall Centre, 2005, p 50). Despite Stern's recommendations, airlines pay no tax on kerosene while new aircraft and international tickets in the EU do not incur Value Added Tax (VAT). The Environmental Change Institute (2006) recommended raising Air Passenger Duty (APD) as a straightforward measure to make flying more expensive. The government did exactly that, doubling APD from 1 February 2007 and making it retrospective to tickets already booked and paid for. In October 2007, it announced its intention of replacing APD with a tax on flights to encourage airlines to fill planes and therefore cut pollution per passenger. It is difficult to disagree with the airlines' complaints that these initiatives owe less to environmental concerns and more to an opportunistic increase in tax income: 'It's bullshit really: They're just raising revenues' (Willie Walsh, CEO BA, quoted in *The Observer*, 2007, p 7).

Yet aviation also delivers social and economic goods although these are frequently exaggerated. It offers direct employment, catalytic spin-offs, contributes to trade and tourism, and is a significant taxpayer (ATAG, 2005). It is estimated that every one million air passengers support almost 6,500 people in air travel-related work, including direct, indirect, induced and catalytic effects (York Aviation, 2004). For what it is worth, Oxford Economic Forecasting (OEF) (OEF, 2006) calculates that the environmental emissions resulting from a full implementation of the 2003 UK White Paper runway proposals would cost £0.7 billion per annum while realising around £13 billion wider economic benefits (at 2006 prices). In terms of the aggregate relationship between aviation and regional economies, OEF (1999, 2002) argues that at both national and regional scales, the sectors most likely to contribute to growth in knowledge-based economies are typically those most dependent on aviation. It can thus be accepted that the positive direction of benefit between air transport provision and regional economic development is relatively clear, if spatially variable, although these economic benefits are achieved at a considerable and as yet unquantified cost. Moreover, all transport linkages work two ways and, while air transport facilitates inbound Foreign Direct Investment and tourism, these benefits have to be offset against losses from outbound investment and tourism. It is estimated that 75% of inbound visitors to the UK arrive by air and contribute 1.1% of Gross Domestic Product (GDP) and support 170,000 jobs. But 'the flow of UK citizens in the other direction is even more substantial' (OEF, 2006, p 27). Residents of the UK made 66.5 million trips abroad in 2005, representing a 61% increase since 1995; two-thirds of these visits were for leisure reasons.

Conclusions

A decade on, both *A new deal for transport* (DETR, 1998) and its core concept of integrated transport seem rather remote. Even such a short time ago, it was not possible to foresee the step-change that would occur on the supply side of UK air transport and its impact on the leisure market. Yet the frequent recourse to the unproven democratisation argument ignores the environmental insanity of encouraging more people to fly more often for leisure reasons. Despite the plethora of studies, we are no closer to integrating air transport into other modes (a few airport–city rail links apart) or at resolving the conundrum of airport (and airspace) capacity for projected growth. No new runways have been built and the airlines, particularly but not specifically the LCCs, are vehement in their objections to paying increased aeronautical charges to privatised companies like BAA to build new runways and terminals. Both Ryanair and easyJet have complained at length about the costs of airport expansion when all they require are 'sheds' in which to process passengers (which is fine for them but less so for the travelling public when their flight is delayed for three or four hours). Meanwhile, the environmental campaign against air transport has markedly escalated, backed by a wealth of scientific studies, which concur in pointing to its dire impact on the attainment of UK carbon reduction targets. Air transport is the fastest-increasing source of atmospheric emissions but international air travel is not included in the UK's carbon targets. If growth continues as forecast – and remember that these trends are fuelled principally by discretionary leisure travel and what is, ultimately, in terms of both its business model and climate change an unsustainable low-cost model – Bows and Anderson (2007, p 109) estimate that the aviation industry will be 'likely emitting in the region of a quarter of the UK's 2050 carbon target by 2012', the result being that '[a]ll other sectors of the economy will need to significantly, possibly completely, decarbonise by 2050 if the [UK] ... carbon-reduction target is not to be exceeded'.

Certainly, while it featured in *A new deal for transport*, the foregrounding of the environment in contesting the policy agenda for air transport was not apparent in 1998. It seems clear that the 2003 White Paper (DfT, 2003), with its focus on capacity growth in the south east and its methodology of reallocating at least some of that growth elsewhere, has stimulated the environmental objections to air transport in the UK in providing ready evidence for accusations of predict and provide. The consultation on Heathrow underlines the government's overriding commitment to the primacy of economic growth at the expense of the environmental dimensions to sustainable aviation. The vested interests are stacked against the environmental lobby: while the government purports to be raising green taxes, it does not spend the revenue on the environment. As the Heathrow consultation underlines, it is in denial over the impact of aviation on climate change, its only solution being to outsource policy to a flawed EU ETS, which has yet even to be negotiated, leavened with an implicit belief that technological advances might somehow deliver a 'carbon neutral' aviation industry. Meanwhile, the national interest is conflated with protecting the short-term profits and shareholders of private sector airport and airline companies. The LCC sector, with its focus on more people flying more often for leisure reasons, is the primary driver of growth in air transport, while its business model depends on creating growth in revenues, not through yields, but in piling in more and more capacity. But, against that, is the government's ideological commitment to private sector solutions and unwillingness to invest in integrated transport so that any 'solution' will be less than optimum for the air transport industry. The likelihood is that, yes, we have the DfT projections and allocations but that sufficient capacity will never be built where it is required to cope with that growth. So, Heathrow aside, is it a case of 'predicting but not really providing', of coming to terms with the environmental dilemma entirely by default through what is, effectively, de facto constraint in failing to build sufficient capacity to meet the projected growth?

Note

[1] Editors' note: the opening of Terminal 5 quickly – and perhaps somewhat predictably – changed from triumph to total shambles as various shortcomings in preparations for the big event revealed themselves. The temporary loss of an estimated 20,000 pieces of luggage left British Airways with egg on its face and two of its senior managers with their marching orders.

References

AEA (Association of European Airlines) (2006) *Yearbook 2006*, Brussels: AEA.

Airline Business (2007) 'The world airline rankings', August, pp 58–85.

ATAG (Air Transport Action Group) (2005) *The economic and social benefits of air transport*, Geneva: ATAG.

Ballard, J. G. (2006) *Kingdom come*, London: Fourth Estate.

Barbot, C. (2006) 'Low-cost airlines, secondary airports, and state aid: an economic assessment of the Ryanair–Charleroi Airport agreement', *Journal of Air Transport Management*, 12, pp 197–203.

Bows, A. and Anderson, K. (2007) 'Policy clash: can projected aviation growth be reconciled with the UK government's 60% carbon-reduction target?', *Transport Policy*, 14, pp 103–10.

CAA (Civil Aviation Authority) (1999) *UK airports 1998*, London: CAA.

CAA (2005) *UK regional air services, CAP 754*, London: CAA.

CAA (2006) *No-frills carriers: Revolution or evolution, CAP 770*, London: CAA.

CAA (2007a) *Air services at UK regional airports: An update on developments, CAP 775*, London: CAA.

CAA (2007b) *Connecting the continents: Long haul passenger operations from the UK, CAP 771*, London: CAA.

CAA (2007c) *UK airports 2006*, London: CAA.

Competition Commission (2008) *Emerging thinking – BAA airports*, London: Competition Commission, www.competition-commission.org.uk/inquiries/ref2007/airports/emerging_thinking.htm (accessed 26 April 2008).

Dennis, N. (2007) 'End of the free lunch? The responses of traditional European airlines to the low-cost carrier threat', *Journal of Air Transport Management*, 13, pp 311–21.

DETR (Department of the Environment, Transport and the Regions) (1998) *A new deal for transport: Better for everyone*, London: The Stationery Office.

DETR (2000) *The future of aviation: The government's consultation paper on air transport policy*, London: DETR.

DfT (Department for Transport) (2003) *The future of air transport*, London: DfT, www.dft.gov.uk/about/strategy/whitepapers/air/ (accessed 16 January 2008).

DfT (2006) *Air transport White Paper progress report*, London: DfT. www.dft.gov.uk/162259/165217/185629/progressreport (accessed 16 January 2008).

DfT (2007) *Adding capacity at Heathrow airport*, London: DfT, www.dft.gov.uk/consultations/open/heathrowconsultation/consultationdocument/ (accessed 16 January 2008).

Doganis, R. (2001) *The airline business in the 21st century*, London: Routledge.

EC (European Commission) (2001) *White Paper: European transport policy for 2010: Time to decide*, Brussels/Luxembourg: European Commission.

EC (2004) *The Commission's decision on Charleroi airport promotes the activities of low-cost airlines and regional development*, IP/04/157, 3 February, Brussels/Luxembourg: European Commission.

EC (2005) Memorandum to the Commission, 'Community guidelines on financing of airports and start-up aid to airlines departing from regional airports', http://europa.eu.int/comm/transport/air/rules/state-aid-consutation-en.htm (accessed 16 February 2005).

EC (2006) *State aid No N 303/2005 – United Kingdom: Air Route Development Funds. C(2006) 1844 final*, Brussels: EC.

Eddington, R. (2006) *The case for action: Sir Rod Eddington's advice to government*, Norwich: The Stationery Office.

Environmental Change Institute (2006) *Predict and decide: Aviation, climate change and UK policy*, Oxford: Environmental Change Institute.

European Aviation Industry Joint Statement on Emissions Trading Scheme (2006) 13 October.

Francis, G., Humphreys, I., Ison, S. and Aicken, M. (2006) 'Where next for low cost airlines? A spatial and temporal comparative study', *Journal of Transport Geography*, 14, pp 83–94.

Frontier Economics (2006) *Economic consideration of extending the EU ETS to include aviation*, London: Frontier Economics.

Givoni, M. and Banister, D. (2006) 'Airline and railway integration', *Transport Policy*, 13, pp 386–97.

Graham, A. (2003) *Managing airports: An international perspective*, Oxford: Butterworth–Heinemann.

Graham, A. (2006) 'Have the major forces driving airline traffic changed?', *Journal of Air Transport Management*, 12, pp 14–20.

Graham, A. and Dennis, N. (2007) 'Airport traffic and financial performance: a UK and Ireland case study', *Journal of Transport Geography*, 15, pp 161–71.

Graham, B. (2003) 'Air transport policy: reconciling growth and sustainability?', in I. Docherty and J. Shaw (eds) *A new deal for transport? The UK's struggle with the sustainable transport agenda*, Oxford: Blackwell, pp 198–225.

Graham, B. and Shaw, J. (2008) 'Low-cost airlines in Europe: reconciling liberalization and sustainability', *Geoforum*, 39, pp 1439–51 (online at www.sciencedirect.com).

Holden, E. (2007) *Achieving sustainable mobility: Everyday and leisure-time travel in the EU*, Ashgate: Aldershot.

MacKinnon, D., Shaw, J. and Docherty, I. (2008) *Diverging mobilities: Devolution, transport and policy innovation*, Oxford: Elsevier Science.

OEF (Oxford Economic Forecasting) (1999) *The contribution of the aviation industry to the UK economy*, Oxford: OEF.

OEF (2002) *The economic contribution of aviation to the UK: Part 2 – assessment of regional impact*, Oxford: OEF.

OEF (2006) *The economic contribution of the aviation industry in the UK*, Oxford: OEF.

Pitfield, D. (2007) 'Ryanair's impact on airline market share from the London area airports: a time series analysis', *Journal of Transport Economics and Policy*, 41, pp 75-92.

Riddington, G. (2006) 'Long range air traffic forecasts for the UK: a critique', *Journal of Transport Economics and Policy*, 40, pp 297-314.

Ruddock, A. (2007) *Michael O'Leary: A life in full flight*, Dublin: Penguin Ireland.

Shaw, S. and Thomas, C. (2006) 'Social and cultural dimensions of air travel demand: hyper-mobility in the UK?', *Journal of Sustainable Tourism*, 14, pp 209-15.

Stern, N. (2006) *The economics of climate change: The Stern Report*, Cambridge: Cambridge University Press.

The Guardian (2007a) 'Heathrow: a closed debate', 23 November, p 38.

The Guardian (2007b) 'Heathrow debate is open and democratic', Letters, 26 November, p 31.

The Guardian (2007c) 'Kelly launches fight for Heathrow expansion', 22 November, p 9.

The Guardian (2007d) 'We'll fight you all the way, airlines warn EU over carbon-trading plans', 19 November, p 26.

The Observer (2007) 'Flying in the face of disaster', 14 October, Business, p 7.

Tyndall Centre (2005) *Decarbonising the UK: Energy for a climate conscious future*, Norwich: Tyndall Centre, University of East Anglia.

Whitelegg, J. and Cambridge, H. (2004) *Aviation and sustainability*, Stockholm: Stockholm Environment Institute.

Wit, R., Dings, J., Mendes de Leon, P., Thwaites, L., Peeters, P., Greenwood, D. and Doganis, R. (2002) *Economic incentives to mitigate greenhouse gas emissions from air transport in Europe*, Delft, the Netherlands: CE Delft.

York Aviation (2004) *The social and economic impact of airports in Europe*, Geneva: ACI Europe.

EIGHT

Economic versus environmental sustainability for ports and shipping: charting a new course?

David Pinder

The UK port system has long been positioned on the crucial interface between the interests of the economy and those of the environment. On the one hand, it is imperative that the national economy is served by ports with both the capacity and the efficiency to ensure the uninterrupted progress of trade. Continuing globalisation strongly underlines this, with the Asian trades currently representing 46% of UK containerised traffic and external energy dependence an increasing feature. On the other hand, however, ports and their associated shipping have been responsible for extensive long-term environmental damage around our coasts. Increasing vessel sizes, driven by the constant search for economies of scale in transport, have generated the demand for new port areas to be carved out of the environmentally sensitive coastal zone. Port-based industries – oil refining, petrochemicals, steelworks – have in their heyday commonly consumed several square kilometres of coast in a single bite, often from the shrinking stocks of wetland (Pinder and Witherick, 1990; Pullen, 2004). Air and water pollution have been driven by both port industries and the upward spiral in shipping movements. And hinterlands have borne the environmental consequences of the swing towards road transport for many imports and exports (Harcombe and Pinder, 1996).

Compared with other facets of the sector, *A new deal for transport* (DETR, 1998) focused only briefly on ports and shipping. Nonetheless, in setting out port policy objectives the document clearly recognised this tension between national economic and environmental interests (1998, p 71):

The aims of our policy will be to:
- promote UK and regional competitiveness by encouraging reliable, efficient distribution to markets;
- enhance environmental and operational performance by encouraging the provision of access to markets by different forms of transport;
- make the best use of existing infrastructure in preference to expansion, wherever practicable;
- promote best environmental standards in port design and operation, including where new development is justified.

Equally importantly, in keeping with the neoliberal spirit of the times, this policy was to be pursued at arm's length. The concept of an overarching national ports strategy was rejected; responsibility for achieving port system development was placed firmly with the numerous private companies, local authorities and trusts that actually owned the ports; and government control was to be limited to that available through the planning system.

Against this background this chapter seeks to address a number of related questions. Despite their poor past environmental record, is there evidence that ports and their associated shipping have entered a new era in which economic growth has been maintained without a high environmental cost? If progress has been achieved, where does the credit lie? And, given that all commentators expect the throughput demands placed on the port system to continue to escalate, is the prospect of future growth consistent with the long-run goal of environmental sustainability? In sum, can it be claimed that we are now charting a genuinely new course in which the inherent conflicts between economic growth and the interests of the environment have been resolved?

To address these questions the chapter begins with an overview of the UK port system's scale, complexity and momentum. Evidence of continuing strong growth then provides the backdrop against which associated environmental trends can be assessed. At this point the analysis concentrates on three major aspects of potential environmental damage: encroachment on coastal ecosystems arising from port expansion; water and air pollution in port and at sea; and the environmental – specifically emissions – consequences of commodity transport in the hinterland. It should be noted that the role of regulation in contributing to any progress observed is not considered at this stage but is held back until the chapter's final section. Here a balance-sheet approach is adopted to assess progress, failure and the allocation of credit.

Scale, complexity and momentum

The UK port system is large and complex. Altogether, more than 80 ports and port groups are recognised by the Department for Transport (DfT), typically handling almost 600 million tonnes a year. Forty of these are equipped to handle containers or roll-on/roll-off (ro-ro) unitised cargoes, with a total throughput of 12 million units or 150 million tonnes each year. As might be anticipated in the current era of high-profile globalisation, around 60% of the system's throughput involves imports.

Although ports are numerous, trade is strongly polarised (Figure 8.1; Table 8.1). Dover (the dominant ro-ro gateway) and Felixstowe (the primary deepsea container port) account for no less than a third of all unitised cargo, and the top 10 unitised cargo ports for three-quarters. When all cargoes are considered, the top 10 ports are similarly responsible for two-thirds of all traffic, led in this case by ports on the Humber, Tees and Thames estuaries. This 'all cargo' ranking, it may be noted, underlines the importance of bulk goods – especially oil and coal – in many ports' traffic. At Sullom Voe and Milford Haven oil shipments are the only significant cargo; and the throughput figures of all the remaining top 10 ports are boosted by crude oil, refined oil products and, in some important instances such as Immingham, coal and ore imports.

Figure 8.1: Top 10 unitised cargo and all cargo ports

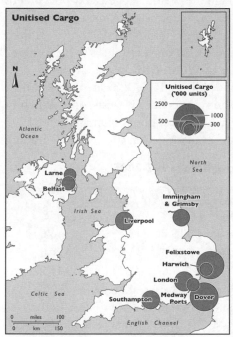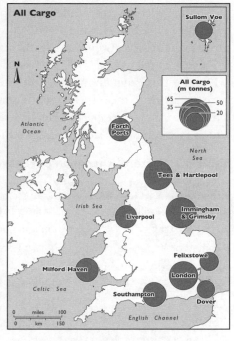

Source: DfT (2006)

Table 8.1: UK port rankings, 2005

Rank		Unitised cargo ('000 units)	Rank		All cargo (million tonnes)
1	Dover	2,047	1	Immingham and Grimsby	60.7
2	Felixstowe	1,945	2	Tees and Hartlepool	55.8
3	London	962	3	London	53.8
4	Southampton	857	4	Southampton	39.4
5	Liverpool	837	5	Milford Haven	37.6
6	Immingham and Grimsby	732	6	Forth ports	34.2
7	Belfast	472	7	Liverpool	33.8
8	Medway ports	413	8	Felixstowe	23.1
9	Harwich	408	9	Dover	21.2
10	Larne	385	10	Sullom Voe	20.5

Source: DfT (2006)

Table 8.2 reviews recent sectoral change in port traffic. Throughput of liquid bulk commodities – dominantly oil and oil products – has declined since *A new deal for transport* was published in 1998, but this reflects the industry's restructuring rather than any port capacity problems. Meanwhile, all other sectors – and particularly container and ro-ro traffic – have recorded significant expansion. This growth, which can be tracked steadily through the period, suggests few port system constraints over the last decade, an interpretation supported by the unitised cargo analysis in Table 8.3. Viewing 1997-2005 as a whole, almost all the top 10 unitised cargo ports achieved impressive traffic increases. In most instances these averaged 5% a year, rising to over 10% for Harwich and Immingham and Grimsby.

Despite this generally positive picture, details in Table 8.3 do suggest a port system starting to meet the demands of a buoyant economy with some difficulty. This is clearest with respect to Felixstowe, where throughput stagnated after 1997 and in fact contracted slightly, despite the fact that this was the country's leading

Table 8.2: Sectoral change in port throughput, 1997-2005

	Unit	1997	2005	Change (%)
Liquid bulk traffic	million tonnes	284.9	265.4	–6.8
Dry bulk traffic	million tonnes	115.7	134.9	+16.6
Container and ro-ro[1] traffic	million tonnes	128.9	154.7	+20.0
of which lo-lo[2] containers '000		3,486	4,573	+31.2
Semi-bulk traffic	million tonnes	21.6	22.8	+5.7
Other	million tonnes	7.5	7.8	+4.0
Total	million tonnes	558.5	585.7	+4.9

Notes: [1] Roll-on/roll-off. [2] Lift-on/lift off.

Source: DfT (2006); MDS Transmodal (2007)

Table 8.3: Unitised cargo growth, 1997-2005

	2005 ('000 units)	Change, 1997-2005 (%)	Average annual change (%)
Dover	2,047	+28.5	+3.6
Felixstowe	1,945	–4.1	–0.5
London	962	+41.9	+5.2
Southampton	857	+44.5	+5.6
Liverpool	837	+47.9	+6.0
Immingham and Grimsby	732	+87.2	+10.9
Belfast	472	+12.6	+1.6
Medway ports	413	+58.9	+7.4
Harwich	408	+86.3	+10.8
Larne	385	+40.5	+5.1

Source: DfT (2006)

container port. Less obvious, but still significant, was Belfast's weak growth rate (1.6% a year). And although Southampton's performance over the complete 1997–2005 period does not ring alarm bells, this changes once recent trends are tracked. Here, in the UK's second-largest container port, an annual average expansion rate of 7.2% shifted abruptly into virtually zero growth after 2003. These developments signal a port system entering transition – moving from a state of flexibility, which enabled the growing demands of the economy to be met smoothly, into an era marked by the prospect of looming bottlenecks and consequent implications for economic sustainability.

While this container port capacity issue is well recognised (Gilman 2003), a second pressure – too recent to emerge from port throughput data – underlines the transition's significance. UK natural gas demand rose by 12% between 1997 and 2005, and is set to rise further as new gas-fired power stations are brought on stream. This has accelerated the depletion of North Sea reserves, output from which fell by almost a fifth between the peak year (2000) and 2005 (BP, 2007). Although partial compensation will take the form of increased imports from politically friendly sources, especially via Norway's recently completed Langeled pipeline, there will also be a growing reliance on Russian gas. This has meant a heightened perception of risk, given the political muscle recently exercised by Russia under President Putin. To limit this risk, and simultaneously provide additional strategic insurance against the emergence of a demand–supply gap in the UK, the import of liquefied natural gas (LNG) has risen rapidly up the agenda.

The implications of this for the national port system are far reaching. Liquefied natural gas can only be imported by ship. Thus, after decades in which the overwhelming paradigm was that natural gas was landed in the UK by pipeline, making no demands on the seaport system, the necessity of safeguarding economic sustainability by developing natural gas ports, plus the infrastructure required to store and re-gasify the liquefied product, has suddenly emerged. More details of this departure are examined later in this chapter. Meanwhile, the key statistic underlining the strategic significance of the new challenge is that four LNG import facilities have already been approved; one of these is fully functioning and three are nearing completion.

While this is the current situation, Table 8.4 highlights the potential for pressures to increase. Particularly high growth is anticipated for LNG and deepsea containers in the next quarter of a century, clearly raising questions concerning this chapter's primary concern: the port system's ability to meet the demands of economic growth at an acceptable environmental price.

Port expansion and coastal ecological degradation: a relationship decoupled?

As the eventual emergence of capacity pressures in the port system implies, for much of the period following the publication of *A new deal for transport* the substantial throughput growth demanded by the economy was accommodated

Table 8.4: Predicted port throughput growth, 2005-30

	2005	2015	2030	Change (%)
Liquid natural gas (imports, million tonnes)	1.1	29.2	38.7	+3,310
International containers (million TEU)[1]	4.4	6.9	11.3	+157
Ro-ro (million vehicles)	5.3	5.8	6.5	+23
Vehicles (million tonnes)	5.3	5.8	6.5	+23
Oil products (million tonnes)	85.9	88.6	90.2	–5
Crude oil (million tonnes)	153.5	129.7	133.4	–13
Coal (million tonnes)	50.2	28.6	40.6	–19

Note: [1] Twenty-foot equivalent units. Because containers are of various sizes, the twenty-foot unit is used as a yardstick to assist throughput analysis between ports and over time.

Source: MDS Transmodal (2007)

without environmentally damaging expansion schemes. To a degree this achievement can be considered a consequence of regulation operating through the physical planning system. Here, a particularly important point is that this regulation was not confined to UK provisions for environmental protection, but also included the extremely wide-ranging requirements of the European Union's (EU's) Habitats Directive (EC, 1992). By the mid to late 1990s these controls ensured that the monetary and other costs of steering major infrastructural schemes through the planning and public inquiry system were well recognised. So, too, was the fact that these costs spiralled upwards as environmental campaigners adeptly deployed the planning system to oppose large-scale projects.

Beyond this, however, seamless growth without extensive ecological damage has also reflected various corporate strategies. In some places capacity existed beyond the immediate needs of the economy. Felixstowe, for example, filled spare capacity by attracting container transhipment trade destined ultimately for continental markets. This trade was gradually squeezed out as the volume of UK-bound freight rose. Elsewhere, parts of the existing port estate were revalued in a different light. By the early 1990s Associated British Ports (ABP) in Southampton had released substantial redundant parts of the early port area to profit from urban waterfront revitalisation projects. But other areas similarly hit by the rapid decline in general cargo were retained for alternative port uses. These now support high throughputs of vehicles, bulk grains and cruise passengers. In Immingham, too, the redundant areas surrounding completely outmoded enclosed docks – which elsewhere might well have been released for waterfront flats, retailing and entertainment venues – have instead been pressed into service again by ABP, and have proved vital to the port's rapid rise in the unitised cargo league table.

In a quite different vein, the pressure for infrastructural growth has also been eased by global economic restructuring initiated in the 1970s. Economic crisis triggered by the oil-price spike of 1973-74 rapidly led to the cancellation of industrial expansion projects – especially in the oil and petrochemicals sector, which until then had routinely taken such large slices of the ecologically vulnerable coastal zone. The second price spike (1979-80) then sparked deindustrialisation, again most marked in the oil sector, which closed no fewer than eight refineries between 1976 and 1986. Subsequently, global competition has continued this trend through, for example, the closure of the Shell Haven oil refinery in 1999.

The valuable consequence of this global restructuring was that it created a large brownfield land bank well suited to the needs of modern ports and ships. As we have entered the transition phase in which expansion schemes can no longer be postponed, it has been possible to draw down reserves from this bank, limiting substantially the level of coastal zone environmental degradation required. In this the pioneer was Thamesport, a well-established development occupying a large part of the former BP (British Petroleum) Isle of Grain refinery in Kent (Harcombe and Pinder, 1996). Soon one of four recently approved container port projects – the London Gateway container port – will similarly take advantage of redundant industrial space, in this case the former Shell Haven refinery. Even more impressively, the three LNG import terminals currently under construction have recycled all or part of former oil refinery sites. The Isle of Grain LNG project is Thamesport's neighbour; and on Milford Haven the sites originally developed for the Esso and Gulf Oil refineries have now been transformed into the South Hook and Dragon LNG ports. What must also be stressed is that these are major new facilities with the capacity to supply almost a third of the UK's gas requirements. This is equivalent to no less than 12% of the country's total primary energy consumption.

When the effects of this brownfield recycling are added to those of projects dependent on strategic reconfiguration within the existing port estate, it emerges that recent and current port expansion schemes entail remarkably little coastal wetland consumption. The Immingham International coal terminal resulted in the loss of just 31 hectares, while for the London Gateway and Harwich's Bathside Bay project the equivalent figures will be fewer than 50 and 69 hectares respectively. Compared with the 20th-century losses noted earlier, these are all modest. Moreover, all these losses have resulted in the provision of compensatory habitat, such as the 138 hectares of wetland created at Hanford Water, eight kilometres from Bathside Bay. The discussion will return to this compensation concept later in the chapter, but at this juncture the key point is that developments such as these give clear cause for optimism that the former strong relationship between port growth and the loss of rich and sensitive coastal environments has indeed been decoupled.

Water and air pollution

Well before the 1990s, trends were established that altered significantly the problem of pollution arising from activities within port areas. Growing environmental awareness tightened the regulatory regime bearing down on potential polluters. And the deindustrialisation that followed the oil crises naturally set in train the alleviation of industrial impacts. This effectively narrowed the port-based pollution problem, centring it increasingly on the impact of ships' water and air pollution in two very different circumstances: enclosed port waters and the open sea.

Water pollution

The most extensive information relating to water pollution by ships in port is that gathered by the Advisory Committee on Protection of the Sea (ACOPS) on behalf of the Maritime and Coastguard Agency (MCA). ACOPS publishes an annual report aiming to provide details of every accidental or deliberate discharge in UK waters and ports. To do so it enlists as reporters diverse land-based organisations – particularly local and harbour authorities – supplementing their work at sea with aerial and satellite surveillance, plus reports from ships and oil and gas installations. The vehicle for reporting is a standardised form, now electronic, that is completed for individual incidents by the reporting organisations.

The resulting data are not perfect. In many cases the report forms are only partially completed, the information requested being unknown or impossible to estimate. In the most recent (2006) report, for example, the discharge volume was unrecorded in 15% of cases, and only half the returns could cite a specific cause for the pollution. Even so, the MCA has not questioned the general reliability of these annual reports, and the indications that emerge from them are extremely clear.

Vessel discharges to port waters

Virtually all vessel discharges are of mineral oil products, mainly fuels and especially diesel. The most serious in 2005 involved 10 tonnes of gas oil lost in London when a barge foundered; and 3.5 tonnes of diesel discharged into Aberdeen harbour by two offshore supply vessels. Despite the fact that causes are frequently unrecorded, it is evident that one major failing is accidental release during bunkering (refuelling) operations. In 2005 this single factor was responsible for 60% of the incidents for which a cause was cited.

Importantly, successive ACOPS annual reports reveal that the number of discharges involving vessels in port fell each year between 2000 and 2005, in total declining by 25%. In consequence, in 2005 only 102 incidents were recorded throughout the entire UK port system. Moreover, serious though the major discharges were, they were a small minority: only 10% of incidents involved the loss of more than 200 litres. Conversely, in 70% of cases fewer than 30 litres were discharged; and in 37% it was fewer than 10 litres. Equally significantly, the types of vessel crucial to the economy – container ships, bulk carriers, tankers, ferries and so on – were not the chief culprits. Nearly half the reported incidents were caused by either fishing vessels (displaying as a group a poor bunkering record) or pleasure craft. Moreover, in many cases the discharges from these fishing and pleasure craft were greater than those from the larger – generally ocean-going – vessels (Figure 8.2). Similarly, the data demonstrate that emissions to water were not concentrated in the larger ports, despite their greater activity. In 2005 Felixstowe experienced no spillages. Milford Haven had seven, but no fewer than six of these involved small fishing boats and occurred in Milford Docks, entirely separate from the high-profile oil port. And although Dover had four major events, the context is that, with more than 24,000 shipping movements a year, this port is by a very large margin the busiest in the country.

Vessel discharges at sea

No such optimism applies to major accidents at sea such as the loss of the supertanker *Sea Empress* at the mouth of Milford Haven in 1996, or the container ship *Napoli* off the Dorset coast in 2007. Statistically significant downward trends

Figure 8.2: Scale of spillages from vessels in UK waters, 2005

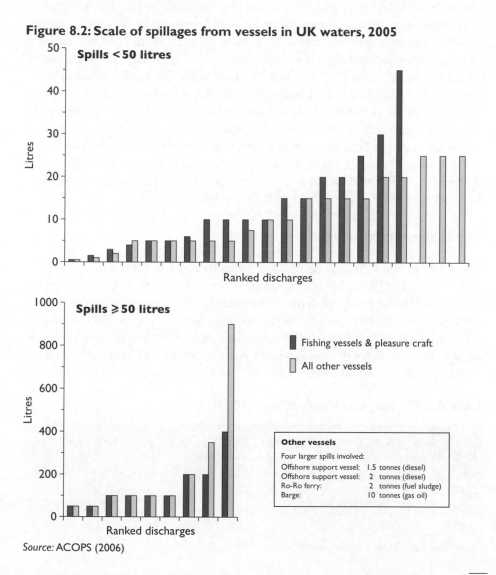

Source: ACOPS (2006)

cannot be discerned, and the circumstances leading up to these incidents can be so complex that improved safety measures applied when 'lessons are learned' may do little or nothing to avert further incidents (NAO, 2002; Pullen, 2004). This problem is clearly associated with the UK's overseas trade, and currently the most promising signs are, first, that incidents' impacts may be ameliorated by measures such as the EU's recent prohibition of vulnerable single-hulled tankers and, second, that high-magnitude accidents are in reality rare despite the intense publicity they receive in the media. For example, prior to the *Sea Empress*, the most recent oil tanker disasters were the *Braer* in 1993 and the *Torrey Canyon* in 1967.

Disasters apart, lower-profile discharges are still generally larger than those in ports. In 2005, for example, one incident in six involved the release of between one and six tonnes of fuel. But while volumes are higher they are, of course, released into a far greater and more active body of water, so that many incidents produce no more than a surface sheen, generally reported by ACOPS as having dispersed naturally by wave action. Moreover, the total number of discharges is again quite limited and the trend through time is downwards, having recently halved to around 50 in 2005 (Table 8.5). Once again, the vessels responsible for most incidents can be readily identified. In 2005, for example, around half were support ships for the offshore oil and gas industry. Half of the remainder were either fishing vessels or naval vessels of various nations. And it was the fishing vessels, most of which sank or ran aground, that caused almost all the large-scale spillages. In contrast to the major disasters, therefore, the ocean-going vessels central to the UK's global trade and prosperity are by no means primarily responsible for this lower-profile degradation of the open seas.

Air pollution in port and at sea

The focus of concern relating to ships' air pollution has been sulphur dioxide (SO_2) emissions. These have been problematic because of the impact the oil industry's response to global demand shifts has had on the quality of the fuel oil used by almost all cargo vessels. As the refiners met growing demand for high-value products by squeezing more and more light fractions from their crude oil, the 'bottom-of-the-barrel' residue – mainly destined to be used as fuel oil – increasingly became the repository for pollutants (Pinder, 1997). Prominent

Table 8.5: Discharge incidents at sea, 2002-05

	Total incidents involving vessels	Incidents involving oil and gas support vessels	Incidents involving other vessels
2002	99	43	56
2003	52	23	29
2004	53	17	36
2005	49	26	23

Source: Successive ACOPS annual reports

among these was sulphur, levels of which were frequently over 3%, producing high levels of SO_x in exhaust gases and worsening ecosystem acidification. Despite past concern, however, all the indicators suggest that this is a problem now under control. In 2007 the North Sea – the most vulnerable UK area because of its intense traffic – became an SO_x Emission Control Area (SECA) in which fuel sulphur content is limited to 0.1%. Similarly, between May 2006 and January 2010 the permitted sulphur content of fuel oil used by ships in UK ports will be reduced from around 2.7% to 0.1%.[1]

This progress does not, however, mean the end of atmospheric emissions problems in UK waters. While attention has centred on SO_x, the realisation is now dawning that other important exhaust emissions – especially the greenhouse gas carbon dioxide (CO_2) – have been overlooked. This neglect is at first sight surprising, given that the Kyoto Protocol recognised the need to control this form of pollution, but responsibility for action was passed to the International Maritime Organization (IMO), which was slow to pursue the issue. This encouraged the assumption that ships' greenhouse gas production was negligible compared with other sources. Recent research, however, strongly suggests that these emissions have been substantially underestimated. Globally, ships may be responsible for 4% of world greenhouse gas output, and the volume released may rise by 75% over 15 to 20 years (Entek, 2005; Vidal, 2007). Here, therefore, is a climate-related issue on which no progress has yet been made beyond problem recognition.

Hinterland integration and sustainability

One form of hinterland integration raises few issues. From day one, LNG ports must be connected to the national gas transmission system by pipelines with adequate capacity; the product simply cannot be distributed in any other way. Provision is, therefore, regarded as a national energy security issue, thus ensuring relatively straightforward passage through the planning approval system.[2] This might suggest that environmental considerations are firmly subservient to economic interests, and this was certainly claimed in the case of the 316-kilometre high-pressure gas main linking the new import terminals at Milford Haven with the strategic network at Tirley in Gloucestershire.[3] Yet buried pipelines do not exact a high environmental price. They offer maximum opportunity for landscape and environmental recovery over time, especially when compared with other transport infrastructure. Few people are able to identify where the UK's trunk gas pipelines run. They are extremely low risk in operation. And they also ensure low-carbon transport by delivering high gas volumes at the cost of very modest energy inputs at the compressor stations.

Much larger issues continue to surround all other forms of hinterland integration. Much is made of the importance of achieving modal shift from road to rail, and impressive examples of rail use can be found. With its capacity to import 15.7 million tonnes of coal a year for use in the electricity and steel industries, and deliver all imports by rail, Immingham is outstanding in this respect. But while other instances appear impressive at first, they are far more questionable on closer inspection. While Felixstowe and Southampton are both served by 20 to 30 freight trains each day, only 22% of the former's containers and 28% of the latter's went by rail in 2006. Nationwide, it is unlikely that more than a fifth of all intermodal traffic is rail hauled from and to the ports. This is despite the stark fact that, per tonne kilometre, road haulage generates five times the CO_2 produced by rail transport (EEA, 2004), a ratio bringing sharply into focus the climate change cost of the current strong bias towards roads.

Reasons for rail's lacklustre share are examined shortly. Here we must note that the performance of two other transport modes frequently assumed to be capable of promoting much more sustainable hinterland integration – coastal shipping and inland waterways – is even more disappointing than that of rail. Coastal shipping opportunities have long been exploited by the oil industry to distribute refined products in small-scale tankers to regional centres. Each year over 11 million tonnes are shipped in this way (MDS Transmodal, 2007). Yet for all commodities coastal traffic amounts to under 5% of all port traffic.[4] This clearly suggests the existence of untapped potential, particularly as maritime CO_2 emissions per tonne kilometre are little more than a tenth of those of road haulage (EEA, 2004). But it is equally evident that the key to unlocking this potential is not simply the technological fix of ensuring appropriate infrastructure provision around the coasts. Saldanha and Gray (2002, p 77) found that attitudinal obstacles among the business and political communities are fundamental. Although more positive attitudes to coastal shipping were detected in their investigation, it was still concluded that the 'secretive nature of the coastal shipping sector could impede joint marketing to promote a mode of transport that is often "invisible" to [decision makers in the standard transport chain]'. From a business perspective, entrenched economic imperatives – the greatest speed and the lowest cost – continue to overshadow the environmental benefits of coastal shipping strategies. Moreover, the investigation offered little prospect of government initiatives overcoming these obstacles. Although the potential to reduce emissions was clear, government was 'only mildly supportive [of coastal shipping] in tangible terms' (Saldanha and Gray, 2002, p 77).

Inland waterways, meanwhile, currently carry only 2.6 million tonnes of freight, a miniscule volume that has in fact fallen by almost 40% since 2000. It might be assumed, therefore, that here there is again substantial untapped potential to promote low-carbon haulage, but from the port system's perspective this is no more than theoretical. Despite navigations such as the Aire and Calder, or the lower Trent, the cost of transforming currently fragmented infrastructure into a network capable of moving substantial flows to and from the leading centres of consumption and production would be exorbitant (Figure 8.3). Moreover, perhaps counterintuitively, inland waterways would not necessarily produce the lowest-carbon transport option. European data show that CO_2 emissions per tonne kilometre on inland waterways are three times those for sea transport and exceed those for rail by almost 50% (EEA, 2004).

Balancing the books: credit, debit and the *New deal for transport*

It is clear that, *in some respects*, recent years have witnessed a very welcome conjunction of rapid growth in port and shipping activity, coupled with much lower environmental impacts than was previously the norm. The UK's strong

Figure 8.3: Major estuarine and inland waterways

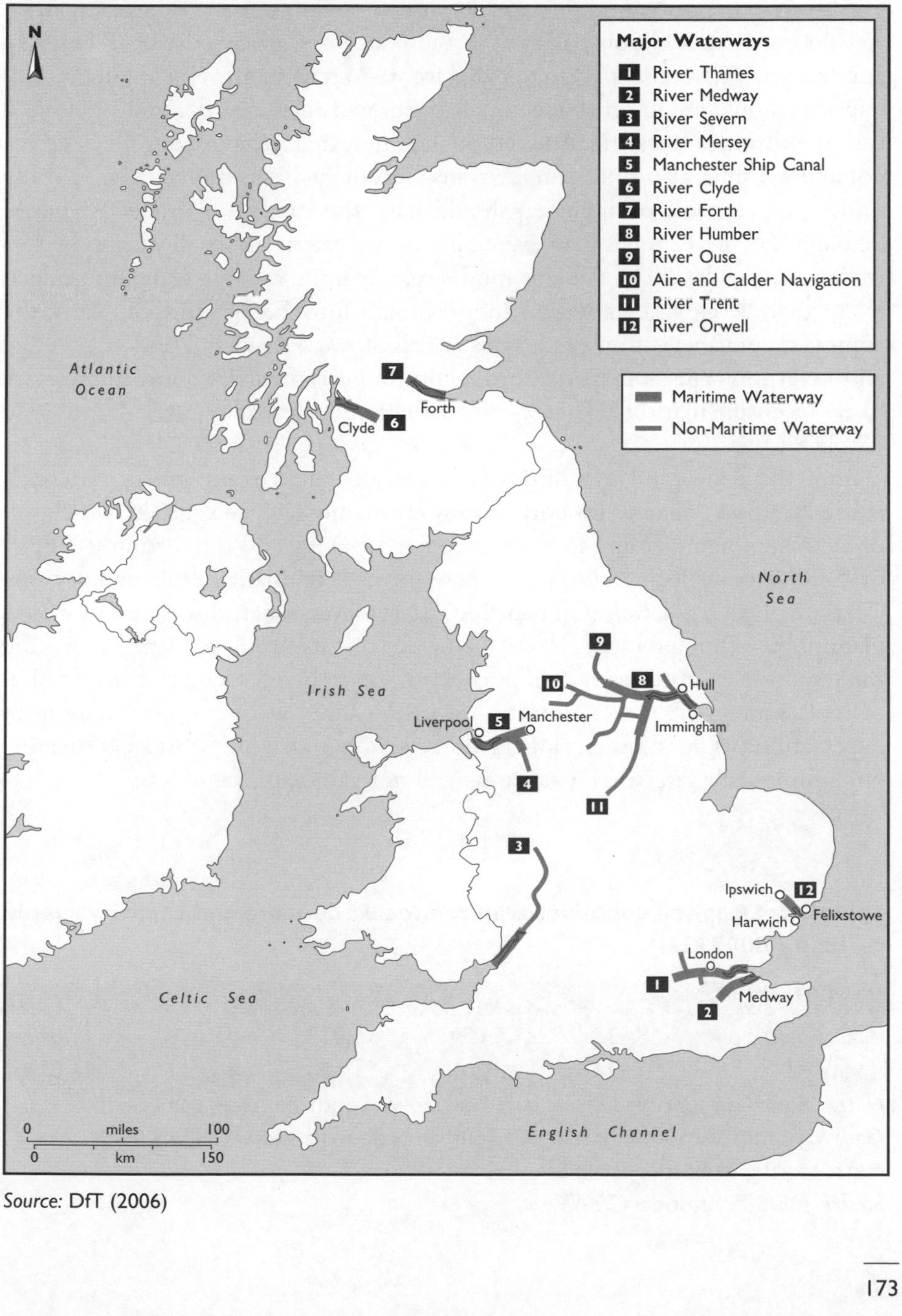
N
Major Waterways
1 River Thames
2 River Medway
3 River Severn
4 River Mersey
5 Manchester Ship Canal
6 River Clyde
7 River Forth
8 River Humber
9 River Ouse
10 Aire and Calder Navigation
11 River Trent
12 River Orwell
Maritime Waterway
Non-Maritime Waterway
Atlantic Ocean
North Sea
Irish Sea
Celtic Sea
English Channel
Forth
Clyde
Liverpool
Manchester
Hull
Immingham
Ipswich
Harwich
Felixstowe
London
Medway
0 miles 100
0 km 150

Source: DfT (2006)

demand growth has been met without recourse to large-scale port expansion of the type that previously inflicted such extensive damage on coastal environments. Although the risk of serious marine accidents is very difficult to ameliorate, the parallel problem of frequent, smaller-scale, spillages has been driven down to low levels in port waters and at sea. The end of serious sulphur emissions to the air is also in sight, a result of the long-established trend for legislation governing water and air pollution, which is likely to be extended further – and applied even more effectively – in future. And forecasts of port throughput growth suggest that, up to 2030 at least, additional port expansion schemes are avoidable (Table 8.4). Modest growth, such as that anticipated for ro-ro traffic and vehicle imports and exports, should be absorbable through continued restructuring and intensified use of existing port estates. And although anticipated growth rates for deep sea container traffic and LNG imports are extremely high, the schemes already under construction or approved should have the capacity to meet envisaged demand. For LNG there may eventually be a capacity shortfall of one or two million tonnes by 2030, but this modest gap is quite capable of being bridged by further developments within the terminals now being built. Similarly, the approved containerisation expansions at Felixstowe, Harwich, London Gateway and Liverpool, plus anticipated throughput improvements at Southampton, are likely to ensure that there is over- rather than under-capacity until almost 2030 (Table 8.6).

But if this is the good news, little of it can be attributed to any 'green' credentials in the *New deal*. The need for port expansion schemes has been curbed by a cluster of factors, prominent among them corporate strategy and the fortuitous effects of deindustrialisation. Only one of these forces – the national planning system – has involved regulation (Gilman, 2003). Moreover, when this facet of physical planning is examined more closely, it emerges that its strongest teeth – including the requirement noted earlier for port expansion to be preceded by the provision of replacement habitat – originate not in the UK but in Europe. There is an expectation (set out most recently in DfT, 2007a, p 8) that new port areas affecting environmentally sensitive coastal areas will not gain approval unless:

Table 8.6: Deep sea container traffic: forecast demand and capacity supply to 2030 ('000 TEUs)

	2010	2015	2020	2025	2030
Capacity supply[1]	8,437	15,029	15,029	15,029	15,029
Demand	7,834	9,578	11,196	13,317	16,029

Note: [1] Based on approved projects at Felixstowe South, Bathside Bay, London Gateway and Liverpool, plus planned Southampton expansion resulting from restructuring of existing facilities.
Source: MDS Transmodal (2007)

- no alternative exists that could deliver the benefits sought by the project;
- there are 'imperative reasons of overriding public interest' (IROPI) in the project proceeding; and
- compensatory habitat is provided, in advance of the development.

These provisions are a direct consequence of the need to adhere to the provisions of the EU Habitats Directive (EC, 1992). Equally significantly, this is a far-from-isolated instance. Time and again, key measures bearing on pollution have been applied nationally by the government, and policed by UK agencies such as the MCA and local authorities, yet are international in origin. Fundamental to the control of marine pollution has been the IMO's MARPOL 73/78 convention, and in particular Annexes I (applying to oil, and in force since 1983) and II (which has regulated noxious liquid substances carried in bulk since 1987) (IMO, 1978). In the same vein, the SO_x pollution problem has recently come under attack from both the IMO and the EU. Annex VI of MARPOL 73/78, covering SO_x, came into force in 2005 (Lloyds Register FOBAS, 2005), while EU action in the form of Directive 2005/33/EC has accelerated the introduction of the drastically reduced fuel-oil sulphur-content limits discussed earlier. And with respect to ships' CO_2 emissions it is the EU that has moved most rapidly, with a commitment to extend carbon trading to the shipping sector (Bounds, 2007; Helsinki Commission, 2007).

Here a note of caution is necessary: in many instances the global dimensions of the shipping industry mean that international action is the most appropriate way forward. It can be extremely difficult for an individual country to act effectively against a ubiquitous problem such as air pollution generated by vessels of many nations. Nonetheless, the principal point is that it would be erroneous to attribute observed progress on the environmental front to actions stemming from the *New deal*. Two processes – increasing environmental protection and overseas trade growth – have operated in parallel with a desirable outcome. But this outcome would very probably have been the same had the *New deal* expressed no environmental aspirations with respect to ports and shipping.

What must also be recognised, however, is that some environmental issues are appropriately addressed at the national level, and that in this context the indications are far from encouraging. One example is provided by the recent emergence of CO_2 emissions as an issue. As with SO_x pollution, controlling ships' CO_2 emissions at sea will require international action beyond the capabilities of any individual government. But CO_2 emissions caused by ships' engines in port are a different matter. Currently, the use of engines to power ships' systems while berthed is standard practice, known in the trade as 'cold ironing'. The government's *Ports policy interim review* (DfT, 2007a) acknowledges that 'substantial' emissions improvements could be made in this context by the provision of shore-side supplies. Yet, even though solutions are not straightforward for technical reasons, the *Review*'s approach is at best disappointing. No specific measures to require emissions reductions are envisaged. Instead, 'we will in future expect newly developed terminals to make advance provision for "cold ironing facilities". We will also expect major ports to formulate plans for introducing such facilities at existing terminals once a standard has been agreed' (DfT, 2007a, p 9). Why ports should perceive any urgency to respond to these exhortations is unclear, and it is hard to resist the suspicion that, once again, the issue will not be addressed before international (probably EU) action is taken.

Easily eclipsing this issue on the climate change front, however, is the failure to address the environmental cost of road-hauled containers that has arisen over the *New deal* years. As we have seen, even the best ports still move less than a third of their containers by rail, even though rail freight's CO_2 emissions are a fifth those of lorry transport. At first sight, the recent policy response to this could be given a positive spin, in as much as there is now a Network Rail strategy for freight capacity improvements (Network Rail, 2007). This not only lists in great detail very significant current limitations – including width and height restrictions, inability to handle longer trains, pinch points, conflicts with passenger services, and capacity caps arising from low speeds – but also presents detailed short- medium- and long-term programmes for their elimination. Yet any attempt to present this as a timely, proactive strategy to drive down emissions collapses rapidly when the Strategic Rail Authority's (SRA's) *Freight strategy*, published in 2001, is placed in the spotlight. Box 8.1 presents this document's major proposals. Although they are less detailed than those of Network Rail, there is a high degree of overlap between the two analyses of the problem, and also their proposed solutions. Moreover, from the timings quoted in Box 8.1 it is evident that the SRA believed that many of the constraints on freight capacity could by now have been relieved. Given the political decision to abolish the SRA, and the saga surrounding the demise of Railtrack, the prime causes of this delay are not difficult to identify (Chapter Four). But this does not alter the fact that, six years after the SRA's strategy appeared, Network Rail has repeated much of the work undertaken by the SRA and is still essentially on the starting blocks.

Most disconcerting of all, however, are the answers that emerge when we explore whether road-haul emissions are viewed as a serious environmental problem set to deteriorate rapidly as container traffic rises by two-thirds by 2015 and almost triples by 2030 (Table 8.4). What is immediately striking across a range of government documents is the absence of willingness to accept ownership of this issue. The DfT's (2007a, p 6) *Ports policy interim review*, for example, recognises ports to be 'just one link in much larger international logistics chains', yet fails to acknowledge that these are also international pollution chains that extend deep into the hinterland where they are a national responsibility. Similarly lacklustre is the White Paper *Delivering a sustainable railway* (DfT, 2007b). While this does discuss current rail freight levels for a variety of commodities, and also recognises the importance of developing the Strategic Freight Network, any sense of urgency with respect to road-haul emissions is completely lacking. And, as with the *Interim review*, at no point does the discussion come close to proposing targets for rail freight growth. The anodyne statement that, in the intermodal context,

Box 8.1: Strategic Rail Authority Freight Strategy 2001: major project summary and timetable

Phase I: Implementation in 2 to 5 years

Incremental freight capabilities to route upgrade for East Coast Main Line

Diversionary routes for network resilience

Enhancement of Felixstowe–Nuneaton: capacity and loading gauge [loading gauge refers to width and height clearance on route, not to track gauge]

Enhancement of Southampton–West Coast Main Line and north west ports: capacity and gauge

Enhancement of London orbital lines

Phase II: Possible implementation around 5 years

Trans-Pennine upgrade: Manchester/Merseyside to north east ports

Manchester capacity

West Coast Main Line north of Crewe

West Midlands capacity and bottlenecks

Gauge enhancement from Channel Tunnel to London

Further gauge enhancements

Phase III: Possible implementation – 5 to 10 years

West Coast Main Line alternative routes

Freight elements of further upgrades

Phase IV: Beyond 10 years

New routes

London routing/bypass

Piggyback programme

Source: SRA (2001)

'rail's contribution is likely to rise, given expansion plans [at Felixstowe] and at Bathside Bay and London Gateway' (DfT, 2007b, p 85) hardly amounts to a call to arms to meet a far-sighted carbon-reduction target.

Does Network Rail's (2007) *Freight: Route utilisation strategy* compensate for this lacuna? At first sight there is cause for optimism since, in addition to the specification and costing of route improvements, this is the one document to estimate (on page 34) rail freight growth trends. By 2015 intermodal traffic carried by rail is predicted to have risen by between 42 and 83%. But in no sense are these figures targets set by the rail industry or any branch of government in the context of accelerating carbon-emission control. Instead they are estimates produced by rail freight users who are under no obligation to seek the environmental advantages of modal shift. Alarm bells ring still louder when the estimated increases in intermodal freight are translated into absolute figures (Table 8.7). Measured in terms of twenty-foot equivalent units (TEUs), and on the most favourable estimate, movement by road is still likely to rise from 4.3 million to almost seven million per year; and if the worst-case scenario proved correct the 2015 total would be 7.6 million. Here it must be noted that TEUs do not equate to individual movements since many containers are longer than the twenty-foot standard. Even so, cautious interpretation means that – despite rail network improvements – at least two million additional road journeys can be anticipated each year as early as 2015. Moreover, this growth will run in tandem with a forecast 35% escalation in ro-ro traffic by 2015, which alone will mean almost a three-million increase in lorry movements (MDS Transmodal, 2007).

Finally, therefore, we are at the heart of the matter. The reality is that the port-related interface between economic and environmental sustainability has many facets. On a number of these, commendable progress has been made towards achieving growth without unacceptable environmental damage. But this progress has not come chiefly through UK policy initiatives, and where UK leadership is required to deal with specific UK problems – most notably in the context of climate change and the control of road freight emissions – it is conspicuously wanting. Yes, there are ambitious national targets to reduce greenhouse gas emissions. But there is a dispiriting dearth of evidence that these have resulted in joined-up thinking in key quarters such as the DfT or Network Rail. Bland documents from these actors communicate no sense of urgency. Organisational

Table 8.7: Predicted trends in intermodal movements by rail and road, 2005-15

		Million TEU
(a)	Deepsea container traffic 2005	5.7
(b)	Estimated movement by rail 2005 (25%)	1.4
(c)	Predicted TEU 2015	9.6
(d)	Best case (b+83%)	2.6
(e)	Worst case (b+42%)	2.0
(f)	Best case (c-d)	7.0
(g)	Worst case (c-e)	7.6

Source: MDS Transmodal (2007); Network Rail(2007)

compartmentalisation dominates, and there is no detectable appetite to challenge the orthodoxy that only the economics of the market can decide how much freight should move off the roads. The pendulum may have swung encouragingly towards better protection of the environment in most spheres, but here we continue to face a heavy and rapidly increasing environmental price.

Notes

[1] Introduction of the North Sea SECA does not, of course, mean that low-sulphur fuel will be used elsewhere. Globally, it is highly likely that traditional fuel oil will remain in common use, not least because it is cheaper than the low-sulphur variety. Outside regulated regions, ships are likely to switch to standard fuel, and sulphur pollution will consequently remain a worldwide problem. Even allowing for some pollution to be transported from elsewhere through the atmosphere, however, control in the North Sea – previously one of the worst locations in the world – should reduce very significantly the localised environmental impact.

[2] This echoes the situation around Milford Haven in the 1960s when, in an outstanding coastal area that would otherwise have been included in the neighbouring Pembrokeshire Coast National Park, four oil refineries with capacities totalling 28 million tonnes were permitted in the interests of national security.

[3] Here the Brecon Beacons National Park Authority was especially vociferous in its opposition to a 25-kilometre section passing through part of the park.

[4] This figure for coastal movements excludes coastwise traffic between the mainland and (1) Northern Ireland and (2) the Isle of Man, Lewis, Orkney, Shetland and the Channel Islands (DfT, 2006). These flows are not included because there is no practical alternative to movement by sea. One-port traffic is also excluded since this is dominated by cargoes such as North Sea oil and aggregates for which there is again no option other than shipment through coastal waters.

References

ACOPS (Advisory Committee on Protection of the Sea) (2006) *Annual survey of reported discharges to vessels and offshore oil and gas installations in the United Kingdom pollution control zone, 2005*, London: ACOPS.

Bounds, A. (2007) 'Clash looms as EU plans shipping emission caps', *Financial Times*, 22 March.

BP (British Petroleum) (2007) *Statistical review of world energy*, London: British Petroleum.

DETR (Department of the Environment, Transport and the Regions) (1998) *A new deal for transport: Better for everyone*, Cm3950, London: The Stationery Office.

DfT (2006) *Transport statistics Great Britain 2006*, Norwich: The Stationery Office.

DfT (2007a) *Ports policy interim review*, London: DfT.

DfT (2007b) *Delivering a sustainable railway*, Cm 7176, London: The Stationery Office.

EC (European Commission) (1992) Directive 92/43/EEC on the conservation of natural habitats and of wild flora and fauna, *Official Journal of the European Communities*, Brussels: EC.

EEA (European Environment Agency) (2004) *Overall efficiency and specific CO$_2$ emissions for passenger and freight transport*, Copenhagen: EEA.

Entek (2005) *Service contract on ship emissions: Abatement, assignment and market-based instruments*, Brussels: European Commission Directorate General Environment.

Gilman, S. (2003) 'Sustainability and national policy in UK port development', *Maritime Policy and Management*, 30, pp 275-91.

Harcombe, S. and Pinder, D. (1996) 'Oil industry restructuring and its environmental consequences in the coastal zone', in B. S. Hoyle (ed) *Cityports, coastal zones and regional change*, Chichester: John Wiley and Sons, pp 83-102.

Helsinki Commission (2007) 'Shipping will enter EU carbon trading scheme', Press Release, 18 April, www.helcom.fi/press_office/news_baltic/en_GB/BalticAnd EUNews420791 (accessed 5 January 2008).

International Maritime Organization (1978) *International convention for the prevention of pollution from ships, as modified by the protocol of 1978*, New York: United Nations.

Lloyds Register FOBAS (2005) *Practical guidelines for handling Marpol 73/78, annex VI regulations 14 and 18*, London: Lloyds Register.

MDS Transmodal (2007) *Update of UK port demand forecasts to 2030*, Chester: MDS Transmodal.

NAO (National Audit Office) (2002) *Dealing with pollution from ships*, London: NAO.

Network Rail (2007) *Freight: Route utilisation strategy*, London: Network Rail.

Pinder, D. (1997) 'Deregulation policy and revitalization of Singapore's bunker supply industry: an appraisal', *Maritime Policy and Management*, 24(3), pp 219-31.

Pinder, D. and Witherick, M. (1990) 'Port industrialisation, urbanisation and wetland decline', in M. Williams (ed) *Wetlands: A threatened landscape*, Oxford: Blackwell, pp 234-66.

Pullen, S. (2004) 'Marine conservation and resource management', in H. Smith (ed) *The oceans: Key issues in marine affairs*, Dordrecht: Kluwer Academic, pp 199-214.

Saldanha, J. and Gray, R. (2002) 'The potential for coastal shipping in a multimodal chain', *Maritime Policy and Management*, 29, pp 77-92.

SRA (Strategic Rail Authority) (2001) *Freight strategy*, London: SRA.

Vidal, J. (2007) 'CO$_2$ output from shipping twice as much as airlines', *The Guardian*, 3 March.

Part Three
Ten years since *A new deal for transport* – signposts to the UK's transport future?

NINE

Transport for London: success despite Westminster?

Peter White

London has always differed in many respects from the rest of the UK. Not only is it the largest conurbation – matched only within Europe by Paris – but it has a far greater dependency on rail systems, and a high level of public transport use. Its economy differs substantially, notably through the major role played by financial and business services. While manufacturing was important in the past, it is now negligible, employment being dominated almost wholly by the service sector. In recent years, these differences have become more marked, with public transport usage growing substantially from an already high level of trips per capita. Car ownership rates have changed very little in 15 years despite significant economic growth. Per capita incomes are high, albeit varying very substantially within different parts of the capital. These differences have been accentuated by contrasts in policy measures, notably the high level of financial support for public transport, and the adoption of congestion charging.

In certain respects, London may be compared with the UK's other devolved territories (Scotland, Wales and Northern Ireland; Chapter Two). In particular, the directly elected Mayor exercises extensive powers, together with the role played by the Greater London Assembly (GLA). At the same time, however, its population of 7.5 million (TfL, 2007a) comfortably exceeds that of the largest other devolved territory – Scotland – and its Gross Domestic Product (GDP) exceeds that of Scotland and Wales combined. In 2006, its gross value added (GVA) comprised 17.4% of the UK total, compared with 8.1% for Scotland and 3.8% for Wales (the per capita figures being £26,192, £17,789 and £14,396 respectively – see National Statistics, 2007).[1] Its boundary is also very tightly drawn. Whereas Scotland, for example, encompasses a largely self-contained urban belt surrounded by extensive rural regions, the Greater London boundary is simply that of the former Greater London Council (GLC), not even encompassing the whole of the contiguous built-up area – it excludes significant settlements such as Watford and Epsom – while the commuter catchment extends much further into south east England. Hence, in areas of similar urban characteristics, very marked differences now exist in public transport services – bus service levels in particular – depending on whether or not a place falls within London's administrative area.

London might also be seen as a model for other major conurbations, which, at the time of writing (early 2008), may gain wider powers through proposals in the 2007 Local Transport Bill. Certainly Transport for London (TfL), an executive agency answerable to the Mayor, has made substantial progress in transforming London's transport system since it was established in 2000, but it has only been able to do so given strong political leadership and very large increases in public expenditure, on a level not matched elsewhere (Chapter Ten). The system is in some respects rather centralised, and there may be scope for giving greater discretion to transport operators and London boroughs in developing transport in the capital, while retaining the benefits of central coordination. Current policies – which by UK and some international standards are radical – could also be subject to sharp changes following the election of a new Mayor in 2008. There are, furthermore, urgent problems relating to the London Underground Public–Private Partnership (PPP), albeit this was policy introduced by central government against the wishes of the former Mayor.

This chapter aims to provide an account of recent developments in London, to consider their relevance to other regions, and also to examine the extent to which further change is desirable within London itself. In any analysis of London's recent transport performance it is first necessary to distinguish between factors that are exogenous and endogenous to the transport system and its supporting policies. For example, overall trends in population and the economy could be seen as exogenous, while factors such as fare levels, service frequency and congestion charging are endogenous. The distinction is not always clear cut, however: car ownership, for instance, is generally seen as an exogenous factor in respect of public transport system use, but its remarkable stability in London in recent years may be due in part to the comprehensive nature of this system, as well as constraints on car use and ownership imposed by limited parking space and road capacity. Equally, while population growth, and that of employment in Central London, could be seen as driven primarily by external economic factors, an adequate transport system is clearly a necessary (if not sufficient) condition for such growth to occur. In particular, the extensive development in Docklands, especially at Canary Wharf, has been dependent on transport links being provided, notably the Docklands Light Railway (DLR) prior to the development of the area.

Major developments under Transport for London

The early 1980s could be seen as a low point in the development of the public transport system in London. Demand for bus services had fallen broadly in line with that in the rest of Britain from a peak around 1950, associated with rising car ownership and changed consumption and activity patterns. Rail use had also fallen, both on the Underground and British Rail (BR); indeed, ridership on the Underground network reached its lowest point of 498 million in 1982 (TfL, 2007a). Overall population had declined, and a reduction in central area employment was deliberately encouraged as a decentralisation policy; traditional manufacturing activity had also fallen away sharply, together with activities such as the docks. This said, a number of positive developments had occurred, notably in rail network investment. Examples are the opening of the Victoria Line in 1968 and the electrification of suburban services north of the capital in the 1970s and early 1980s. The first phase of the DLR opened in 1987, serving at first very modest passenger flows (and not justified on traditional economic evaluation criteria) but providing a base for more extensive development; this system alone now carries 61 million passengers per year (TfL, 2007a). Free bus travel for pensioners had also applied from the early 1970s, increasing ridership as a result. Retention of a centralised system did enable some network-wide marketing initiatives to be adopted more easily, such as the (paid) bus pass for regular users.

The trend towards reduced employment in the central area began to reverse in the early 1980s on account of strong growth in certain service industry sectors – notably tourism and financial and business services – that offset some continued decline elsewhere (Evans and Crampton, 1989). The fare structure of the bus and underground networks was also greatly simplified by the introduction of the Travelcard and the associated zonal system. This followed the GLC's 'Fare's Fair' initiative in 1982 to heavily subsidise the cost of bus and underground travel, and although this had to be abandoned after a successful legal challenge from Bromley Council on the grounds that its residents were paying extra towards the running of a system (that is, the Underground) that did not run through their borough, the zonal structure remained intact even after fares were forced to rise. The Travelcard structure was later extended to the BR system, albeit only for period tickets, while a very complex structure remained for other fare types. In combination, growth in the economy, central area employment, and the stimulus through simplified pricing structures resulted in a substantial growth in rail use during the 1980s, reaching a peak around 1989, such that congestion on the network became significant. Bus use fluctuated, but remained much more stable than in the other conurbations affected by deregulation and sharp reductions in subsidy from 1986 (Chapter Five).

The dispute over Fares Fair, although legally between the GLC and a London borough, epitomised the nature of relations between the GLC and the Conservative UK government at Westminster. The latter would ultimately abolish the former – which left Greater London without a unified governance structure until the creation of the GLA in 2000 – but in a precursor move wrested control of London Transport from the GLC under the 1984 London Regional Transport Act. Control of the new London Regional Transport (LRT) passed to a management board appointed directly by central government at Westminster. While making few changes to the management of the Underground, the LRT board pursued a policy of gradually opening the bus network to competitive tendering, commencing with services in the outer suburbs. This contrasted with the much more dramatic deregulation of services elsewhere from 1986 and initially produced lower average unit cost savings, but it did allow the benefits of a coordinated network and fare structure to be retained. The London boroughs continued as locally accountable democratic institutions, but with limited functions, especially in respect of public transport.

A recession in the early 1990s reversed some of the growth in rail use, although also reducing peak congestion as a result. Within BR a shift from the previous regional structure to management based on three main passenger sectors enabled a more comprehensive view of the London commuter market to be taken (although there was never much coordination in investment policy between BR and the Underground). Network South East covered the whole region within and around London, and scope was realised for the reopening of the Farringdon–Blackfriars tunnel to create the 'Thameslink' cross-London service. Network South East did not survive the sale of BR, however, and a somewhat short-term approach to investment was adopted post privatisation, especially in the cutbacks to planned peak capacity growth on routes to the south east of London. Those bus operations remaining in the public sector were privatised by selling off directly LRT's subsidiary companies. Initially, a number passed to management buy-outs, but, as in the rest of Britain, came to be owned by larger groups (Chapter Five). By then considerable changes in working conditions and pay had enabled reduction in unit bus operating costs, in addition to savings resulting from tendering of specific routes. In consequence, a point was reached in 1999/2000 where the bus network operated with virtually no subsidy apart from compensation for concessionary fares.

Notwithstanding the setbacks of Fares Fair and the loss of democratic accountability and strategic rail planning potential, by the mid-1990s a much more positive picture in public transport was evident than at the start of the 1980s. Bus use had held up far better than in other conurbations, while unit costs per bus kilometre were being reduced by a similar percentage, and the Travelcard had encouraged greater use of public transport, notably for off-peak periods. In respect of the road system, an approach has developed from the 1970s of allocating space more effectively, notably in expansion of the bus priority network. Major construction of urban motorways had been abandoned in the early 1970s, and public reaction to corridor studies around 1990 indicated little support for substantial new construction. Car use was constrained mainly by parking policy and while some new road schemes were built, notably the Hayes bypass in west London, little growth in capacity occurred.

Transport for London under Transport for London

The 1999 Greater London Authority Act created the GLA and the post of a directly elected Mayor with extensive powers, especially in the fields of transport and land-use planning, and established TfL. The latter took over not only the role of LRT but also assumed a wider range of functions such as managing the principal road network, taxi and private hire vehicle and driver licensing, and river services. In contrast to the deregulated environment elsewhere in Britain, TfL has responsibility for providing the vast majority of scheduled local bus services within

Greater London, and also acts as the regulatory body in granting permission for other operators to run services within, or to and from, the capital through London Service Permits (LSPs). It subsequently took control of the Underground after complex PPP deals to fund significant upgrades to the system were signed (see below). The road network under control of TfL comprises some 580 kilometres, principally the major radial 'A' roads and some orbital routes, as compared to the total London road network of 14,926 kilometres (TfL 2007a). It is worth noting that this new structure did not arise in a vacuum: the continued role of planning and research functions within LRT provided a base of expertise, together with statistical and data analysis functions that had continued through collaborative arrangements since the demise of the GLC. In other words, TfL was well equipped with an existing skills base – albeit one on which it built considerably – as it sought to develop and apply new policies.

Transport for London is unique in terms of its funding settlement from central government. Whereas the Treasury's Comprehensive Spending Review process, which allocates money to the devolved territories and Whitehall departments, operates over a three-year cycle, TfL was awarded a five-year settlement in 2004. This 'settlement was announced ahead of other transport spending review allocations in order to meet the timetable required for London's Olympic bid … [and] will allow TfL to make a step change in its approach to investment in London's transport infrastructure' (DfT, 2004, para 5). As a result, TfL was able to publish a financially balanced five-year business plan consisting of a £22 billion operating plan and a £10 billion capital investment programme (see TfL, 2005). The importance of this innovation was not only that it transformed the level of certainty with which TfL was able to plan for the longer term – the Department for Transport (DfT) even recognised this, noting that 'planning and investment in transport infrastructure is a long term business and this settlement has allowed TfL to plan and prioritise its investment priorities for the rest of the decade with certainty about government funding level' (DfT, 2004, para 3) – but also that it acknowledged the substantial degree of trust that government had developed in TfL's capacity to deliver (MacKinnon et al, 2008).

The establishment of the GLA also involved recreating a two-tier structure of elected government within London. The 33 London boroughs (including the City of London Corporation) continue to be responsible for the great majority of the road network, together with parking policy determination and enforcement. This can result in some conflict with TfL policy, notably over bus priority measures. Through their joint body – London Councils (formerly the Association of London Government) – the London boroughs are responsible for funding the concessionary fares scheme for older and disabled public transport users. In contrast to the Local Transport Plans (LTPs) applicable outside London (Chapter Two), somewhat simpler Local Implementation Plans (LIPs) are prepared by each borough. Local Implementation Plan funding is very much dependent on TfL, and the sums of money involved are relatively modest in contrast to the spending undertaken by TfL directly, especially within the public transport sector.

Since assuming its powers in 2000, TfL has developed a radical suite of new policies aimed at improving the transport experience in the capital. Indeed, Ken Livingstone made transport his 'number one priority' in his Mayoral campaign and continued to pursue an approach – articulated in *The Mayor's transport strategy* (GLA, 2001) – based on managing demand for congested roadspace and significantly enhancing public transport services and walking/cycling experiences. As TfL Commissioner Peter Hendy likes to point out, London is in fact the only jurisdiction in the UK to have met the aspirations of *A new deal for transport: Better for everyone* (DETR, 1998). The remainder of this chapter reviews progress in three key policy areas, two of which – bus transport and the congestion charge – TfL has been responsible for driving forward. These are generally (although not unanimously) regarded as having been successful. The third, the Underground PPP – a complex means of procuring an upgrade to the system over the coming 30 years – was designed and pursued by central government against the wishes of TfL, and has produced sharply differing outcomes from the two companies awarded 'infraco' contracts, with ramifications for future transport investment in London and beyond.

Soaring bus use

Although the demise of the open rear platform 'Routemaster' type of bus (by then a very small proportion of all operations in any case) in December 2005 received enormous press coverage, and more recently a dislike of 'bendy buses' (that is, articulated vehicles) has become fashionable, there has been a story of quite remarkable growth in bus provision and use in the capital. Much of this can be seen as a direct consequence of policy measures applied in London itself, on a scale and a type not possible elsewhere in the UK (see White, 2007).

Total passenger stages rose from 1,296 million in 1999/2000 to 1,880 million in 2006/07, a rise of 584 million, or 45% (TfL, 2007a).[2] This growth in fact offset an aggregate decline in the same period in the rest of Britain (DfT, 2007), and thus the aggregate net growth witnessed nationally was almost entirely attributable to London. The most noticeable difference between London and elsewhere in the country was with the other large conurbations (White, 2008), while a number of smaller centres have displayed substantial growth and the introduction of free travel for all pensioners throughout England from April 2006 undoubtedly explains much of the growth outside the main urban areas in the most recent year (Chapter Five). As already noted, in London free travel for pensioners and disabled people has applied for many years, and as such is not a factor in recent change.

The strongest explanatory factor for the large growth in patronage is the number of bus kilometres run, which increased from 348 million in 1999/2000 to 458 million in 2006/07 (TfL, 2007a), a difference of 28%. This contrasts with a general decline elsewhere in England and Wales during the same period, notably in the Passenger Transport Executive (PTE) areas (there was no decrease in Scotland). An increase in bus kilometres run typically represents a proportionate increase in service frequency, but it is also noticeable that many services have been substantially improved during evenings and/or Sundays (in some cases where journeys were not previously offered at such times), and all-night operation has been greatly expanded. Many trunk radial routes and a number of major inter-suburban routes now offer a 24-hour service. Thus the increase in bus kilometres in London has greatly widened the range of travel opportunities, consistent with more flexible working patterns, the growth in Sunday shopping and so on. Conversely, in deregulated areas, services are often good in the daytime on Mondays to Saturdays, but very poor at other times.

The other usually quantified endogenous factor is the real fare level. This may be influenced by operators' commercial decisions or, as in London, by those of controlling authorities. An index of changes in real terms is produced by the DfT (bus fares across the country have generally risen – Chapter Five). As the proportion of off-bus ticketing has increased, the traditional cash fare is a less reliable indicator of real fare levels than before; indeed, in London, such payment is no longer permitted within most of the central area, and even outside is very limited, comprising only about 4% of all passenger boardings. A weighted average of the cost to the user of all bus trips is a better guide, therefore, and between 1999/2000 and 2005/06 the average revenue per passenger trip fell by about 9.8% (the extension of free travel to children towards the end of the period is probably a major factor in the reduction in average revenue per trip).

It is possible to estimate the expected change in patronage from alterations in bus kilometres and fares levels by applying established demand elasticities.[3] A typical 'short-run' – that is, one year – elasticity of +0.4 in response to the increase of bus kilometres run (Balcombe et al, 2004) would produce a ridership growth of about 11%, and this figure increases to around 16% if a higher, medium-run elasticity of +0.55 is applied (reflecting the six-year period over which change has been assessed). In respect of price, an elasticity of –0.4 would indicate that a net passenger growth of about 4% can be explained by the drop in real terms fare levels. A higher medium-term elasticity of –0.55 can also be applied (White, 2007) to produce a slightly higher expected growth. What becomes clear from these calculations is that the *expected* increase in patronage from the combination of increased bus kilometres and real fares reductions – around 22% – is only around half of the 45% *actual* growth. A number of other factors are thus contributing to the increase in bus patronage being experienced in London. Key among these are:

- *The adoption of a completely low-floor fleet by the end of 2005.* Typically, such conversion produces a ridership growth of about 5% due primarily to additional off-peak use by shoppers with trolleys and parents with small children in buggies.
- *Implementation of the congestion charge* (see below). This caused dramatic growth at the charging cordon itself, the bus share of the inward morning peak flow by all modes rising from 6.6% in autumn 2000 to 10.4% two years later. Rail

actually remains dominant in this role – a share of 78.2% in autumn 2006 (TfL, 2007a) – and most bus use is wholly outside the central area, where in turn most growth has occurred. As a proportion of the overall growth in bus use over the period 1999/2000 to 2005/06, the contribution from this source was modest, at around 6%. Furthermore, the expansion of bus services coincident with implementation of the charge (reflected in the growth in bus kilometres) has already been accounted for through its contribution to the ridership growth mentioned above, although, having said this, substantial ridership growth on buses within the charging area may well have occurred anyway due to improvements in reliability and speed in addition to changes measured at the cordon itself. Wiseall (2007) shows that very marked improvements occurred in reliability (measured through the 'excess waiting time' indicator) on routes within the charging area.

- *The high proportion of off-bus ticketing.* This results in very low marginal boarding times – around 2.0 to 2.5 seconds per passenger for routes where all users are required to pass the driver and some passengers still pay in cash, and around one second per passenger on 'bendy buses' where parallel boarding through three doorways is permitted (Lizon, 2004). The effects of such low boarding times are lower dwell times at stops (which speeds up services) and greater reliability (because less variability in running time occurs).

- *Better provision of passenger information.* A comprehensively-planned network makes it easier to provide updated information, evident for example in much better displays at stops and real-time displays.

In addition, there are identifiable exogenous and other factors in observed bus use growth:

- *London's population is growing.* Between 2001 and 2006 the number of residents in London rose from 7.32 million to 7.52 million (about 2.6%) (TfL, 2007a) and this trend is projected to continue. This would be expected to produce an approximately pro rata growth in transport demand for all modes. It is also possible that bus use has been further stimulated by the nature of the incomers, if they have low car ownership levels.

- *Stable car ownership rates.* Growth in car ownership is undoubtedly a major factor in declining bus use in Britain as a whole, especially when a no-car household becomes a one-car household (Balcombe et al, 2004). A striking feature of London is that per capita car ownership has changed very little in recent years, rising from 0.324 in 1996 to 0.330 in 2006 (derived from TfL, 2007a), a growth of only 1.8%. In contrast, the total number of cars licensed nationally rose by 13% between 1999 and 2004. Another notable feature is the low proportion of households with two or more cars in London – 17% in 2005/06 compared with 32% nationally (TfL, 2007a). Car ownership is generally seen as being determined by factors such as real incomes, but it may also be influenced by running costs and availability of parking. London may also be an example of a city in which the high level of available public transport acts as a discouragement to additional car purchase.

Thus, although the most obvious explanatory factors such as the increase in bus kilometres run and real fares levels clearly explain about half[4] of the observed growth in London since 2000, a substantial 'unexplained' element remains (the stability in car ownership represents the absence of a negative factor, rather than a positive factor in its own right). Still further factors to those outlined above are likely to include: the extensive provision of bus priorities, aided by red routes (for all traffic types), which assists both speed and reliability; and the comprehensive nature of the Travelcard and other off-bus ticket types that enables most interchange to take place without financial penalty. A noticeable feature in London is the high ratio of bus-to-bus interchange (which may itself result in some exaggeration of per capita trip rates when bus boardings per head are the indicator); in addition to enabling trips to be made where a through bus route would not be feasible, passengers are also able to optimise their journeys by taking the first bus to arrive, then interchanging en route rather than waiting for a less frequent through service.

An issue sometimes raised is the extent to which capacity constraints on the Underground resulted in some of the bus growth simply being a continuation of overall growth that would have occurred on the public transport system as a whole. There is some truth in this: as indicated above, the net diversion to bus following the congestion charge was associated with expansion of services in and around the central area. It should be borne in mind, however, that the great majority of bus trips do not involve the central area at all, and within the suburbs only a few sections apply where bus and Underground are direct substitutes. For example, in 2001/02, 78% of all bus trips did not involve Zone 1 (TfL, 2002) while in 2006/07 the percentage was 77% (TfL, 2007a). These were equivalent to about 1,115 million and 1,445 million trips respectively. Hence, of the net growth in trips of 450 million over that period, about 330 million (about 73%) occurred wholly outside Zone 1.

Before moving on to discuss other transport policies in London, it is worth noting that a net revenue loss normally occurs when changes to bus services occur 'across the board'. For example, a 10% service level increase would generally be expected to increase total costs pro rata, while revenue would rise by only 4 to 5.5%. A substantial increase in public funding is thus required to fund the better service, and in London this has been possible because the Mayor chose to use his financial powers accordingly. This said, because the network is planned as a whole, it is possible to optimise the allocation of additional resources. Outside London, by contrast, authorities' powers are limited largely to purchasing tendered services to augment the core commercial network (Chapter Five), and this can make it difficult to maximise the impact of service improvements.

It is questionable whether the position attained by 1999, where the bus network operated with very little subsidy beyond concessionary fares reimbursements, would have been sustainable owing to increasingly tight labour market conditions and concerns about service quality. Nevertheless, the improvements outlined above will have contributed significantly to a real terms increase in net operating costs per bus kilometre of 26% between 1999/2000 and 2005/06 (another factor is the specification by TfL of new buses in many contracts, aiding rapid conversion to low-floor layout, but increasing costs borne by operators). Total operating costs actually rose by about 70% whereas revenue rose by slightly less than patronage (due to the drop in real revenue per trip), leading to the amount of subsidy being required rising to about £640 million. Such a level of subsidy in proportion to farebox revenues is not untypical of that found in Europe as a whole, but very much higher than in the rest of Britain. The use of competitive tendering for bus service provision would be expected to keep costs down, but in a tight labour market all operators will be affected by the need to improve wages. In addition, the degree of competition between potential operators may have been limited by the difficulty faced by newcomers in securing sites for operating bases, since existing depots were sold off with the London Buses' subsidiaries when they were privatised in the early 1990s. One lesson here is for the government to retain the freehold on bus garages; another, and one far more significant, is that if Westminster (or Holyrood, Cardiff Bay and Stormont) politicians require very high-quality bus services, they must be willing to pay considerably more for them than is currently the case throughout most of the UK.

Congestion charging

The implementation of 'congestion charging' (a term that has been used in London in preference to 'road pricing') is perhaps the strongest example of powers being used in London, which have yet to be applied elsewhere in the UK. The discretion to introduce congestion charging is only one element of the equation, however; the local determination to actually apply it is quite another. Although a separate referendum has not been held on the subject (unlike Edinburgh, where similar proposals were defeated – see Gaunt et al, 2007), Ken Livingstone made clear in his Mayoral manifesto that such charging would be implemented. It is also noteworthy that while the 1999 Greater London Authority Act granted the necessary powers to introduce road pricing, central government support for such a policy in general has often been fluctuating, or lukewarm, in response to generally hostile public and press opinion (Chapter Three); indeed, Labour ministers quite openly opposed Livingstone's plans. Notwithstanding arguably unique governmental and geographical factors in his favour (Chapter One), there should be no doubt that applying this policy in London required significant political courage on the part of the former Mayor.

The economic case for road pricing has been established over many years. Essentially, more vehicles on a stretch of road can cause the traffic flow to be slowed down. While the utility of a journey to drivers in congested conditions may still exceed the cost (in terms of fuel, running costs, time and so on) to these drivers of making it in the first place, their decisions to make that journey do not take into account the delays imposed on other traffic. The idea behind a congestion charge is to reflect the resultant 'marginal social cost' of making a given journey, in an effort to ensure that additional vehicles will only join the traffic flow where the benefits their users derive exceed the total cost incurred. It is not the aim of such charges to wholly remove congestion from the roads – that is, to produce speeds associated with 'free flow' conditions – but to produce an 'optimal' outcome where journeys in private cars that are not worth the marginal social cost reflected in a charge imposed, are either not made at all or are made by a different mode of transport. In practice, across a whole network it is delays at junctions that produce much of the delay experienced by road users, and an area-wide pricing scheme enables these to be reduced substantially. Thus, in quantifying benefits it is important to look not only at changes in average speeds, but also those in journey time variability. While these are of benefit to all road users, they especially help those operating scheduled services (such as buses) or running throughout the day and making a series of successive trips (for example, taxis or goods deliveries). In such cases, direct financial benefits to operators – such as using fewer buses and drivers to offer a given service level – may be evaluated, as well as user time savings.

A limitation of area-wide schemes is the technology available, especially in a large city such as London in which many road vehicles are used only occasionally to visit the central area (or, indeed, originate from areas or countries well outside the city itself). In the absence of standard national technology, the fitting of on-board units (as in Singapore) may be impracticable, and indeed in London Automated Number Plate Recognition – in which a digitised image is produced of each number plate – has been installed. Automated Number Plate Recognition allows the comparison of those number plates photographed going through the cordon with registers of exempt vehicles and those for which payment has been made, to ensure compliance. Offenders are then identified and penalty charges applied. Such technology is, however, very costly to operate and, as we shall see, absorbs a substantial part of the revenue obtained.

The London congestion charging scheme was introduced in February 2003, covering the whole of the City, an area to the south of the River Thames, and much of the West End. At first the western boundary was drawn very tightly, along Edgware Road, Park Lane and Vauxhall Bridge Road, excluding parts of the West End and important shopping areas such as those in Kensington. A charge of £5 per vehicle per day was levied, irrespective of the number of times the cordon was crossed. Various vehicle types were exempted, such as buses and emergency vehicles, and discounts of 90% were given for residents with cars based within the zone. From February 2007, the original scheme was extended substantially westward, to a boundary following the Earls Court Road and the West Cross Route, encompassing not only the rest of the West End but also substantial residential areas (Figure 9.1).

Figure 9.1: The London congestion charge area, including the western extension

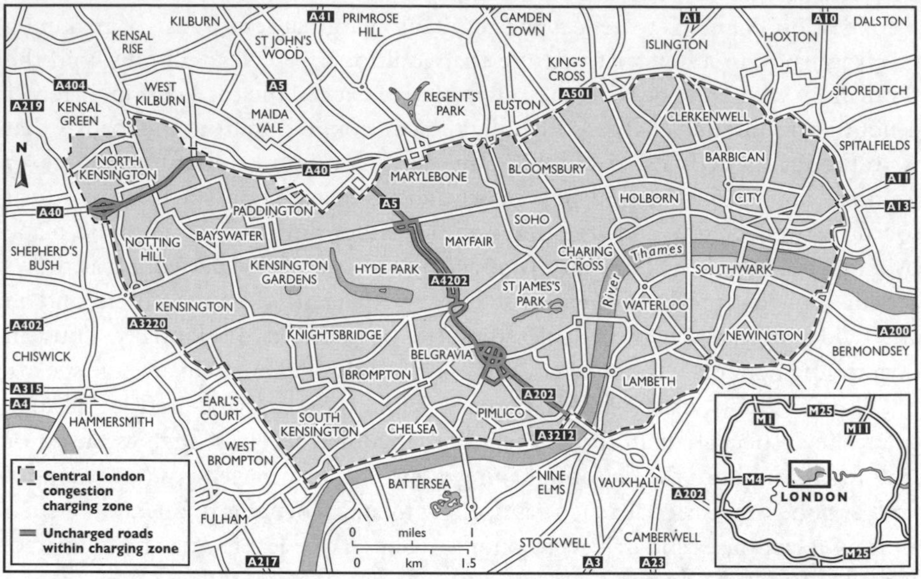

Source: Adapted from MacKinnon et al (2008)

Impacts have been monitored regularly by TfL, available through reports placed on its website (TfL 2007b). In addition a number of commentators have assessed the economic implications of the charging scheme. (With regard to its political implications, Livingstone was re-elected after the introduction of the scheme, and in this sense its successful implementation demonstrates that such charging schemes are operationally feasible, and can be accepted by the majority of the population.) Following introduction of the congestion charge in February 2003, car traffic fell by 33%, substantially more than anticipated, producing an overall reduction in traffic volumes of 15% (TfL, 2007b). This in turn produced considerable benefits through improvements in average speeds and reduced travel time variability. The larger than expected traffic reduction resulted in less revenue being generated than forecast, however, and an increase in the charge to £8 from July 2005 produced little further impact on traffic volumes, thus increasing net revenue obtained.

The high cost of collection results in a relatively small net financial surplus being produced – approximately £120 million in 2006/07. This only covers about one-fifth of the net support to bus services, for example, and thus a policy based on the ability of revenues from congestion charging to cover costs of greatly expanded bus services may be of limited effect.[5] It is noteworthy that some reduction in car travel into Central London in the morning peak (a three-hour period from 7am to 10am) had already been observed prior to the introduction of congestion charging, from 135,000 occupants in autumn 1999 to 105,000 three years later. Following the introduction of charging, this fell further to 86,000 in autumn 2003, with another slight fall to 78,000 in 2006. Average car occupancy has varied little, changing from 1.36 in 1999 to 1.38 in 2005 (TfL, 2007a). It can thus be debated whether the net reduction observed was wholly attributable to charging or whether it at least in part represented a continuation of an existing trend associated with policy measures such as parking controls, although economic evaluations of the effects of congestion charging generally attribute the whole net reduction to new intervention. In terms of car and minicab traffic entering the zone during the whole period of charging hours (7am to 6.30pm) the reduction was more marked in the early phases, from about 200,000 in spring 2002 to about 130,000 in February/March 2003, and remaining at a similar level subsequently (TfL, 2007b).

An evaluation of effects by Prud'homme and Bocarejo (2005) suggested that congestion costs had been largely eliminated by the charge. They noted that charge proceeds were about three times greater than the value of congestion, but the yearly amortisation and operational costs of the charging system appeared to be significantly higher than the economic benefit produced. While an operational success, the outcome in terms of net economic benefits was questionable. In response, Mackie (2005) suggested that a wider range of benefits could be considered, referring to TfL's evaluation, which produced a benefit–cost ratio (BCR) of 1.3. A subsequent further study (Evans, 2007) examined the outcome after the £8 charge was introduced, but before the western extension. Including benefits of reliability and time savings to road users, accidents and pollution, but offset by other impacts on road users and system operating costs, Evans estimated a BCR of 1.5 with a £5 charge and up to 1.7 with an £8 charge. A 'London weighting' of 1.385 was applied to values of time, based on higher earnings in the London area.

The closest parallel with London is the cordon pricing scheme in Stockholm, first introduced experimentally in 2006 and then on a long-term basis from August 2007. A lower charge than in London, and varying significantly by time period, was applied. The reduction in total traffic in the experimental phase was about 22%, although car traffic as such fell by less than in London. Broadly similar effects in traffic speed were observed and, again like London, the scheme incurred a large operating cost in relation to revenue. The London case thus presents an example where the operational and user benefits of charging have been demonstrated, but a somewhat crude system based on a flat rate per vehicle per day and a high cost of collection are found. A shift towards more sophisticated charging technology will, hopefully, enable costs of collection to be reduced, and greater variability by time period.[6]

Railways and the Public–Private Partnership

The rail system in London is primarily geared to serving the central area through a network of radial links. The Underground tends to serve this function to the north and west of the central area, surface railways (the privatised Train Operating Companies; TOCs) to the south and east, primarily for historical reasons. In addition, the Underground provides an intensive network within the central area.

Contrasting with the roles of bus and car, rail use is far more strongly focused on the central area journey-to-work market and hence fluctuates with its volume. Operators do, however, have a strong incentive to increase off-peak traffic, which incurs low marginal costs.

Unlike with buses and the road system, the influence of TfL and the Mayor has been limited with respect to rail transport. Franchises for TOCs have been let by the DfT and the transfer of infrastructure provision for the Underground to the private sector by way of a PPP scheme was, as we have seen, very much driven by central government against the wishes of the former Mayor and TfL. In general, historic service patterns have been maintained in respect of local services within London and relatively little innovation has occurred, although in November 2007 a significant change took place. TfL became the franchising body for 'London Overground' (primarily the North and West London lines, previously run by Silverlink), and immediately began upgrading the service. New trains are now on order and the Overground concept is being extended through the incorporation of the East London line with the goal of creating an orbital rail service to serve Inner London (Figure 9.2). Note that the section in the east between Dalston and Queen's Road Peckham, New Cross, and New Cross Gate is currently being rebuilt, incorporating the East London Line of the Underground. When complete, trains will then run through, over existing infrastructure, to Clapham Junction, Crystal Palace, West Croydon and New Cross.

The London Underground was somewhat unusual among urban rail systems in covering all of its direct operating costs until relatively recently (2000/01) (Knowles and White, 2003). Thereafter, operating costs, notably labour, rose rapidly, while revenue increased little, given modest traffic growth in part constrained by peak capacity. Total revenue rose from £1,256 million in 1999/2000 (at 2006/07 prices) to £1,417 million in 2006/07, or by 12.8%. Passenger trips grew from 927 million to 1,040 million over the same period, by 12.2%, implying very little change in real revenue per trip (DfT, 2007). The Underground and DLR volume in the three-hour morning peak grew more modestly from 564,000 in autumn 1999 to 591,000 in autumn 2006 (TfL, 2007a), by 4.8%, constrained by available capacity.

London has been the main UK recipient of new transport infrastructure in the last decade, notably the Jubilee Line extension (JLE), with substantial impacts on economic and social activity in the areas served (Jones et al, 2004). An economic evaluation of the JLE (Colin Buchanan and Partners, 2007) indicates a BCR of 1.75 (an encouraging figure, given that there was a very large cost overrun). Because of its age, however, much of the investment in the Underground is in renewal of the existing system. This creates opportunities for enhancing capacity – for example through resignalling to permit closer headways, new trains with higher performance, and station works to improve passenger flow – and TfL estimates that between 2006 and 2025 peak capacity into Central London on the existing network could be raised by 28.5% through measures forming part of the PPP. At the level of individual lines, this typically takes a 'step' form, as

Figure 9.2: The London 'Overground' network

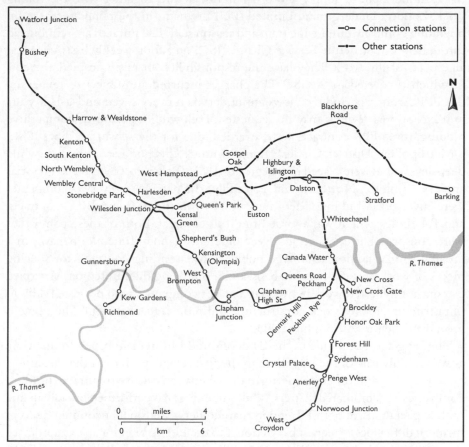

Source: Adapted from MacKinnon et al (2008)

fleet renewal and associated infrastructure work take place within a short period (TfL, 2006).

Strategies such as the PPP offer the scope for a much longer-term approach to investment than the previous year-to-year financing, enabling more efficient scheduling of work to be done (Knowles and White, 2003). A whole-life costing approach can be adopted in which optimal trade-offs are made between initial specification of work and long-run maintenance costs. New companies may bring innovative methods of working in a very traditional engineering sector. On the other hand, the high costs of capital for the private sector – both in interest rates for borrowing and investors' expectations for equity capital returns – can push up total costs, unless offsetting efficiency gains are attained. These gains, it should be noted, are substantial given estimates that net savings of about 20% in the direct costs of undertaking a given volume of work would be necessary in order to offset higher financing costs.

Under the PPP, 30-year contracts were given to infrastructure companies ('infracos'), which would assume responsibility for maintenance and renewal of track, tunnels, power supply and other infrastructure, together with the rolling stock. London Underground Limited (LUL) remains in the public sector as an operating company, employing train and station staff. The infracos are reimbursed through an Infrastructure Service Charge (ISC) on a four-weekly basis, covering all aspects of this work. They have the responsibility for raising capital, the cost of which is covered in the ISC. The charges incurred are subject to review by the PPP Arbiter; periodic reviews are undertaken every seven-and-a-half years but exceptional reviews may be requested. Following a period of competitive bidding, three PPP contracts were awarded, one for the subsurface lines (SSL) – Metropolitan, District, Circle, Hammersmith & City and East London – while deep-level tubes were placed in two groups: BCV (Bakerloo, Central and Victoria) and JNP (Jubilee, Northern and Piccadilly). In practice, only two companies were involved in bidding: Metronet, which won the SSL and BCV contracts, and TubeLines, which was awarded the JNP contract. Both of these companies were consortia but operated in a very different manner. Tubelines behaves in a broadly similar fashion to a large public body, awarding contracts for specific pieces of work on a competitive basis, and monitoring their outcome. Metronet, by contrast, allocated work between its partner companies who possessed skills in infrastructure, rolling stock construction and project management. The infracos took over their roles from July 2003.

The long-term outcome of the Underground PPP remains open to question, as we are only part of the way through the first review period. In the meantime, however, the difference in performance between the two infraco holding companies has dominated matters. While TubeLines has performed broadly in line with expectations, of both TfL and its shareholders, Metronet encountered severe financial difficulties. A request by Metronet to the PPP Arbiter for an extraordinary review of its 'underlying' ISC of £22.1 million per four weeks led to an award of a higher ISC from January 2008, but of a volume and timescale insufficient to meet the company's needs (PPP Arbiter, 2007); the company went into administration in July 2007 with large debts. In April 2008 the PPP administrators confirmed that they had reached agreement to transfer Metronet's business to TfL (Metronet, 2008). Because TubeLines is still able to honour its contract, a comparator will continue to be available. In the midst of all of this it is worth mentioning that there are also concerns about the performance of LUL itself, particularly in relation to passenger service quality and unit operating costs. Whereas substantial penalty and incentive payments are applied to the infracos, LUL is not subject to the type of regime applicable to the private TOCs on national rail in respect of passenger service quality, as examined by Walton (2007).

Total operating costs – including depreciation, renewals and severance – for the Underground system at 2005/06 prices rose from £1,502 million in 1999/2000 to £2,176 million in 2002/03 (an increase in cost per train kilometre rising from £24 to £33 in real terms – DfT, 2006). More recent data indicate that operating costs (including PPP payments, which now comprise about 34% of all costs) were £2,230 million in 2006/07, or about £2,150 million at 2005/06 prices, thus possibly falling slightly in real terms since 2002/03 (*Transit*, 2007), albeit some elements of depreciation and renewals may not be defined consistently. In 2006/07, at 2005/06 price levels, the cost per train kilometre was about £31, although it was towards the end of this period that Metronet was unable to stay in business at the level of PPP payment it then received and this figure is highly likely to rise given the high levels of funding that have had to be injected into Metronet to sustain its activities. Whereas in 1999/2000, revenue (principally from passengers) covered about 93% of all costs (derived from DfT, 2006), by 2006/07 this had fallen to about 62% (derived from *Transit*, 2007). Although the quality of the Underground will surely increase as a result of such additional expenditure, the principal lesson might not be the same as that which arose from a similar change in the ratio of farebox revenue to public support in the bus sector. Whereas London's better bus services are broadly a result of TfL getting what it pays for, here it may well be that good money is being thrown after bad to support an overly ambitious scheme of public private financing that would have been better avoided.

Some concluding observations

Recent experience in London clearly offers examples of where the devolution of power to the GLA and the Mayor has enabled radical changes to occur on a scale not seen elsewhere in the UK. These have provided benefits for London, and offer examples that may in certain circumstances apply in other regions. Notable instances include the successful implementation of congestion charging, and measures that have resulted in a rapid rise in bus provision and use. Some of the most serious short-run problems have arisen in relation to the Underground PPP which was a Gordon Brown, rather than a mayoral, initiative.

The pro-bus and congestion charging policies fall into a wider framework within London, in which a general encouragement has also been given to modes other than the car, promoting more efficient use of energy and a more socially inclusive pattern of travel. This includes measures to promote walking and cycling. While such trips are generally very short, and hence could be seen as influenced by policies mainly at the borough level, TfL has pursued initiatives to introduce more extensive cycling priorities on roads which it controls, and to improve pedestrian conditions in the central area, such as the redesign of Trafalgar Square. The City of London Corporation has also made notable efforts to improve walking and especially cycling conditions within its area. While the 'ring of steel' was introduced some years ago primarily for security reasons, the reduction in vehicle traffic thus produced has enabled more space to be allocated to other modes.

TfL's efforts and those of others such as the City of London Corporation are paying off not only in achieving higher patronage of individual public transport modes, but also the sense that they can be seen to be promoting modal shift. Estimates of the daily average number of journey stages by TfL (2007a) show a 7% increase in the total, from 25.8 million in 2001 to 27.6 million in 2006. This is in part explained by population growth of nearly 3% over the same period. The bus and tram total grew from 3.9 to 5.2 million, but in contrast car stages fell marginally from 11.0 to 10.9 million (and thus from 41.6% to 39.5% of all stages). A striking growth has occurred in cycling, associated with supporting policy measures, increasing by about 17% per year from 2003 onwards, after stability over the previous 10 years (Steer Davies Gleave, 2008).

One interesting question is the extent to which current trends in London may continue. Forecast population growth, from 7.5 million in 2005 to 8.3 million in 2025, and associated economic growth, will create a further growth in demand for transport (TfL, 2006) – and concomitant growth in congestion on both public transport and the road system. There is strong evidence for agglomeration economies – a greater output per head – in areas such as the City of London, leading to a continued emphasis on physical concentration of activity in sectors such as finance and business services (Ormerod et al, 2006). This can also be seen in the continued rapid growth of employment at Canary Wharf, which, while a new location of such activity, is in many respects a 'traditional' form of city-centre employment.

Of obvious significance, therefore, is the question of possible substitution for travel by changes such as teleworking from home. As yet, however, its likely impacts appear limited. A recent review indicates that much teleworking is of an informal, part-time nature – typically one or two days a week working at home, not the full-time displacement sometimes advocated. In London and the south east about 7.5% of the labour force work from home at least once a week, representing about 3.5% of all days worked (White et al, 2007). This seems to be increasing, but only slowly. Greater impacts may emerge from home-based travel planning initiatives, but the extent to which peak demand is reduced or shifted will clearly be critical in terms of system capacity.

The extent to which the London experience may be transferable to elsewhere in the UK will depend partly on underlying economic and population trends, not to mention governance arrangements and the existence of determined political leadership. These, along with the stability in per capita car ownership witnessed in London, may be largely exceptional, yet the operational feasibility of road pricing is clear. What may be required is a policy framework elsewhere in which substantial improvements to public transport can be made prior to its introduction, which can be difficult under deregulated bus systems, and limited investment in rail networks. The bus experience in London suggests substantial benefits from coordinated network provision, comprehensive information and off-bus ticketing – and these might be achieved more easily through quality contracts, more comprehensive quality partnerships, or at least the less rigid interpretation of competition law: the current Local Transport Bill may assist in this respect (Chapter Five).

In finishing, it should be pointed out that there may also be some questions about the structure within London itself. The very strong powers given directly to the Mayor enable radical policy changes to be made (notably the introduction of road pricing) but also can result in abrupt changes when an election occurs. Direct mayoral powers over public transport fares, rather than their determination by the TfL board, could also be questioned. Londoners have clearly benefited from improved bus services, but at some point there is likely to be concern about the high unit operating costs (even taking into account the nature of the local labour market) of both buses and the Underground. A high proportion of congestion charging revenue is also taken up by operating costs. The restrictive nature of the Greater London boundary creates some difficulties – for example, greater powers over TOCs on the national rail system in the London area have been given to the Mayor, but authorities in adjoining regions also wish to influence the services they receive. Finally, the comprehensive Travelcard system applies only within the GLA boundary, and does not cover adjoining areas of a very similar nature, in contrast to the wider coverage of, for example, the *Carte Orange* in the Paris region.

Notes

[1] Gross value added measures 'the contribution to the economy of each individual producer, industry or sector in the United Kingdom.... GVA is used in the estimation of Gross Domestic product' (National Statistics, 2008, unpaginated). Note that the GVA figures given here are based on residential location.

[2] These figures may be revised upwards in future years given the better data on ridership now available through the 'Oyster' smartcard system. Note that data quoted here are those published by TfL, which differ slightly from those published by the DfT (White, 2008).

[3] 'Demand elasticity' refers to the rate of change in the amount of a good or service demanded, in response to a change in another variable (commonly price). In this case these other variables are the number of bus kilometres operated, and real fare levels.

[4] Further analysis to cover the 2006/07 year, using the DfT data for comparability with trends eleswhere, gives a somewhat greater growth in Londoon bus trips, and a slightly smaller proportion of that growth explained by real fare- and service-level changes – see White (2008).

[5] One should bear in mind, however, that most of the bus service expansion in London has been outside the central area, representing the manifestation of a policy decision to greatly improve bus services over the capital as a whole, not only in the areas directly affected by congestion charging.

[6] This could be important in addressing potential impacts on the retail sector. Quddus et al (2007) found that the Oxford Street branch of John Lewis was achieving sales 5 to 8% below those that might be expected from trends elsewhere in the London region, although the extent to which this finding would apply to other shops is unclear.

References

Balcombe, R., Mackett, R., Paulley, N., Preston, J., Shires, J., Titheridge, H., Wardman, M. and White, P. (2004) *The demand for public transport: Practical guide*, Technical Report TR593, London: Transport Research Laboratory.

Colin Buchanan and Partners (2007) *Reappraisal of the Jubilee Line extension*, Final Report to Transport for London, June, London: Transport for London.

DETR (Department of the Environment, Transport and the Regions) (1998) *A new deal for transport: Better for everyone*, Cm 3950, London: The Stationery Office.

DfT (Department for Transport) (2004) *Five year funding settlement for transport for London*, www.dft.gov.uk/pgr/regional/policy/lt/fiveyearfundingsettlementfor3724 (accessed 12 January 2008).

DfT (2006) *Transport statistics Great Britain 2006*, London: DfT.

DfT (2007) *Public transport statistics bulletin GB: 2007 edition*, Statistics Bulletin SB(07) 22, London: DfT.

Evans, A. and Crampton G. (1989) 'Myth, reality and employment in Central London', *Journal of Transport Economics and Policy*, 23, pp 89–108.

Evans, R. (2007) *The Central London congestion charging scheme: Ex-post evaluation of the quantified impacts of the original scheme*, London: TfL.

Gaunt, M., Rye, T. and Allen, S. (2007) 'Public acceptability of road user charging: the case of Edinburgh and the 2005 referendum', *Transport Reviews*, 27, pp 85–102.

GLA (Greater London Authority) (2001) *The Mayor's transport strategy*, London: GLA.

Jones, P., Eyers, T., Bray, J., Georgeson, N., Powell, T., Paris, J. and Lane, R. (2004) 'The Jubilee Line Extension Impact Study: Main findings and lessons for future appraisal of major public transport investments', Paper presented at the European Transport Conference, Strasbourg, October.

Knowles, R. and White, P. (2003) 'Light rail and the London Underground', in I. Docherty and J. Shaw (eds) *A new deal for transport? The UK's struggle with the sustainable transport agenda*, Oxford: Blackwell.

Lizon, R. (2004) 'Articulated buses on route 18', Master of Science in Transport Planning and Management dissertation, University of Westminster.

Mackie, P. (2005) 'The London congestion charge: a tentative economic appraisal. A comment on the paper by Prud'homme and Bocarejo', *Transport Policy*, 12, pp 288–90.

MacKinnon, D., Shaw, J. and Docherty, I. (2008) *Diverging mobilities? Devolution, transport and policy innovation*, Oxford: Elsevier.

Metronet (2008) *Statement from the PPP administrators in relation to the Mayor's approval of transport schemes*, www.metronetrail.com/default.asp?sID=1208891778343 (accessed 26 April 2008).

National Statistics (2007) *Regional, sub-regional and local gross value added*, www.statistics.gov.uk/pdfdir/gva1201.pdf (accessed 15 December 2008).

National Statistics (2008) *Guide to gross value added*, www.statistics.gov.uk/cci/nugget.asp?id=254 (accessed 9 January 2008).

Ormerod, P., Cook, W. and Rosewell, B. (2006) *Why distance doesn't die: Agglomeration and its benefits*, Economics Working Paper 17, London: GLA.

PPP Arbiter (2007) *Reference for directions from Metronet Rail BCV Ltd: Draft Directions*, 16 July, London: Office of the PPP Arbiter.

Prud'homme, R. and Bocarejo, J. (2005) 'The London congestion charge: a tentative economic appraisal', *Transport Policy*, 12, pp 279–87.

Quddus, M., Bell, M., Schmoecker, J.-D. and Fonzone, A. (2007) 'The impact of the congestion charge on the retail business in London: an econometric analysis', *Transport Policy*, 14, pp 433–44.

Steer Davies Gleave (2008) *Cycling in London*, London: TfL.

TfL (Transport for London) (2002) *London travel report 2002*, London: TfL.

TfL (2005) *The TfL business plan 2005/06 – 2009/10*, www.tfl.gov.uk/assets/downloads/corporate/business-plan-05(1).pdf (accessed 12 January 2008).

TfL (2006) *Transport 2025: Transport vision for a growing world city*, London: TfL.

TfL (2007a) *London travel report 2007*, London: TfL.

TfL (2007b) *Central London congestion charging: Impacts monitoring: Fifth annual report*, London: TfL.

Transit (2007) 'LUL delivers first operating profit for eight years despite £73m cut in revenue grant', *Transit*, 24 August, p 17.

Walton, S. (2007) 'The comparative effectiveness of the performance regimes in surface and underground rail', Master of Science in Transport Planning and Management dissertation, University of Westminster.

White, P. (2007) 'Factors behind recent patronage trends in Britain and their implications for future policy', Paper presented at the 'Thredbo10' (Tenth International Conference on Competition and Ownership in Land Passenger Transport), Hamilton Island, Australia, August.

White, P. (2008) *Factors affecting decline of bus use in the metropolitan areas*, Leeds: Passenger Transport Executive Group (www.pteg.net).

White, P., Christodoulou, G., Mackett, R., Titheridge, H., Thoreau, R. and Polak, J. (2007) 'The role of teleworking in Britain: its implications on the transport system, and economic evaluation', Proceedings of the European Transport Conference, Leeuwenhorst, the Netherlands, October.

Wiseall, A. (2007) 'Bus usage inside the London congestion charging zone', Master of Science in Transport Planning and Management dissertation, University of Westminster.

TEN

Mind the gap! The UK's record in European perspective

Tom Rye

The purpose of this chapter is to consider the changes in transport 'on the ground' in the 10 years since *A new deal for transport* (DETR, 1998), in comparison with what other European countries have achieved. In other words, at the local and national scales, what real changes to transport have there been that people notice and hence that influence their travel behaviour? How far have policy objectives such as reduced congestion and cardon dioxide (CO_2) emissions been achieved? In answering such questions, the chapter marshals a range of evidence. It first outlines factors that are widely considered capable of promoting travel behaviour change, before discussing recent transport developments at the local level in the UK using an analysis of a sample of English Local Transport Plans (LTPs). These are compared with equivalent jurisdictions in mainland Europe. Discussion then turns to comparing the UK's transport progress with that elsewhere in Europe at the national level. On these bases it is possible to comment on the extent to which the UK has in any way 'closed the gap' in transport provision with its main northern and western European counterparts; the Commission for Integrated Transport (CfIT) found in 2001 that as a proportion of Gross Domestic Product (GDP) Britain had been spending 40% less than its competitor countries on transport infrastructure for 40 years (CfIT, 2001; Docherty, 2004; see also the Preface and acknowledgements).

A key challenge in writing this chapter has been obtaining reliable comparative data. Even within the UK, this is a problem: discussion of changes at the local level concentrates mainly on changes in England because of the much greater availability of monitoring data compared with Scotland, Wales and Northern Ireland. European comparisons are even more difficult given that the different territorial scale at which many transport schemes are delivered means that there is no consistent country-by-country summary of what has been achieved. Thus, it has been necessary instead to use a variety of sources, from DG TREN statistics, through national statistics and annual reports of organisations such as Netherlands Railways to Spanish mobility observatories, site visits and personal communications with local and regional authorities.

The CfIT *Study of European best practice in the delivery of integrated transport* (CfIT, 2001) is also a valuable source of data. A follow-up report was published by CfIT in 2007. The two draw rather different conclusions; while the 2001 report highlighted significant gaps in public transport, the latest offering (CfIT, 2007, p 1) argued that:

> Far from being at the bottom of the league, our evidence shows a narrow range of performance between the UK and other large European nations. In some aspects the UK leads the way – we have among the safest roads in Europe, and, while there is still more to do, we have to date been more successful than many other nations in reducing ground transport emissions.

Whether or not the generally positive change claimed in the 2007 report really exists is a key question for this chapter (and indeed the book as a whole). At the outset, some sleight of hand is apparent, since the difference in conclusions is in part due to the different approaches taken in the two documents. Crucially, there is less consideration in the later report of key variables such as the quality, cost to the user and extent of public transport systems in different European countries, and nothing on the significant historical differences in public spending on transport between the UK and other Northern European countries. It is also the case that the 2007 report bases its conclusions on a selection of headline outcomes, including 'a vibrant aviation industry' and 'more efficient car use' (due to slightly higher average occupancy and kilometres per vehicle when one is owned). In addition, its conclusions regarding road safety do not assess accident risk per kilometre travelled by walking and cycling, an approach that may have the effect of making the UK's roads appear safer than they actually are.

Factors that bring about a change in people's travel behaviour

The general consensus among researchers is that people's propensity to use a particular mode of transport is closely related to their perception of the 'utility' of that mode in comparison to other modes, *when they are in a position to make a choice between modes* (in the way that someone without access to a car is not) (see Stradling and Anable, 2008). The utility is composed of money cost, journey time and a factor that bundles together all other aspects of the way that mode is perceived, good or bad, such as crowding, associations with feelings of security, status, independence and so on. The money cost and journey time (including reliability) of a mode relative to other modes have historically been seen as the factors that play the greatest role in people's mode choice. Therefore, other things being equal, measures that make car travel more expensive and/or slower, and measures that make alternatives cheaper and/or faster or more reliable, are likely to bring about modal shift away from car – and vice versa (Barker and Connolly, 2005).

Of course, things have not remained equal. Car ownership, for example, has grown in all European Union (EU) member states, and fastest in the new member states, but within the 'old' EU15 the UK's rate of ownership per 1,000 people grew faster (at 28%) than any other country except Portugal and Spain (56 and 29% respectively) between 1995 and 2000. Slowest of all was France, with a growth of only 4% over this period (Eurostat, undated). Thus, in those countries with the greatest rates of growth in car ownership, policies to reduce car use or its negative effects face more difficulties than in those with lower rates of growth or, put another way, these policies need to be more effective even to maintain the status quo.

Evidence from cities and city-regions that have reversed the growth in car use and increased the proportion of trips made by cycling, walking and public transport, shows commonalities in their experiences. They have to a greater or lesser degree:

- improved their public transport systems' speed and coverage with network simplification and increased network length;
- kept public transport prices down, especially for multi-journey (season) tickets;
- promoted easy interchange between modes and services;
- bought new higher-quality rolling stock and/or refurbished existing vehicles;
- improved walking and cycling conditions; and
- made car travel slower and more costly through traffic and parking management measures.

In addition, in some cases, careful land-use planning to manage the demand for travel and to focus high trip-generating land uses around public transport stops has also contributed. There also appears to be a relationship between the presence of rail-based urban public transport (for example, metro, tram, S-Bahn) and a high mode share for public transport (see CfIT, 2001; Scottish Executive, 2003; HiTRANS, 2005). Broadly, these sources conclude that the reason why these cities and regions have been able to bring about such changes is because they have had the requisite political will and financing mechanisms (both capital and revenue) available to them.

An example of such a place is Munich, a city of 1.3 million people in a wider region of 2.7 million. In spite of high economic growth and rapid formation of new, smaller households, it has held its car mode share constant over the past 20 years. It has done this by:

- investing over £2.5 billion (1996 prices) in its S-Bahn, tram and (especially) underground network;
- enforcing 30 kilometres per hour (20 miles per hour) zones on all minor roads;
- providing excellent, segregated cycle routes on main roads;
- integrating public transport services and fares across its region; and

• having sufficient faith in its planning system to actually control development and to integrate parking strategies effectively in the wider policy context.

It has been able to do this because of the availability of large capital and revenue funding from the *Land* government, but also – crucially – because its politicians have demonstrated sufficient political will. Much of the public transport network was in place before 1990 (the core S–Bahn tunnel across the city centre was built in time for the 1972 Olympics), but in recent years it has significantly extended its rail-based public transport and integrated its bus services therewith, in order to fully capitalise on the value of costly fixed infrastructure. In contrast to most British cities, Munich started from a very good position in terms of the quality, extent and cost of its public transport network, and in terms of conditions for walking and cycling, and it has continued to build on this good position over the past 10 years and thus maintain the proportion of trips carried by non-car modes (CfIT, 2001; HiTRANS, 2005).

Changes in local transport planning and funding

In the context of examples of cities like Munich, the UK government's approach to improving local transport in England was less about immediate investment in substantial infrastructure improvement, and more about the kind of institutional tinkering often associated with British policy making (Chapter Two). 1999 saw the replacement in all of England except London – which acquired its own new arrangements (Chapter Nine) – of the former Transport Policies and Programmes (TPP) system of local transport funding with the introduction of LTPs. In these documents local authorities are required to set out their policies and objectives for transport, including a programme of capital and revenue projects. Local Transport Plans are produced by every transport authority from tiny Rutland to the largest cities such as Birmingham and Leeds; thus, they vary in their coverage from the completely urban, such as Manchester, to the deeply rural, such as Cumbria. The documents must be aligned with central government's policies yet somehow reflect distinctive local character and needs. In addition, some authorities with recognised congestion problems must include indicators of traffic flows, congestion and air quality. Residents of English local authority areas would thus expect to see measurable changes in core indicators, many of which imply a need for actual changes in the safety of the road environment as well as in the quality, speed, availability and price of alternatives to the car.

The LTP was also to act as a bidding document to central government for transport capital funding: in the UK, local authorities have little flexibility to raise funds themselves and must instead depend on central government for most of their finance. Under the first round of plans ('LTP1', 2001 to 2006), there was a basic funding level for capital schemes in what was termed the 'Integrated Transport' category. This could be varied by plus or minus 25% depending on the quality of the LTP and its implementation, as judged by central government civil servants on the basis of annual (now biennial) LTP progress reports from the local authority. Further funding was received for maintenance and, under a separate but related approval process, for schemes of over £5 million. The last year of LTP1 was marked by the publication of Monitoring Reports for the entire five-year period, summarising what was implemented and achieved in each area. In this section of the chapter I have taken a random selection of 10 English local transport authorities – Cardiff, Cheshire, Derbyshire, Essex, Lincoln, Nottingham, Plymouth, Stockton-on-Tees, Surrey and West Yorkshire – to form a view as to the typical range and extent of new measures that inhabitants of these areas will have seen over the LTP period. The authorities chosen vary in size, economic buoyancy and urbanisation, but all have in common that they were judged by central government to have at least a 'good' LTP.

Typical LTP content

An LTP typically includes measures over which the local transport authority has direct control, but also identifies schemes and other measures for which implementation responsibility lies elsewhere. For example, traffic injury reduction has been a key government objective for many years, but increased in importance with a measurable national target set in 1999. In order to deal with this, some local authorities have introduced area-wide traffic calming and other safety schemes to the benefit of (child) pedestrians in particular. Safety camera partnerships have allowed local authorities to raise revenue from speeding offences at accident blackspots to put back into further road safety campaigns. As a result, there have been sharp reductions in injury accidents and deaths involving pedestrians, in some instances already exceeding government targets of a 40% reduction in killed and seriously injured (KSI) casualties and a 50% reduction in child KSI casualties by 2010 compared to 1994-98. Pedestrians are also likely to have noticed improved footway surfaces and many more dropped kerbs, while road surfaces have also been improved much faster than in the years before the LTP system due to the importance placed by central government on maintenance. Almost all LTP areas will have seen more pedestrian crossings and, in certain areas, the replacement of 1960s subways with surface crossings; some have also implemented extended pedestrian zones.

Improvements to bus services have formed a key part of all LTPs, as bus patronage is a core indicator of LTP performance. Local authority control of bus services is, of course, limited (Chapter Five), but under the auspices of the LTP system there has been growth in local authority and bus operator voluntary partnership working, where the former have improved infrastructure (new bus stops and shelters, bus lanes, and sometimes bus stations), and the latter have introduced new vehicles, route branding and restructured route networks, sometimes resulting in spectacular increases in ridership (mostly in smaller towns and cities that previously had very low bus ridership per head – see CPT, 2004). In spite of this, on aggregate, bus ridership has continued to fall in England outside London – by 7.2% between

2000/01 and 2005/06. But while it is legally possible for authorities – with the permission of central government – to control bus fares, routes and schedules, in practice this has not occurred (Chapter Five). Very few effective multi-operator tickets are available outside the Passenger Transport Executive (PTE) areas of the UK (the largest urban areas) and in all areas they are more expensive than single operator tickets. In contrast, due to local authority, bus operator and national initiatives, the availability of information (paper and electronic) has improved immensely.

Local authorities have also put considerable sums into cycling during the LTP years, generally to install new on-road cycle lanes, or shared footways for pedestrians and cyclists, and/or advanced stop lines. Linked to this has been the development by a charity, Sustrans, of a national cycle route network including many off-road sections (Chapter Six). Cycle infrastructure has therefore improved in most towns and cities in the past 10 years but overall it remains of highly variable quality and therefore usefulness. Certain cities have witnessed measurable increases in numbers of their residents who are cycling, although the overall national trend in cycling continues downwards.

There has also been a considerable increase in the number of towns and cities in Britain that have decriminalised parking to take over its enforcement from the police. This has led to larger areas being covered by controlled parking zones, more effective enforcement and also, for some councils, it has become an important income stream. In tandem, authorities in the more economically buoyant parts of England have adopted maximum parking standards for all new developments – backed up by national maximum standards since 2001 for all large developments – which have led to reduced parking supply at larger new offices, hospitals and residential developments. Related to this, increased emphasis has been placed on voluntary travel behaviour change (so-called 'smart' measures) such as travel plans, travel awareness campaigns and personalised travel planning (Chapter Eleven). Many authorities employ travel plan officers, and promote school travel plans, and state in their LTPs that a large proportion of the employees in their areas work in organisations that have a travel plan in place.

It is worth noting that the LTP regime has *not* spelt the end of local road-building in England. Atkins' report for the Department for Transport (DfT) (Atkins, 2006) lists 58 major schemes completed during LTP1, of which 35 were roads schemes, mainly bypasses and inner-city relief roads. But while many LTPs include aspirations for improved rail services and new rail stations, English local authorities have no direct powers over the railway network or services and the most that local authorities can do is to lobby for, and provide input into, the non-rail-related aspects (such as station car parking or bus stops) of the rail improvements to which they aspire.

An important point about LTP finances is that they are capital monies – that is, they can only be spent on building things, or on capital maintenance. Revenue spending is granted separately to local authorities, and the amount received is largely independent of the quality of the LTP. The total amounts spent in the LTPs reviewed for this chapter are shown in Table 10.1. It is notable that the amount spent on new demand management, public transport, safety and walking/cycling schemes is still much lower than the amounts spent on maintenance (although this includes footway maintenance) and, in some cases such as Essex County Council, on new road schemes. Many councils spent additionally from general capital and revenue funds, by 'prudential borrowing',[1] and/or from developer contributions. Southampton, for example, supplemented its £20.5 million LTP settlement with a further £60 million of capital and revenue funding, mostly from internal sources (Southampton City Council, 2006). Suffolk's £150 million of LTP allocation was more than doubled with an injection of £170 million in revenue and capital from the authority's general funds (Suffolk County Council, 2006). A general and important point to note is the large increase in transport capital spending made available to English local authorities by the government since 1997, which has helped to address a backlog in road and bridge maintenance. According to the *2000 Local Transport Plan settlement* (DfT, 2000), the £1.3 billion (cash terms) of transport capital spending allocated to English local authorities for the 2001/02 financial year represented an almost 100% increase on previous years; this level of funds increased to around £1.6 billion in 2006/07.

Continental experience in local transport

This experience in English local transport can be contrasted with changes that northern continental European citizens might have seen in their transport systems over the past 10 years. Straightaway I should caution that these comparisons are less easy to carry out than might be hoped, in part because there is no easy access to LTP equivalents for many other countries, so examples have instead been drawn from those towns and cities for which it has been possible to find useful and reliable information. These include Gent, Belgium (personal communication and site visit); Bremen and Berlin, Germany (a combination of personal communication and research on official Internet sites); Lund, Sweden (personal communication; Lund Kommune, 2005); Burgos, Spain (from the local authority's website and from the EU website for its CIVITAS project); and Graz, Austria (personal communication). Because these cities have made available information it is likely that they represent better rather than average practice, but their experiences are an important comparator to those in the UK, nonetheless.

In general, these towns and cities have seen the application of measures similar to those in LTPs, but in many cases on a greater scale, and also starting from a different baseline position. Thus, for example, all except Burgos and Lund have pre-existing tram networks, all of which have had some extensions built during the past 10 years. Cities such as Gent, Graz and Lund have seen significant enhancements to service frequencies of core public transport routes, typically from every 10-15 minutes to every 5-7 minutes – in Lund, for example, new direct frequent bus services to major employment sites have been introduced and have played a key role in its transport plan, which has seen car use decline by 2-3%

Table 10.1: LTP spending 2000/01 to 2005/06 (costs in £ million to the nearest £0.5 million)

Area	Population	Rural or urban	Public transport infra-structure	Cycle schemes	Walking schemes	Road safety	Traffic calming and manage-ment	Travel plans/ Safer routes to school	Mainten-ance	Local road schemes	Other	TOTAL	Spend per capita
Bristol	1,000,000	Urban	18.83	4.05	6.38	15.53	20.63	8.03	67.00	1.65	0.00	142.08	£142.08
Cheshire	672,400	Mixed	8.50	2.50	0.50	6.00	17.50	0.50	73.00	6.50	1.00	116.00	£172.52
Cumbria	496,200	Rural	4.00	1.00	3.50	12.80	0.00	1.28	48.00	4.80	6.56	81.94	£165.14
Essex	1,320,000	Mixed	9.13	5.22	5.22	10.43	24.12	3.91	90.10	262.50	7.17	417.80	£316.52
Nottingham	630,000	Urban	14.00	4.50	7.50	12.50	11.00	4.00	39.50	2.00	10.00	105.00	£166.67
Plymouth	250,000	Urban	2.50	1.00	2.00	3.00	4.50	3.50	11.50	10.50	3.50	42.00	£168.00
Southampton	217,000	Urban	3.65	1.23	2.05	1.19	0.00	0.21	8.55	0.86	2.71	20.44	£94.19
Stockton	187,000	Urban	2.16	0.80	1.28	2.24	1.28	0.24	5.00	28.41		41.41	£221.44
Suffolk	684,000	Rural	40.00						70.00	21.30		131.30	£191.96
Surrey	1,076,923	Mixed	17.50	3.00	5.80	22.30	17.00	1.10	70.00	5.70		142.40	£132.23
Thurrock	145,689	Mixed	1.84	0.65	0.45	3.42	1.51	0.35	6.18	8.54	0.72	23.65	£162.35
West Yorks	2,200,000	Urban	54.29	5.80	12.70	14.10	34.24	6.06	179.00	8.30	9.50	324.00	£147.27
England	52,000,000	Mainly urban	806.8	175.6	191.7	524.4	570.7	33.6	3586	297.1	542.1	6728.00	£129.38
England % by category			11.99%	2.61%	2.85%	7.79%	8.48%	0.50%	53.30%	4.42%	8.06%	100.00%	

Note: Where gaps are shown this does not necessarily mean that nothing was spent in this category, only that is was not listed in the Delivery Report in this category.

Source: Individual authorities' LTP delivery reports; Atkins (2006)

between 2001 and 2004 (Lund Kommune, 2005). In all these cities, local public transport is under public sector control, although not necessarily the control of the city administration. All cities other than Burgos have integrated tickets that are valid on all modes of public transport in the area and which offer significant discounts over single fares. Pedestrianisation has been carried out but to a wider extent than would be seen in a typical English city – for example, in the past 10 years Gent has pedestrianised almost all its historic core, making it one of the largest pedestrian areas in Europe.

When looking at the changes in Spanish cities, we see the introduction of trams in several, including Alicante, Barcelona and Madrid, the construction of a new metro line in Seville, and the reorganisation and enhancement of frequencies on bus services in cities such as Pamplona and Seville. Madrid has also seen the extension of metro lines 1, 2, 3, 4, 5 and 11 by 49 kilometres between the years 2003 and 2007, and now has a 100% low-floor bus fleet, 125 of which run on natural gas. Finally, a new 8.4 kilometre city-centre tunnel for suburban trains was completed to link the northern and the southern networks, at a cost of €169 million (Centro de Investigación del Transporte, 2005). In France, the urban realm of many cities has been transformed by the introduction of new tram and metro systems, nearly always linked to extensive pedestrianisation and traffic reduction strategies. The example of the reinvigoration of the centre of Nantes cited in Chapter Six is one of the very many in France stimulated by that country's significant investment in the city-centre public realm as part of tram and metro projects; another is Strasbourg, a city perhaps more profoundly changed in 'feel' by a deliberate combination of major public transport investment and better environments for walking than any other in Europe over the last decade (Figure 10.1).

Cycling is also a mode of transport that receives more resources in northern continental Europe than in most British cities. Traffic calming and the widespread use of streets that are one-way for car but two-way for cyclists have both been used to improve safety and relative journey times for cyclists significantly (700 one-way streets in Gent have been converted in this way in the past 12 years, for example), as have investments in new cycle bridges to cross waterways and railway lines, to make routes continuous. In Lund, too, there has been significant investment in cycle paths (Lund Kommune, 2005). Outside core areas, it is much more typical in these cities to find well-designed segregated cycle paths than in the UK, while bikes enjoy priority in German (speaking), Dutch and Scandinavian town and city centres. These cities have all also seen extensions to those parts of their area covered by controlled parking zones, although not to the same extent as UK equivalents. Equally, until very recently, less attention has been paid by French, German and Spanish cities to 'smart' measures than by their UK equivalents.

Figure 10.1: Pedestrians and cyclists as equals with the modern tramway in Strasbourg, France

© Iain Docherty

Comparisons at the national level

Using EU and other statistics it is possible to make some important comparisons between the UK and its northern European counterparts in terms of aggregate transport statistics. Table 10.2 shows the change in rail network length over the period 1996–2004 in the EU15, and Table 10.3 the change in motorway length. These two tables show the general trend of modest expansion and slight contraction of the UK road and rail networks respectively; and very great expansion of motorway networks in other EU countries. Table 10.4 shows the number of new (and extended) stations, railway lines, tramlines and metros opened in various European countries between 2000 and 2006. In this table a new tramline is an entirely new line in a city, or a new line in an existing system. A tramline extension is when an existing line is lengthened. New railway lines include short sections of route such as new chords at junctions, or multitracking, as well as entirely new routes such as the Channel Tunnel rail link or other high speed lines. Reopened rail lines, as the name suggests, are those that were formerly closed to passenger traffic but have been reconditioned and opened. New or extended metro or light rail includes schemes such as Madrid's Line 6 metro, and the Tyne and Wear Sunderland extension. It should be noted that some of the largest rail schemes in the UK, such as the upgrading of the West Coast Main Line or of Leeds and Edinburgh Waverley stations, do not fall into any of the categories in this table.

Table 10.2: Change in rail network length, 1996-2004

Country	Kilometres 2004	% change 1996-2004
Denmark	2,785	18.56
Belgium	3,536	4.62
Netherlands	2,811	2.63
Italy	16,236	1.39
Sweden	11,050	0.78
Spain	14,395	0.71
Luxembourg	275	0.36
Austria	5,675	0.05
Portugal	2,849	−0.04
Ireland	1,919	−1.79
Finland	5,741	−2.01
UK	16,514	−3.23
France	29,246	−8.18
Germany	34,732	−14.93

Source: DG TREN (2006)

Table 10.3: Change in motorway network length, 1995-2003, ranked by change in kilometres per 1,000 people

	Population (million)	Total kilometres of motorway			Kilometres per 1,000 people		
		1,995	2003	% increase	1995	2003	% increase
Portugal	10.5	687	2002	191.4	0.0654	0.1907	191.4
Ireland	4	72	176	144.4	0.0180	0.0440	144.4
Finland	5.2	394	653	65.7	0.0758	0.1256	65.7
Spain	45	6,962	10,296	47.9	0.1547	0.2288	47.9
Sweden	9	1,141	1591	39.4	0.1268	0.1768	39.4
Denmark	5.5	796	1027	29.0	0.1447	0.1867	29.0
Luxembourg	0.2	115	147	27.8	0.5750	0.7350	27.8
France	63	8,275	10,379	25.4	0.1313	0.1647	25.4
Netherlands	16	2,208	2,541	15.1	0.1380	0.1588	15.1
UK	60.5	3,307	3,609	9.1	0.0547	0.0597	9.1
Germany	82.5	11,190	12,044	7.6	0.1356	0.1460	7.6
Austria	8.5	1,596	1,670	4.6	0.1878	0.1965	4.6
Belgium	10.5	1,666	1,729	3.8	0.1587	0.1647	3.8
Italy	59	6,435	6,487	0.8	0.1091	0.1099	0.8

Source: Eurostat (undated)

Table 10.4: New rail-based infrastructure in western Europe, 2000-06

Country	New tramlines	Tramline extensions	New stations on existing rail lines	New rail lines	Reopened rail lines	New or extended metro or light rail
Belgium	0	5	1	6	1	0
Denmark	0	0	4	5	0	5
France	22	5	1	8	6	8
Germany	38	21	9	43	19	13
Great Britain	2	4	13	3	4	1
Italy	5	6	8	27	7	5
Netherlands	6	2	8	5	0	5
Portugal	0	0	0	0	0	10[1]
Spain	6	6	10	18	0	17
Sweden	0	2	0	0	0	4
Switzerland	4	1	5	6	1	1
Other	3	1	6	12	< 3	< 4

Note: [1] New system in Porto.

Source: Adapted from Phillip and Versteeg (2007)

We can see quite clearly that the UK has lagged behind, in particular, Germany, Spain and Italy in rail and metro openings, and behind Belgium, France and Germany in terms of new tram provision. Only in opening new stations on existing lines has the UK led in Europe, but this is a modest achievement (see also European Rail Research and Advisory Council (ERRAC), 2004, 2006; Grant Thornton, 2008). The provision of rail-based public transport is important in terms of changing people's travel behaviour, since railways, metros and trams have more potential than buses to achieve higher average speeds compared to cars. It is often politically more feasible to give priority to trams than to buses when road space has to be shared – and the priority given is an important determinant of speed (Semaly and Faber Maunsell, 2003). The availability and speed of rail-based public transport has been shown by Kenworthy and Laube (2002) to be an important determinant of mode share for passenger transport in a city.

Table 10.5 considers the issue of the costs of using transport. Unfortunately there are few countries that publish indices of bus and rail fares, although the UK is one of these. The table thus compares trends in costs in the UK with those in the (pre-2007) EU25 as a whole. The table shows that, in the UK, car ownership and running costs have risen more slowly, and bus and rail fares more quickly, than in the EU as a whole. The European Environment Agency (EEA) (EEA, 2000) presents data on similar trends in Denmark, the UK and Finland between 1980 and 1998, suggesting that in the two former countries, the costs of car use remained stable during this period, while public transport fares rose much

Table 10.5: Indices of prices and transport costs, EU25 and UK (2000 = 100)

	EU25				UK		
	All items	Private transport operating costs	Passenger transport by railway	Passenger transport by road	Car operating and ownership costs	Rail fares	Bus fares
2005	111	117	116	121	112	121	125
2004	109	110	112	117	110	114	116
2003	107	105	108	113	108	109	110
2002	105	102	105	108	107	105	106
2001	102	100	103	105	104	102	103
2000	100	100	100	100	100	100	100
1999	98	92	98	96	98	98	96
1998	96	88	96	93	97	94	93
1997	94	88	93	90	96	91	89
1996	92	85	91	86	93	88	84

Source: DfT (2006); DG TREN (2006); RAC Foundation (2006)

faster than inflation. Note that neither the EEA data nor Table 10.5 shows the absolute level of these costs, although CfIT (2001) found that there are significant differences in these levels in the UK compared to other EU15 countries (Figure 10.2).

The various data would support the contentions that in the UK over the past 10 years, in comparison to other Northern European countries, public transport has continued to become more expensive than the car; that there has been less investment in new or extended local rail, metro or tram services; and that the road network has expanded more slowly. As argued earlier, in terms of the provision of tram and metro networks, British cities started from a very low base in 1997 compared to many of their Northern European counterparts, but the trends over the past few years have not done much to close this gap. Unfortunately there are no consistent congestion indices for western Europe so it is difficult to draw any firm conclusions as to how this important indicator has changed in the UK compared to its counterparts on the continent (although CfIT, 2001, reports that the UK has the most congested roads in Europe).

All of these trends should only be of concern, however, if there are significant and diverging differences in travel behaviour between the UK and other Northern European countries with mature economies. Tables 10.6 and 10.7 show the mode share (in passenger kilometres) and car use per capita in the EU 25/15 and in the UK. This shows clearly that the UK has a higher reliance on the car, but that there has been a reduction in the proportion of travel undertaken by this mode

Figure 10.2: UK public transport fares compared

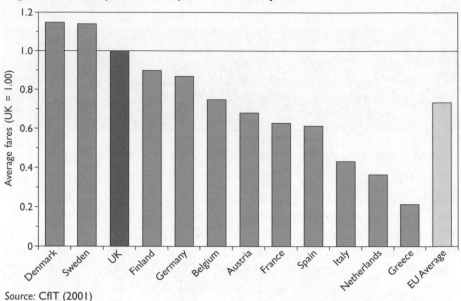

Source: CfIT (2001)

over the last decade. In the EU25 it has remained stable. The average increase in the total amount of travel between 1996 and 2004 was 13% in the EU and 12% in the UK, to a 2004 total of 4,610 billion and 796 billion passenger kilometres respectively (DG TREN, 1998, 2006). Yet when the economies that have grown and motorised very rapidly over this period (Spain, Ireland and Portugal) are removed from the EU25 figures, the average growth rate drops to only 7%. In Table 10.8, these data are considered further in terms of the change in passenger kilometres by mode and by country over the same period. This shows the UK towards the lower end of the range of growth in car kilometres, although from a higher base; around average for bus use (a growth accounted for almost entirely by Greater London – see Chapters Five and Nine); and very much out in the leading group when growth in rail use is considered (Chapter Four). On the basis of these data, it can be argued that the UK is a more car-dependent society than many of its Northern European counterparts, but becoming less so in relative terms because of increasing rail use, although this change is modest in overall terms. In any event, total passenger kilometres are also increasing quite strongly.

Differing cultures, policies and vested interests?

The comparative data laid out in this chapter reinforce the general theme of the book, that 10 years of Labour's 'sustainable' transport policy has done little to make Britain's transport genuinely more sustainable by influencing how we travel, despite having put significantly more money into the transport system against a backdrop of sustained low investment. Compared to its Northern European counterparts, the UK remains more car dependent, and its rate of growth in total surface travel has been among the highest in the older EU member states. The biggest change has been growth in rail use, but there is some doubt about this being a result of government policy as opposed to general economic growth (Chapter Four). At the same time, the cost to the passenger of using the British rail network has continued to increase at well above the rate of inflation, with the January 2008 round of increases seeing double-digit rises in many fares, much to the displeasure of passengers (*The Guardian*, 2008).

Table 10.6: Mode share, EU25 and UK (% of total passenger kilometres)

	EU25					UK			
	Pass-enger cars	P2W[1]	Bus and coach	Railway	Tram and metro	Pass-enger cars	P2W	Bus and coach	Rail, tram and metro
2004	80.6	2.6	9.1	6.4	1.3	85	1	6	8
2003	80.7	2.6	9.1	6.3	1.3	85	1	6	8
2002	80.7	2.5	9.1	6.4	1.3	86	1	6	7
2001	80.2	2.5	9.3	6.7	1.3	85	1	6	8
2000	80.0	2.5	9.4	6.8	1.3	85	1	6	8
1999	80.1	2.5	9.5	6.6	1.3	86	1	6	7
1998	80.0	2.5	9.7	6.5	1.3	86	1	6	7
1997	79.8	2.5	9.8	6.6	1.3	86	1	6	7
1996	79.6	2.5	9.8	6.7	1.4	87	1	6	6
1995	79.4	2.5	9.9	6.8	1.4	87	1	6	6

Note: [1] Powered two-wheeler

Source: DG TREN (1998, 2006), DfT (2006)

Table 10.7: Car kilometres per capita, larger old member states

	Population (million)	1995 kilometres per capita	2004 kilometres per capita (ranked)	% change
Italy	59	10,419	12,137	16.5
France	64	10,002	11,514	15.1
UK	60.5	10,215	11,207	9.7
Sweden	9	9,644	10,778	11.8
Belgium	10.5	9,283	10,631	14.5
Germany	82.5	9,882	10,532	6.6
Netherlands	16	8,213	9,150	11.4
Spain	45	5,564	7,886	41.7

Sources: DG TREN (1998, 2006)

Table 10.8: Change in passenger kilometres travelled, by different modes, 1996-2004 (%)

	Cars	Bus/coach	Tram/metro	Rail
Austria	13.5	2.3	10.2	3.2
Belgium	10.6	28.6	12.3	31.1
Denmark	5.7	−5.4		15.2
Finland	20.9	−4.9	30.8	3.0
France	13.5	0.2	29.5	23.8
Germany	6.5	−0.8	3.6	3.5
Ireland	51.5	23.6		28.4
Italy	14.1	12.5	16.0	5.9
Luxembourg	27.1	40.0		−7.8
Netherlands	10.3	−2.5	9.4	6.2
Portugal	52.3	−2.6	56.9	−19.4
Spain	37.0	21.5	29.2	18.6
Sweden	11.4	2.3	1.9	27.1
UK	9.0	8.6	29.9	22.7

Source: Eurostat (undated)

In considering the reasons for this, it is worth highlighting some key differences between the UK and elsewhere in Europe in the ways in which transport is approached. One major factor is the existence of a deregulated bus market throughout much of the UK. With the exceptions of London and Northern Ireland, the bus industry – the mainstay of most public transport – has not, on aggregate, enjoyed success during this period, when measured in changes in passenger numbers and passenger kilometres (Chapters Five and Nine). This contrasts starkly with the average European picture, which has been one of growth. Perhaps even worse is the UK's unwillingness to invest significantly in fixed modes such as the tram (Chapter Five) compared with many EU countries, and to integrate them with buses. The lack of political appetite to reregulate, despite the rude health of the bus network in London and the successes of other European networks, immediately raises the question as to whether vested interests are at work. It is possible, although difficult to prove, that the strong lobbying power of major bus groups in Westminster and Holyrood is at play here, since they have long been vocal champions of the deregulated status quo. The situation is potentially most acute in Scotland, where two of the UK's major bus groups – First and Stagecoach – are headquartered, and where considerable press interest was generated by the disappearance from the Scottish National Party's (SNP's) legislative programme of its earlier commitment to reregulate following the £0.5 million donation to the Party from Brian Souter, Chairman of Stagecoach (see, for example, *Sunday Herald*, 2007).[2]

Another reason is the complexity of planning and appraising schemes in the UK compared with many of its EU15 counterparts. Partly this is because of the UK's complex governance structures (Chapter Two) compared with countries such as Belgium and France (Priestley, 2005). To illustrate, the general fuzziness of the LTP system becomes apparent in comparison with a much stronger continental equivalent, the *Plans de Déplacements Urbains* (PDU – Urban Travel Plan) regime in France. PDUs are holistic transport plans designed to integrate with other strategic policy objectives including better environmental sustainability and urban regeneration and renewal, managed by local governments at the city-regional level. The original stated objectives of the PDUs were unambiguously to support a more rational use of the car, and to ensure integration between the needs of pedestrians, cyclists and public transport users. These were refined in 1996 to stress the need to manage the demand for mobility to safeguard the environment and improve public health. Policies were to deliberately favour the development of the least-polluting and most energy-efficient transport modes, and to make them compulsory in urban areas with a population greater than 100,000. The 1996 legislation also identified six *obligatory* objectives for each PDU (of which John Prescott would be proud):

- a reduction in the amount of road traffic;
- the development of public transport and other less polluting modes;
- management of the principal road network in each conurbation;
- a surface and underground car parking strategy, which is to privilege less polluting vehicles;
- freight transport management; and
- the development of 'green transport plans' by major employers.

Further legislation in 2000 supplemented these provisions, adding social and urban cohesion to the policy objectives, and extending the statutory powers of the PDUs to include parking policy, taxi management, urban freight management, road safety and integrated ticketing.

The details of the UK planning system are also problematic. Even the implementation of simple schemes such as parking and loading restrictions or a new bus lane can be held up or even stopped by the statutory right to object, notwithstanding evidence that the views of objectors are not representative of the population in the local area (IHT, 1999). In contrast, in Flanders in Belgium, for example, there is no statutory right to object to a traffic management measure such as a one-way street or bus lane and the non-statutory consultation period lasts two weeks instead of the 10-12 weeks (combined non-statutory and statutory consultation period) typical in the UK. Even in Sweden, there is no statutory right to object to the installation of a traffic management measure such as a bus lane (Storstockholmslandstrafik, personal communication, 2003). This is not to argue that consultation is necessarily a bad thing but that, rather, the scale and nature of the consultation should relate to the scale of the project, and that objectors in the UK may at times have too great an influence on scheme outcomes. The need to obtain Private Acts of Parliament or go through lengthy Transport and Works Act procedures to gain permission to build a new busway or rail scheme, and the complexity of financing and project structures for such ventures, slows down and makes more expensive the promotion of projects like this. This has been recognised by the National Audit Office (NAO, 2004), among others, and has been incorporated in plans for planning reform in the UK.

It is also the case that central government is much more involved in the (detailed) planning and approval of major schemes in the UK than is the case in other Northern European countries, where such matters are the exclusive concern of municipalities or regional government – even if funding is in part provided by national government. In Sweden, for example, the finance for, say, a regional tram scheme is raised largely at regional (county) level, and the decision on whether to approve the scheme and the financing for it rests with the county and with district councils (since they grant planning permission to use the land). Approval at county and municipal level tends to run in parallel to reduce planning times, such that schemes can be planned and approved within two to three years, and built within a further two (Storstockholmslandstrafik, personal communication. 2003). The same is true in France, where the PDU structure generates genuinely integrated, multimodal planning, finance for investment is forthcoming from local, regional and national governments, and major schemes, such as the Lyon tramway, can be delivered in impressively short timescales (see Chapter Five). In contrast, each English LTP scheme costing more than £5 million requires the involvement of DfT civil servants and is now appraised using the New Approach to Appraisal (NATA). The adoption of NATA is a positive change, since schemes are considered in relation to wider policy objectives, and not only on the basis of their net present value, but the methodology does not address overcentralisation of decision making and seems to have done little to change the overall balance of investment, or to increase the pace of development.

On top of all this there is a sense in which it is in the interests of the transport consultancy industry and the financial sector to make scheme planning and project management structures more complex than those of our continental partners in order to ensure higher revenues (NAO, 2004; see also the Foreword). This may help to slow project delivery and raise costs above those seen on the continent. For example, transport modelling is a much less important (and therefore time-consuming) part of tram scheme planning in France than it is in the UK (SYPTE, 2003).

The increase in transport funding in the UK will not have the intended effect if it is absorbed in increased implementation costs. There is evidence to suggest that, for major transport schemes, the latter is sometimes the case. Project cost inflation has recently dogged road schemes (Chapter Three); with regard to public transport, Table 10.9 sets out some costs of recent or planned tram schemes in various other EU countries, and for two planned schemes in the UK (one of which, in Edinburgh, is now under construction). Evidence from the rail sector

Table 10.9: Comparative costs of tram schemes, UK and continental Europe[1]

City	Name of scheme	New or extension	Length (kilometres)	Cost (€)	Cost/ kilometre (€)	Opening year	Source/notes
Barcelona	Trambesos	New	14	200	14.29	2004	www.lightrailnow.org/news/n_lrt-europe_2004-01.htm
Barcelona	TramBaix	New	17	251	14.76	2006	www.lightrailnow.org/news/n_lrt-europe_2004-01.htm
Freiburg	Line 7	Extension	2.4	50	20.83	2006	www.freiburg.de/servlet/PB/show/1173142/AB_SS_2002-1004.pdf
Bilbao	Line A	New	5	18	3.60	2002	www.tramvia.org
Madrid	Tram Line 1	New	5.4	262	48.52	2007	www.tramvia.org 70% in deep tunnel
Malaga	Velez Malaga	Tram train	4.6	18	3.91	2006	www.tramvia.org. Largely a tram-train scheme
Erfurt	5 new lines 1997-2007	Extension	13.5	100	7.41	various	City of Erfurt, personal communication (2007)
Bremen	Lilienthal Line 4	Extension	5.6	41	7.32	2010	Axel Kuehn, personal communication (2007)
Graz	Line 4	Extension	1.3	12	9.23	2005	City of Graz, personal communication (2007)
Graz	Line 5	Extension	0.75	13	17.33	2005	City of Graz, personal communication (2007)
Graz	Line 6	Extension	1.85	20	10.81	2006	City of Graz, personal communication (2007)
Augsburg	Line 6	New	5.2	49.2	9.46	2009	City of Augsburg, personal communication (2007)
Amsterdam	Ijtram 26	New	8.5	170	20.00	2005	www.ijtram.amsterdam.nl/live/main.asp and City of Amsterdam, personal communication (2007)
Rotterdam	Carnisselande	New	8	76	9.50	2004	www.ret.nl/uploads/files//downloadbestanden//ret_jaarverslag_2004.pdf

Table 10.9: Comparative costs of tram schemes, UK and continental Europe[1] (continued)

City	Name of scheme	New or extension	Length (kilometres)	Cost (€)	Cost/ kilometre (€)	Opening year	Source/notes
Average cost per kilometre of continental schemes					14.07		
Edinburgh	Line 1a	New	19	500.5	26.34	2011	CfIT (2005) (for proportion of total costs accounted for by utilities, depot and vehicles); CEC (2007) (for total scheme cost). Excludes utility diversion costs, vehicles and depot
London	West London Tram	New	15	396.825	26.455	Not known	TfL (2004). Excludes utility diversion costs, vehicles and depot

Note: [1] All include utilities diversions but exclude cost of vehicles and depot unless otherwise stated.

suggests that costs are much higher in the UK than on the continent. For example, the German Halle–Willem line was reopened in 2005. This 27 kilometre line was closed to passengers in 1981 and freight in 1992, and the track mothballed; one 600 metre stretch was covered by a new motorway. For reopening in 2005, all track and signalling was replaced and upgraded to a line speed of 80 kilometres per hour, a structure built under the motorway, 13 stations were completely renovated and four entirely new stations constructed. This scheme was completed in 18 months and of the 23 kilometres that lie in the state of Lower-Saxony, the construction costs were €16.3 million. Another example is the Achterhoek region of the Netherlands, where approximately 80 kilometres of railway was renovated and capacity enhanced to increase line speeds from 100 to 130 kilometres per hour and permit a half-hourly as opposed to hourly frequency, for a total of €17.4 million (in 1999), excluding vehicles (HiTRANS, 2005). A key factor in these cases appears to be that the local authorities in the regions concerned are able to purchase the infrastructure from the rail infrastructure owner at a very low cost; they then become the owner and franchise operations. Compare these examples with the cost of reopening and upgrading the 21 kilometres of single track railway and one new station in Scotland that comprises the Stirling–Alloa–Kincardine project. This scheme, which had an initial estimated cost of £30 million, ended up costing around £90 million, and has been accused of governance failings that betray the continuing internecine warfare of the British rail industry (*The Scotsman*, 2007; Audit Scotland, 2008; see also Chapter Four).

Conclusions

This chapter has reviewed some of the available data on changes in transport infrastructure and services in the UK (and England in particular) over the past 10-12 years, and compared this with experience in continental Europe. It has shown that, outside London, the average English person will not have observed much change in their local or regional transport system: it is likely to have become slightly safer, some short stretches of new local and trunk road may have been built, there will be limited new cycling infrastructure, perhaps more frequent off-peak trains (in garish liveries) stopping at the occasional new or refurbished station, roads will be better maintained, and buses on the whole will be cleaner, newer and more user friendly, and operating on routes with better stops, and more bus lanes. But there has been minimal attempt to engineer step-change by building major urban transport tram or metro networks, and seemingly one of the most simple of transport policies, that of ensuring through-ticketing between public transport modes, still remains a wistful aspiration in many places due to the deregulated bus market. Overall, the key variables that affect mode share – the relative journey time and journey cost by car and by public transport, and to a lesser extent the quality and reliability of public transport – have changed little in most places during this period and so the UK's greater reliance on the car in comparison to its European neighbours has not reduced. It is likely that there are cities in the UK that have done much more than is implied by this overall summary, but the difficulties of obtaining comparative data for countries are even more acute when trying to make city-level comparisons. This data availability problem must be borne in mind when considering the conclusions presented here.

In terms of bringing about significant changes in mode choice, the presumption against investing in faster rail-based public transport (especially in England outside London) stands in stark contrast to countries like Belgium, France, Germany, the Netherlands and Spain, where lower costs and different governance and delivery structures have seen far greater numbers of projects of all sizes delivered over the last decade. It is clearly the case that New Labour's approach to transport planning and delivery has brought *some* benefits, but there remain very significant structural problems in the system that make it very difficult for cities and regions to bring about major changes to their transport networks and services. Although aware of these structural difficulties, Labour has chosen not to address them, or even worse, to add to the institutional 'clutter' by creating more new (usually weak and/or voluntary) organisations that add to the governance mess (Chapter Two). Added to this are vested interests that rally against more proactive intervention in the transport marketplace to achieve sustainability objectives (despite the genuine success of London), and which strive to justify and maintain fantastically complex delivery mechanisms and a culture of 'death by appraisal' that can so often be self-defeating (Chapter One).

And so it remains difficult for the UK to deliver the transport improvements that many of its northern and western European counterparts manage routinely, and with much greater purpose, regularity and efficiency. This means that the additional resources that Labour has rightly put into transport after so many years of underspending have not been able to achieve as much change and produce as much benefit as they might. Even the apparent matching of European levels of investment falls short of what is required, since at the headline level, this merely stops the gap between the UK and its European counterparts and competitors getting any worse (Docherty, 2004), but also because the constrained purchasing power of the transport pound in the UK means that this money buys less than it should. Ultimately, therefore, the UK has seen 10 years of limited improvement on the ground; because the majority of the grander plans, policies and strategies have not been implemented, it is left no nearer the position of its continental peers than in 1997. Perhaps the biggest issue is the cultural difference between the UK and its continental neighbours when it comes to transport investment. On mainland Europe, government enthusiasm for the planning, delivery and management of major transport schemes is mainstream, and their success has bred public demand for more (see the decision in December 2007 to build a second automatic metro line in Rennes, an urban area of half a million people; Rennes Métropole, 2007). The comparison with the UK, where the sheer complexity of governance structures, together with the political power of vested interests, the fetish for complexity where none is required and, above all, government suspicion of transport as a 'too-difficult' problem best ignored if at all possible, could not be more acute.

All of this highlights the unease with which many people read the conclusions of the CfIT's (2007) *Comparison of transport in Europe* report, which, as noted at the start of this chapter, was surprisingly upbeat about the performance of UK transport in relation to that of its continental neighbours. It seems that the CfIT is now content to think that its evidence is sufficient to dispel 'the myth that we are bottom of the league' (2007, p 26) – and perhaps this is true in a literal sense – but the problem is that its view is based on partial evidence that does not appear to have been gathered to address the main concerns raised by its own equivalent report of six years earlier. It is interesting to note how the Commission, which was stripped of its responsibility to monitor government performance by ministers concerned about its increasingly critical tone in the early 2000s, has rather moved the goalposts of the debate, focusing on secondary (and perhaps spurious) measures such as 'efficiency' and 'vibrancy' while the fundamental issues remain resilient and unresolved.

Notes

[1] Prudential borrowing is the mechanism whereby local authorities (and Transport for London) are allowed to borrow without the consent of central government, as long as they remain within defined borrowing limits, with future revenue streams used as security. See CIPFA (2004).

[2] Stagecoach had previously engaged people in dinosaur costumes to protest outside the House of Commons in response to the Transport Committee's positive analysis of reregulation. See Stagecoach Group (2006).

Acknowledgements

I gratefully acknowledge the assistance of the following people in the researching for and writing of this chapter: Dr Jonathan Cowie and Carlos Arranz, Napier University, Edinburgh; Yves van de Baets and Peter Vansevenant, City of Gent; Storstockholmslandtrafik, Stockholm; Axel Kuehn, Karlsruhe, Germany; and the cities of Erfurt, Kassel, Amsterdam, Augsburg and Bremen for tram costing information kindly provided.

References

Atkins (2006) *Delivering better local transport: key achievements and good practice from the first round of Local Transport Plans*, London: DfT, www.dft.gov.uk/pgr/regional/ltp/capital/ltpsettle06/pdfatkinsreport (accessed 15 January 2008).

Audit Scotland (2008) *Review of the major capital projects in Scotland: How government works*, Edinburgh: Scotland.

Barker, L. and Connolly, D. (2005) *Scottish Household Survey topic report 2005: Mode choice*, Report to the Scottish Executive, Edinburgh: Scottish Executive.

CEC (City of Edinburgh Council) (2007) Minutes of council meeting, 25 October, Item 8.1, 'Edinburgh tram: presentation by tie Limited, TEL and City of Edinburgh Council', www.edinburgh.gov.uk

Centro de Investigación del Transporte (2005) *Observatorio de la Movilidad Metropolitana.* Madrid: Ministerio de Medio Ambiente.

CfIT (Commission for Integrated Transport) (2001) *A study of European best practice in the delivery of integrated transport*, London: CfIT.

CfIT (2005) *Affordable mass transit: Guidance*, London: CfIT.

CfIT (2007) *Are we there yet? A Comparison of Transport in Europe*, London: CfIT.

CIPFA (Chartered Institute of Public Finance and Accountancy) (2004) *Up, up and away*, London: Cipfa, www.cipfa.org.uk/publicfinance/features_details.cfm?News_id=22318 (accessed 11 January 2008).

CPT (Confederation of Passenger Transport) (2004) *'04 on the move: The changing face of the UK bus industry*, London: CPT.

DfT (Department for Transport) (2000) *2000 Local Transport Plan settlement*, London: DfT.

DfT (2006) *Transport statistics Great Britain*, London: DfT.

DG TREN (1998) *EU transport in figures – statistical pocket book*, Brussels: European Commission.

DG TREN (2006) *Energy and transport in figures: Part 3, Transport*, Brussels: European Commission.

Docherty, I. (2004) 'You get what you pay for', *Holyrood Transport Quarterly*, 2, pp 12-13.

EEA (European Environment Agency) (2000) *Are we moving in the right direction? Indicators on transport and environmental integration in the EU: TERM 2000*, Environmental Issue Report no 12, http://reports.eea.europa.eu/ENVISSUENo12/en (accessed 27 April 2008).

ERRAC (European Rail Research Advisory Council) (2004) *Light rail and metro systems in Europe*, Brussels: ERRAC, www.errac.org/docs/LRailandMetroinEU-042004.pdf (accessed 27 April 2008).

ERRAC (2006) *Suburban and regional railways landscape in Europe*, Brussels: ERRAC, www.errac.org/docs/Suburban%20and%20Regional%20Railways%20Landscape%20in%20Europe.pdf (accessed 28 April 2008).

Eurostat (undated) *Transport*, http://epp.eurostat.ec.europa.eu/portal/page?_pageid=1996,45323734&_dad=portal&_schema=PORTAL&screen=welcomeref&open=/&product=Yearlies_new_transport&depth=3 (accessed 27 April 2008).

Grant Thornton (2008) *Connecting for competitiveness: The future of transport in the UK city regions*, London: Grant Thornton LLP.

HiTRANS (2005) *Public transport – citizens' requirements*, Report on Strand 5 of the HiTRANS project, HiTRANS: County of Rogaland, Stavanger, Norway.

IHT (Institute of Highways and Transportation) (1999) *Roads and traffic in urban areas*, London: IHT.

Kenworthy, N. and Laube, G. (2002) 'Travel demand management: the potential for enhancing urban rail opportunities & reducing automobile dependence in cities', *World Transport Policy & Practice*, vol 8, no 3, pp 20-36.

Lund Kommune (2005) *Lundamats – awareness and effects 2004*, Lund City Council: Lund, Sweden.

NAO (National Audit Office) (2004) *Improving public transport in England through light rail*, London: NAO.

Phillip, B. and Versteeg, M. (2007) 'Railway lines opened since 2000, and to be opened', www.xs4all.nl/~mmverst/rinbad/ (accessed 2 April 2008).

Priestley, A. (2005) 'How to fast track Edinburgh's trams', MSc dissertation, Napier University.

RAC (2006) RAC know-how: Owning a car: running costs, www.rac.co.uk/web/know-how/ (accessed 2 April 2008).

Rennes Métropole (2007) 'Le conseil adopte l'extension du réseau de metro (Council votes for the extension of the metro network)', www.rennes-metropole.fr/detail-d-une-actualite,145705,fr.html?newsParam[newsref]=147109 (accessed 11 January 2008).

Scottish Executive (2003) *Transferability of best practice in transport policy delivery*, Edinburgh: Scottish Executive.

Semaly and Faber Maunsell (2003) *Comparative performance data from French tramway systems*, Sheffield: South Yorkshire Passenger Transport Executive.

Southampton City Council (2006) *Local Transport Plan 2006-2011*, www.southampton.gov.uk/transport/transportplanning/localtransportplan/default.asp (accessed 26 April 2008).

Stagecoach Group (2006) 'Stagecoach attacks "Gwyneth and the dinosaurs"', Press Release, 26 October, www.stagecoachgroup.com/scg/media/press/pr2006/2006-10-26/ (accessed 10 January 2008).

Stradling, S. and Anable, J. (2008) 'Individual transport patterns', in R. Knowles, J. Shaw and I. Docherty (eds) *Transport geographies: Mobilities, flows and spaces*, Oxford: Blackwell, pp 179-95.

Suffolk County Council (2006) *Suffolk County Council Local Transport Plan 2006-2011*, www.hopfensperger.co.uk/docs/20062011FullLTP.pdf (accessed 26 April 2008).

Sunday Herald (2007) 'SNP donor in £3.3m hovercraft subsidy plea', www.sundayherald.com/news/heraldnews/display.var.1807832.0.snp_donor_in_3_3m_hovercraft_subsidy_plea.php (accessed 24 December 2007).

SYPTE (South Yorkshire Passenger Transport Executive) (2003) *Comparative performance data from French tramways systems: Final report*, Sheffield: SYPTE.

The Guardian (2008) 'Fare increases of up to 15% anger rail passengers', 1 January, http://politics.guardian.co.uk/homeaffairs/story/0,,2233770,00.html (accessed 10 January 2008).

The Scotsman (2007) 'Costs going like a runaway train...', 24 September, http://thescotsman.scotsman.com/ViewArticle.aspx?articleid=3329866 (accessed 10 January 2008).

ELEVEN

Traffic jam? Policy debates after 10 years of 'sustainable' transport

Phil Goodwin

There seems little doubt that in the last decade the UK government has made, or overseen, or put in place new institutional arrangements for, many sensible improvements to travel arrangements in British cities and across the country as a whole. At the same time, it is also unarguable that even many of those accepting this view make very sharp criticism of the pace, consistency, logic and cost-effectiveness of what has been done. And this is also unarguably not only a criticism that 'the government should do more and explain itself better': there is also criticism of the direction of change. Above all, there is not a single voice – in government, in opposition, among stakeholders or in academia – who would say that an extrapolation of the vagaries of the last decade indefinitely into the future can be described as 'sustainable', in any of the disputed senses of the word. Almost a decade after the publication of *A new deal for transport* (DETR, 1998), Ruth Kelly, then Secretary of State for Transport, wrote that her new 'discussion' document 'begins a process of debate about how we best ensure that our investment and policies result in real-world improvements that are both sustained and sustainable. And I urge people to join in the debate and have their say' (DfT, 2007, p 6). The authors of this book would raise their eyebrows at that first word – 'begins' – asserting that contributions to assessment of experience – failures as well as successes – have been earlier and should have been taken more seriously.

There are always, of course, challenges about whether policy analyses produced by academics are truly representative, or complete, or consistent with each other, or realistic, or salient, or true. If this book makes the waves that its authors clearly intend, no doubt all those aspects will be picked over by its critics. In this final chapter I intend briefly to summarise the central core of the arguments that run through the book, and then put forward the case that they must be taken very seriously indeed. The book's criticisms of why the UK finds itself stuck in a transport policy traffic jam are entirely valid, and they come at a time when the government stands to waste further resources and opportunities if they are not addressed. The authors all have singular voices, and have not come together to pursue a predefined manifesto or party line. Nevertheless, the prevailing mood is unmistakeable: impatience, bordering on exasperation, that a government which started off with such a clear aim has frittered away goodwill and time by taking its eye off the ball.

Shaw and Docherty – whose editorship is observed throughout the book – discuss what is, in effect, the abandonment of the precepts of sustainability in favour of a form of pragmatism, one that is not only devoid of principle or consistency, but which also descends further into little more than shopping lists of transport projects, many of them abandoned as their escalating costs come into conflict with their expected achievements. In their chapter, MacKinnon and Vigar describe the compromises that have dogged devolution – sometimes opaque, usually overcomplicated and with transparency, responsibility for policy and democratic accountability that is questionable. While there may be reasons to move the institutional furniture around, not least the wider constitutional and good governance issues that underpin the debate, all too often devolution has failed to generate the institutional capacity and leadership essential to good policy making, detracting from successes such as the London congestion charge and rail line reopenings in Scotland.

Parkhurst and Dudley discuss roads and traffic, the central territory of policy debate, both complex and divisive. They characterise the government's approach as 'timidity, reactiveness and excessive faith in future technologies', although with the positive comment that experience in London 'may be a vital, missing ingredient for paradigm shift at the UK national level'. Global oil price remains a threat, but may also be a promise in creating space for radical leadership and real policy change. With regard to public transport, Preston starts with the observation that 'railways under New Labour seem a runaway success' but rapidly concludes that this will remain superficial as long as there remains a key fault-line between commercial and social objectives in the rail sector. Rail can have a sustainable future but the nature of that future, and how it fits in with other modes, is not yet fully (or in some cases even partially) articulated.

Knowles and Abrantes consider buses and light rail – buses bedevilled by the specific way in which deregulation was implemented at the expense of strategic consistency, and opposition to trams oddly out of key with the manifest experience in so many cities throughout other parts of the world. They comment that *Transport 2010* 'briefly heralded a new dawn for light rail', but this was eroded in stages and abandoned completely in 2007. Tolley's chapter deals with walking and cycling, being careful to avoid treating the two together since this would risk the nonsense of thinking of them as a single mode of transport, which has rendered most orthodox transport modelling almost completely useless in this area. 'There have been green gains for walking and cycling under Labour', he says, but 'they are set in a sea of red losses', with no clear sign that the government is prepared to take them as seriously, and centrally, as they need to be.

Graham's chapter is on air travel, and some of the 'myriad contradictions' that stand in the way of coherence or consistency: 'A decade on, both *A new deal for transport* (DETR, 1998) and its core concept of integrated transport seem rather remote'. He introduces a recurrent theme of 'the government's overriding commitment to the primacy of economic growth at the expense of the environmental dimensions to sustainable aviation ... it is in denial on the impact of aviation on climate change'. Pinder enters territory that is less well trodden in the policy discussions: how do ports and shipping fit into sustainability? He comments that strong demand growth has been met without extensive damage to coastal environments, but the good news has little if anything to do with any green credentials in Labour's policies, with the combination of fortuitous factors saving what could have been much more negative. And in a classic example of ministers' ostrich mentality, a critical issue for shipping – what happens to the road-hauled containers that have dominated recent growth? – is simply wished away.

London is (in some but not all respects) the exception that precisely proves the rule. White records the increase in bus use, the radical initiative in congestion charging, the sensible use of such devolved powers as have been transferred – but devastatingly high costs on the rail side, not least due to the complexities of financial arrangements that were imposed on the London Underground. Finally, from a European perspective, Rye records that other cities and countries have for whatever reason done more, and more quickly, than our own. He comments also on the somewhat bizarre way in which at least in some circles the policy discourse seems to have shifted gear from 'how badly we are doing' to 'how well we are doing' without any obvious change in the underlying data that could explain such a thing.

There is a key phrase in all the chapters, repeated and implied over and over again – '10 years'. Every one of the authors acknowledges and explains the sheer complications of the transport policy task. Nobody says it is simple (and I acknowledge that my own brief summaries above inevitably do not give credit to the subtlety of the various analyses), but 10 years is long enough, they all imply, to have got it sorted, or closer to sorted than it has been. From the point of view of historical narrative, each chapter does not chart successive improvements to clearer and clearer policies, but a halting process of reversal and lost momentum, each report never saying that the previous one was either wrong and to be withdrawn, or right and to be implemented. It is as though successive ministers have been locked in a time-loop, doomed to repeat the same platitudes – and, let us acknowledge, the same truths – but without ever any feeling of forward progress.

Looking in the rear-view mirror merely serves to highlight the extent of the policy jam that has built up in these 10 years, since things could only really get better. The exercise of helping to write the 1998 White Paper *A new deal for transport* – which is spoken of in broadly favourable terms in most of the chapters – left me with a feeling that the government's original commitment to complete a radical rethinking of the whole thrust of transport policy was genuine and backed by some calculation of how it might be done. That there was and would continue to be a battle was already clear from the beginning, but the government's determination to join in that battle and win it was impressive. And in some important areas of policy development since then – notably on road pricing and on the 'smart' measures of influencing travel behaviour (see below) – my own research positioned me to see that commitment, at various times, at its best.

So the questions have to be posed: have the authors made their case? Is it just a set of academics for whom irritation is a mode of life, or is something deeper going on? Let us consider the provenance of this debate, and some of the most immediate policy priorities, and the extent to which the consensus of the period after *Roads for prosperity* (DoT, 1989) collapsed has strengthened, or disappeared (Chapter One).

Policy provenance

It is obvious that for virtually any conceivable policy proposition, there will exist some academic somewhere who can be cited in its support, and whose research will be cited by his or her supporters. But it is notable that the theoreticians who had helped to define how to design and deliver a roads programme in the 1950s and 1960s, mostly in the government's Road Research Laboratory and the civil engineering departments of universities, moved away from this position in the 1970s and 1980s. When Margaret Thatcher launched *Roads for prosperity* in 1989, its research base was weak (and irrelevant), and one of the first substantial breaks in the intellectual underpinning of 'predict and provide' was launched from the professionals and academics in the Institution of Civil Engineering in the 1980s. These were brought together in an exercise sponsored by the prescient Rees Jeffreys Road Fund started at about the same time as *Roads for prosperity* and culminating in a report, *Transport: The new realism* (Goodwin et al, 1991), which was one of the early statements of the shift in view.

The 'new realism' was not, of course, the first to argue the case for its separate policy prescriptions,[1] but it did put these together in a quite different way from its predecessors by constructing a narrative whose essential points were: (a) a policy logic about why *Roads for prosperity* was bound to fail and be abandoned; (b) an account of shifts in opinion among those involved in the transport policy debate suggesting that a new consensus was already being built; and (c) a suggestion that the combined effects of the proposed policies could in fact be both acceptable and successful. At the core of the argument was the proposition that unrestricted traffic growth would grow faster than any feasible road programme, hence without demand management the choice between a large road programme and a small one would be the choice between conditions getting worse quickly, or getting worse slowly. Since 'vote for me, I will make things worse more slowly than the opposition' is not a credible political manifesto, the shift away from predict and provide was both a political and a technical necessity.

In opposition, Labour made use of academic and think tank advice as a substitute for the civil service advice unavailable to them (BBC, 2008). In preparing for the 1998 White Paper (DETR, 1998), the Deputy Prime Minister put together an advisory group broadly following the 'new realism' agenda, which involved academics and other 'outsiders', even in the internal discussions, to an unprecedented extent (with some quite bitter resentment of this, I should say, from those outside the circle). The proposition that a coalition of the willing could be put together in support of demand management – or, to put it more crudely, deliberate government intervention to reduce car use – was crucial to the White Paper, and early responses to it bore this out.

So it was instructive that the first attempt to make a collective expression of academic opinion was in 2002, around the halfway mark in the 10 years, already expressing concern that the policy was going adrift:

> Many politicians would like to be advised that a programme of selective road building, together with promised improvements to alternative methods of transport, will be sufficient to improve travel conditions. The evidence is that if traffic growth continues at the rate of recent decades, such a package will not in practice achieve its desired results ... we have a range of different views about the scale of road building that should be undertaken, some of us advocating more, and others less, than is currently planned. But we all agree that effective road planning depends on a clear understanding that there will have to be active policy intervention to manage the demand for road space at congested times and spaces. (Transport Planning Society, 2002)

Twenty-eight professors[2] signed this letter, out of about 40 in total of whom eight, as I remember, were away or sent messages of support in principle but felt unable to sign for reasons of politique or conflict of interest. It was fair to say that this represented as close to a consensus as one would ever get in a controversial area. It is particularly significant that the scale of infrastructure building, especially roads, was explicitly not in the consensus, but demand management was at its heart. The divisive character of the road programme was noted then and that, it seems, has not changed: what has developed is that the scale of infrastructure provision for air travel – hardly mentioned at all in 1998, or in 2002 – has joined it in the non-consensus category. And the central point of agreement on intervention to influence demand remains the most difficult one for the government to swallow. That needs examination below.

There is a notable difference between the 2002 professors' letter and this 2008 academics' book, in that there has been something of a change of generation. Among the authors of this book only Peter White and I remain from the 2002 letter. That is not (as far as I know) because the old guard has changed its mind, but because the argument now is being conducted mostly by an energetic new generation that refers to our work but is naturally more focused on its own, and the policy environment in which it finds itself. This is of potential importance to the government. At present there are signs of a divergence between officialdom and key parts of academic thinking analogous to what was happening in the 1980s: this is unnecessary and in the long run unhelpful and unfortunate for both sides.

The strange characteristic of the evolution of government policy statements over the decade has not, in my view, been a series of U-turns, but instead a series of what might be called 'J-turns', or *uncompleted* U-turns – a series of statements, each of which pleases or displeases now one group of stakeholders, and now another, but there is no feeling that there is an overarching vision. As the decade progressed, it seemed to commentators at the time that the 2000 Transport Act, the launch of Smarter Choices and discussion of the importance of 'locking in' any benefits of new infrastructure by related demand management, and intermittent ministerial speeches supporting road pricing, were broadly in line with the 'new realism' and *A new deal for transport*. On the other hand, the *Transport 2010* (DETR, 2000) plans for motorway widening, Heathrow expansion and intermittent ministerial speeches opposing road pricing seemed to be much closer to the ideas underpinning *Roads for prosperity* (DoT, 1989).[3]

Towards a sustainable transport system: the current crossroads

We might detect three changes in the current debate, compared with the earlier period. First, the territory of argument has widened, from the urban transport policy and inter-urban road building controversies where it started, to encompass other sectors of transport as well. The argument about Heathrow expansion in early 2008, whose scale and intensity clearly took the government aback, may prove to be as important in rethinking the thoughtless presumptions about the future of air transport as the debate about motorway-building was for the roads argument in the 1970s and 1980s.

Second, the degree of consensus that had been built up has, to some extent, been frittered away, the loss of momentum resulting in some fractiousness. In the final days before delivery of the first complete draft of this typescript to the publishers, an issue of *Local Transport Today* (24 January 2008) arrived in which the main headlines included:

- Controversial HA bypass inquiry adjourned for the fourth time
- Curbs on car-based development ditched in bid to boost economy
- Look beyond road-building solutions, study tells ministers
- CO_2 targets can't determine planning applications – DCLG
- Pressure for TIF referendum grows with Bury vote to reject congestion charging
- Angry editorials highly critical of rail network's management
- Guardian columnist labels DfT as 'tarmac tendency'
- Global warming queried but fears about air travel continue
- Does the UK bus industry have a platform for growth or is it doomed to decline?

There could hardly be a more intense demonstration of a sort of fractious, almost despairing, instability and incoherence of policy thinking than this. (The fact that a previous, or subsequent, issue would have had a different balance of stories does not undermine this point, but reinforces it.)

Third, there has definitely been some movement in at least two areas: smarter transport instruments of policy at the local level and climate change at the global level. The structure of this book, based as it is on a mode-by-mode treatment of the issue so as to be inclusive of several expert and experienced voices, by necessity diverts attention away from one of the most important examples of the opposite side of the case. This is the development of thinking on what used to be called 'soft measures' (and renamed on ministerial insistence 'smart' policies). This is important since at exactly the same time as many key issues of sustainable transport policy have (as the authors here argue) crumbled, government has given much greater importance to a previously almost unknown or derided policy approach.

Smarter Choices (Cairns et al 2004) is the name of a set of policy tools (and the report assessing them) using methods other than price and bans to discourage car use. They include workplace and school travel plans, use of web-based alternatives to some trips (e-shopping, teleconferences and so on, although our long-term understanding of whether virtual mobility replaces rather than generates new mobility remains in its early stages), personalised travel information at the level of the individual or household and various new types of marketing. They had been dismissed as of almost trivial importance by policy makers until a very detailed analysis of the experience in many countries demonstrated that in fact they are quite astonishingly effective, with reductions in car use in the order of 10% or so achieved swiftly and cheaply with little resistance to well-planned initiatives, and an estimate of around 20% reduction in peak period total traffic volume to be achieved by vigorous implementation of a combined package of measures building up over a 10-year period. The Department for Transport (DfT) has set up a unit whose job is to encourage such initiatives, and there can be no doubt of the commitment of those involved in this territory of work. If the implementation of road pricing is far short of the intended achievement in 1998, the application of smarter measures is progressing at a greater rate than anybody then expected.

Indeed, the development of Smarter Choices has to be seen as one of the most important counter-examples to the theme of the book. Yet, at the same time, it also illustrates the same deep flaw pointed out by the authors. There are two great lessons from the experience of Smarter Choices. First, travel choices and behaviour are very much more flexible and changeable than was thought. Travel behaviour does change, and therefore it can be changed – for the better, and with people being happy at the results. But second, in conditions of congested networks, voluntary and painless behaviour change of this sort can be rapidly eroded by the equal but opposite flexibility of other people to increase their car use. (It is a version of the same 'induced traffic' phenomenon seen when new roads are built in congested conditions, which occasionally makes things worse rather than better and nearly always means that the benefit is less than hoped for.) The dilemma is that, when used in combination with other, more restrictive measures such as pricing, bans, rationing or allocated priority, Smarter Choices can make policies more effective and more acceptable. But on their own, they are likely in the long run to have invisibly small effects overall, especially since the alternatives to the car in the UK are often much less well developed and attractive to use than they are in the places where Smarter Choices has been seen to work.

A different example, but also demonstrating that successful policy can only be achieved if two different areas of policy are consistent with one other, is illustrated most strongly in a report that came out, also during the preparation of this book, under the auspices of the RAC Foundation, and with a strong, although flawed, technical base (Banks et al, 2007). The policy argument was a reverse of the approach of the 'new realism' and *A new deal for transport*: the best outcome would be if there were both road pricing and an expanded road programme, but the focus should shift because the choice, they argued, is between a big road programme with road pricing and an even bigger one without. Since road pricing, although supported by the report's authors, is uncertain, better get on with the road programme in either case. It is offered as the candidate for the consensus 'core' policy, demand management becoming a supported, but secondary, element. This is not the place to debate the specific technical flaws in this argument, which in any case will have moved on by the time this book is published. Yet there is a central fault-line in policy consistency, which reflects in part the government's own split personality on the issue of the relationship between infrastructure capacity and demand management. The prescription is for an expanded inter-urban road programme but (in broad terms) an acceptance that there should not, or in any case will not, be a substantially expanded provision of new road capacity within towns. The two are treated as completely independent of each other. But the encouragement of large volumes of inter-urban traffic to pour off the ends of motorways onto unexpanded, congested, urban road networks is just bad planning.

The argument on sustainable transport policies, intriguingly, did not historically stem from arguments about globate climate change, but predated them. As I have noted, the core of the argument was that if current trends in the volume of travel were allowed, or encouraged, to continue, then any feasible infrastructure programme would at root have the character of slowing down the pace at which conditions got worse, rather than making them better. The alternative strategic trajectory, focusing on influencing travel behaviour, was shown to be potentially more effective in delivering improvements in quality of life. If this basic proposition is true, then the false choice of 'the economy or the environment' is a badly misleading way of taking decisions, as noted by several of the contributors here. Where the authors of this book will undoubtedly find support is in their patient (but only just) description of the last 10 years as being – at best – a disappointment. The central choice remains, as it was in 1998, the extent to which present trends in travel behaviour are seen as a given, or a variable. A policy paradigm that starts out by extrapolating the current trends for one or two or six decades, and then considering what policy instruments might be implemented by the end of that period to counter their dire consequences, is doomed to failure. That would not be 'towards' a sustainable future, but inexorably away from it.

That is why it is so interesting that in the early months of 2008, there has been heightened discussion of two developments: the October 2007 government statement preparing for Green and White Papers called *Towards a sustainable transport system* (Dft, 2007),[4] and the 2008 Climate Change Bill, which sets the basis for legally enforceable targets for carbon reduction (a 60% reduction is set, with work to prepare for 80%). The tone of both of these is positive and serious, and they raise again, from the viewpoint of carbon, the set of policy prescriptions that had emerged already from the viewpoints of congestion and transport efficiency. The statement started with a list of what has been achieved:

> A lot has been achieved over the past decade to deliver a transport system which can support a growing economy whilst helping us to live within carbon emission limits. The decline in use of the railway has been reversed. The energy efficiency of cars has improved. Local authorities have made much progress in delivering successful local transport packages, though experience, particularly in terms of bus patronage, has been varied across the country. London has shown what can be done to promote bus use and cycling, as part of a co-ordinated package of congestion-charging and investment. And transport demand is not growing as fast as it used to. Meeting the transport needs of a modern economy whilst delivering CO_2 reductions is still a challenge, but not an insuperable one ... we need a new approach to strategic transport planning. (DfT, 2007, p 8)

As in any government document, a close scrutiny of ambiguity and caveats can reveal loopholes and ambivalence to a suspicious mind, but on the other hand there is no reason to dismiss ministers' intentions and sincerity automatically. That the recognition that 'transport demand is not growing as fast as it used to' is included in a list of successes rather than a list of problems is a step forward in thinking, albeit a hesitant one. And the statement is consistent with the argument in the new realism and *A new deal for transport* that the right policies to pursue are those which deliver benefits in improved access to goods and activities without relying on increasing vehicle movement.

There is no reason why this approach should not be successful other than determination and political will. The authors of this book, I suspect, will be in the frame of mind of simply not knowing whether they now dare to believe what they have felt so let down on before. For what is now not-so-new Labour, this may indeed be the last chance saloon for a credible and coherent transport strategy.

Notes

[1] Pedestrianisation, traffic calming, traffic management used to optimise rather than maximise traffic flow, the reallocation of scarce road space to the most needy or efficient claimants on it, the promotion of walking, cycling and public transport, the use of land-use planning to reduce unnecessary travel, the use of prices that reflect the cost of congestion and environmental effects, and tackling the psychological or 'soft' influences on travel attitudes and choices.

[2] Professors Allsop, Banister, Bell, Bielefeldt, Cole, Goodwin, Grieco, Hamilton, Hills, Hine, Jeffery, Jones, Kirby, Lesley, Lowson, Lyons, Maher, May, McDonald, Metz, Nash, Smyth, Stradling, Urry, Vickerman, White, Wigan and Wright.

[3] If it were possible to treat policy evolution in the form of mathematical relationships, I would suggest that there seem to be two cycles, one of ebb and flow of support for infrastructure expansion to meet demand with a period of around 10 years (probably due to the timetable of institutional forgetfulness), and the other of demand management with a period of about four years (perhaps due to election timetables), the offsetting reinforcement causing a resonance effect such that competing 'parties' within the Department for Transport hold temporary eminence within their sectors.

[4] Nearly the same title as my chapter in the predecessor to this book: 'Towards a genuinely sustainable transport agenda for the United Kingdom' in Docherty and Shaw (2003).

References

Banks, N., Bayliss, D. and Glaister, S. (2007) *Motoring towards 2050: Roads and reality*, London: RAC Foundation.

BBC (British Broadcasting Corporation) (2008) 'Just what is a think tank?', http://news.bbc.co.uk/1/hi/magazine/7189094.stm (accessed 15 January 2008).

Cairns, S., Sloman, L., Newson, C., Anable, J., Kirkbride, A. and Goodwin, P. (2004) *Smarter choices: Changing the way we travel*, London: Department for Transport.

DETR (Department of the Environment, Transport and the Regions) (1998) *A new deal for transport: Better for everyone*, Cm 3950, London: The Stationery Office.

DETR (2000) *Transport 2010: The 10-year plan*, London: DETR.

DfT (Department for Transport) (2007) *Towards a sustainable transport system*, Cm 7226, London: DfT.

Docherty, I. and Shaw, J. (eds) (2003) *A new deal for transport? The UK's struggle with the sustainable transport agenda*, Oxford: Blackwell.

DoT (Department of Transport) (1989) *Roads for prosperity*, Cm 693, London: HMSO.

Goodwin, P., Hallett, S., Kenny, P. and Stokes, G. (1991) *Transport: The new realism*, Oxford: Transport Studies Unit, University of Oxford.

Transport Planning Society (2002) Letter of 28 transport professors to Secretary of State for Transport, www.tps.org.uk (accessed 14 December 2002).

Index

Page references for notes are followed by n